Beanie Mania™ II

The Complete Collector's Guide

1st Edition
All Rights Reserved
An Unofficial Collector's Guide

Beanie Mania™ II

The Complete Collector's Guide

Becky Phillips and Becky Estenssoro

First Edition: October 1998

Library of Congress Card Catalog Number: 98-093023

ISBN 0-9659036-1-3

For information write:

Dinomates, Inc.
710 E. Ogden Avenue, Suite 545
Naperville, Illinois 60563

www.beaniemania.net

Printed by Royle Communications Group, Inc., Sun Prairie, WI

We dedicate this book to our children

Michelle, Michael and Caroline Phillips;

Christopher, Audra and Matthew Estenssoro.

It was because of  them that our

journey began into the world

of Beanie Babies – a journey

that has changed our lives forever!

ACKNOWLEDGMENTS

We express our gratitude to those who have helped in so many ways:

To H. Ty Warner, the creative genius, whose Beanie Babies were the inspiration behind this book.

To Vicky Krupka, friend and contributing author of featured articles: Beanie Baby Mistakes, Years in Review, McDonald's Teenie Beanies and Counterfeits.

To Sara Nelson (BeanieMom) whose hard work and dedication has created a web site that is a safe haven for all Beanie Baby collectors.

To Steve Misewicz of Steven Designs, Inc., whose creative talent has brought this book to life.

To Tiffany Stark, Joe Cullen, Chris Swenson, Mark Lindner, Frank Gibson, Ernie Childress, Paul Buechner and Russ Allen, the dynamic, hard working crew from Royle Communications Group, Inc. They were there for us every step of the way until the completion of this project.

To Carlton Bjork, whose Beanie Baby artwork captures the imagination.

To Rich Seidelman, whose humor and artistic talent has contributed to the enjoyment of the McDonalds Teenie Beanie craze.

To Ed, Kathy and Dylan Siasoco, friends and fellow Beanie Baby collectors who helped with our research on the counterfeits.

To Kathy Reed for her creative Beanie Baby descriptions.

To Joni Blackman, whose exceptional writing style and reporting has captured a moment in time.

To Herb Shenkin, our photographer, who is always there when we need him.

To all of our Beanie Baby friends who have supported us throughout the years.

To all the Beanie Baby collectors who have unselfishly allowed us to photograph their prized Beanie Babies, so other collectors could enjoy them.

TABLE OF CONTENTS

BEANIE BABIES ARE BORN

Mr. H. Ty Warner, sole owner of Ty Inc., is the creator of Beanie Babies. Mr. Warner established Ty Inc. in 1986, in Oak Brook, Illinois (U.S). The company's original products included a complete line of full sized (12" to 20" long) plush animals. With offices in England (Ty UK), Germany (Ty Deutschland), Mexico (Ty Mexico), and Canada (Ty Canada.) Ty Inc. was a successful international enterprise long before Beanie Babies.

Mr. Warner came up with the idea to design less expensive versions of his original stuffed animals. He wanted them to be priced low enough so kids could afford to buy them with their allowance. The lower price led to the small size - small enough to be held in the palm of a child's hand. He wanted them to be squishy, so he used the PVC pellets he was using in the feet of his larger animals. Soon, the Beanie Babies were born. The first nine Beanie Babies were introduced at a toy exposition in November 1993. These first nine were designed after the best patterns of his larger animals.

Beanie Babies debuted in stores in 1994 and took a while to get going. Mostly that's because there were only 9. Every six months, another 9 to 12 were added and as the group grew, their popularity did too. It was late 1995 when Beanie Babies first got too popular to keep up with demand.

Beanie Baby mania began in the western suburbs of Chicagoland, not too far from Ty Inc.'s corporate headquarters. Eventually, Beanie Baby mania spread throughout the United States, and into other countries, most notably Canada and England.

Ty's marketing strategy for Beanie Babies has been to limit their availability, in order to create a sense of scarcity and stimulate demand. Ty avoided the more common marketing plan of selling through mass market stores. Instead, Beanie Babies are only sold through small retail stores, such as card shops, specialty gift stores, small toy stores and airport gift shops.

Another important part of Ty's strategy to create scarcity, and to insure that the Beanies are not just another short lived fad, has been to periodically discontinue, or "retire," a select number of the Beanies. These "limited editions" have become highly prized by collectors and have helped to heighten the demand for all types of Beanie Babies.

It's been five years since they were born, and Ty's little beanies are still one of the biggest success stories in retailing and collecting history.

"Some companies are in it for a quick buck – I want longevity," says Warner (with an armful of his cuddly creations).

TY WARNER
THE MAN AND HIS MAGIC

An exclusive interview with the creator of Beanie Babies
By Joni Blackman

The July 1, 1996 issue of People Magazine featured a brief article about H. Ty Warner and his hot toys, Beanie Babies. The article was based on a rare interview with the elusive Mr. Warner. The interviewer, Joni Blackman, spent several hours talking to Ty, in his office and then later at his home. Much of what they talked about wasn't in the People article, due to space limitations. In Joni's words, "He told me lots of things that never got into the story." We are pleased to bring you the rest of Joni's story:

He was named after his dad's baseball hero, Ty Cobb, and Harry S. Truman. That is, Truman's middle initial didn't stand for anything and Warner, whose given name is H. Ty Warner, also has no explanation for the H.

"The nurses thought my mom was crazy," he told me. "Two names with a total of just three letters!"

His mother was a homemaker and his father sold jewelry. He has one younger sister.

Warner attended St. John's Military Academy in Delafield, Wisconsin. At St. John's he played baseball, football, and basketball. He was a member of the Star and Circle Club. The club membership consists of those cadets who have been awarded the highest scholastic average in the upper school.

He attended Kalamazoo College in Michigan, where he majored in drama. He worked in summer stock after college and then moved to Los Angeles, planning to become an actor.

But after a year of pumping gas, stocking grocery shelves and selling cameras door to door, Warner decided he'd rather make money than wait for a call that might never come.

He returned home to Illinois and began working for Dakin, the stuffed animal company. He stayed with the San Francisco-based company for 18 years, working both as a sales rep. in Illinois, Indiana and Ohio and in product design.

Knowing that it is hard for any salesman to get store owners interested in their products, Ty drew from his drama background and created a character for himself, someone that buyers would want to see.

He wore a long fur coat, a top hat, carried a cane and drove a white convertible Rolls Royce.

"It was all to get in to see the buyer," he told me. "I figured if I was eccentric-looking in Indiana, people would think, 'what is he selling? Let's look in his case!' I wanted people to pay attention to what I had, then it was easy to sell."

Ty Warner attended St. John's Military Academy in Delafield, WI.

Ty Warner Center Field

Ty was given his unusual name by his father whose favorite baseball hero was the legendary player Ty Cobb.

TY WARNER: THE MAN AND HIS MAGIC

They may have been disappointed to see just stuffed animals, but they bought plenty.

"I learned marketing, impulse items - I learned this company (Ty) from Dakin," said Warner of his old employer that closed in 1995 after 40 years as a plush toy leader. "They were the best."

But in 1980, Warner got tired and burned out and left the company, took some time off and moved to Sorrento, Italy, where some friends lived.

> ## He wore a long fur coat, a top hat, carried a cane and drove a white convertible Rolls Royce.

"It's the opposite of what we do here," said Warner. "Everyone knows each other. They have a three-hour lunch, swim, lay in the sun. It's a very enjoyable lifestyle. For three years I played tennis, swam, and ate."

But Warner couldn't keep out of card and gift stores and couldn't stop noticing that the Italians produced some really nice stuffed cats.

"I decided to come back and do something that no one has done - make a good cat. If you carry cats, they'll really make you money," said Warner, himself the owner of two live cats, a mixed gold Persian named Nokomis and a white Persian called Yoda.

He returned to the states in early 1984 and by 1985 had incorporated as Ty, Inc. He then traveled to Seoul, Korea to find a source to make a good cat. When he found one, he took it to some of the old accounts he trusted and asked their opinion. They told him it was the best stuffed cat they'd ever seen and they'd buy as many as he had.

"I knew I had a winner," said Warner of the $20 Himalayan cat. And he did. I knew how to market, what to make. I did everything myself."

The appeal of the cats was not only how realistic they looked, but that they were posable. They were understuffed animals with tiny PVC pellets in the paws that helped keep them sitting up or laying down. "No one had put the combination of understuffed with beans. All the animals were stiff and hard."

Himalayan Cats

"At the very beginning, everyone called them 'roadkill' and told me I was cheap - that I hadn't stuffed it enough. They didn't get it. The whole idea was that it looked real because it moved."

Warner got a $20,000 second mortgage on his small condo in Hinsdale, Illinois, to finance his company and he worked out of the condo. He shipped his goods in from Korea and trucked them to his condo.

"I pushed the furniture to the sides and unpacked the boxes, mixed the merchandise to fill orders and re-packed everything back into the same boxes and shipped them out, carrying them out to the UPS driver. I did that twice before the manager of the complex told me that this was a residential complex and I was running a business," said Warner.

Meanwhile, his cats were selling out locally. He went to the Atlanta gift show and put his cats on a table he rented from another wholesaler and sold $30,000 worth of cats in one hour - 10 colors of the same cat, each with its own name.

"Kids identify with names. In the beginning, I thought of the cute names. Now I take them into the office and everyone makes suggestions," said Warner, who asks everyone he knows for input on names and colors for his Beanies.

After the Atlanta gift show, Warner rented 12,000 square feet of warehouse space in Lombard, Illinois and put the furniture back where it belonged in his condo. He hired two employees through ads - Anne

Who would have thought that eventually this upstanding cadet would be selling stuffed animals while riding in a white Rolls Royce?

Ty's previous office.

His current business residence. Quite a change.

Nickels (who is his public relations person now, but answered an ad on a community college bulletin board for data entry) to work on invoices and Patricia Roche, who did everything else. Both still work for him.

His tiny company moved on to producing dogs, monkeys and bears. Then on to farm animals, and jungle animals. By 1992, Ty had a catalog full of dozens of animals, simply priced at $5, $10 and $20 wholesale (typically marked up 100 percent for retail sale), which Warner says made his company popular with retailers who liked the fact that all of the animals of the same size were the same simple, rounded price.

In 1993, Ty introduced Beanie Babies.

"At that time, there wasn't anything in the $5 retail range that I wouldn't consider real garbage," said Warner. "It was a tough category - everything was either plastic or hard stuffed."

He knew what price he wanted, which brought him to the small size. He knew he wanted it to be squishy and he thought of the PVC pellets he was using in the feet of his larger animals. He found some soft material he was using on his larger animals' paws and put the pellets in it.

"It was great," said Warner.

He started out with 9, copying designs from the best patterns of his larger animals.

Beanie Babies debuted in stores in 1994 and took a while to get going, he admits. Mostly that's because there were only 9. Every six months, another 9 to 12 were added and as the group grew, their popularity did too. It was late 1995 when Beanie Babies first got too popular to keep up with demand.

Three years later, Ty and his little Beanies are still one of the biggest success stories in retailing.

'93-'95
Year in Review

1993 INTRODUCTIONS

Brownie and Deep Fuchsia Patti

1994 INTRODUCTIONS
"ORIGINAL NINE"

*l-r, top to bottom: Cubbie, Chocolate, Pinchers, Spot without a spot, Squealer
Splash, Raspberry Patti, Legs and Flash*

1994 MID-YEAR INTRODUCTIONS

l-r, top to bottom: Old face Teddys: Jade, Violet, Teal, Cranberry, Magenta and Brown
Blackie, Chilly, Peking, Daisy, Goldie
Ally, Quackers without wings, Bones, Gray Happy, Humphrey
Fine-mane Mystic, Web, Orange Digger, Tan Inky without a mouth
Seamore, Speedy, Trap, Lucky 7 dots and Slither

OTHER 1994 INTRODUCTIONS

These Beanie Babies were introduced throughout the year.

Spot with a spot, Quacker without wings and Punchers

1995 INTRODUCTIONS

l-r, top to bottom: New face Teddys: Violet, Cranberry, Teal, Magenta, Jade and Brown Valentino, Zip with white face and belly, Nip with white face and belly and Quackers with wings

OTHER 1995 INTRODUCTIONS

These Beanie Babies were introduced throughout the year.

l-r, top to bottom: Magenta Patti, Spook, Nana
All Gold Nip, Tan Inky with a mouth and All Black Zip

1995 MID-YEAR INTRODUCTIONS

l-r, top to bottom: Stripes black and orange, Rex, Steg, Bronty, Velvet, Ziggy thin stripes,
Waddle, Tabasco, Caw, Bongo tan tail-b/w tush, Royal blue Peanut, Magic light pink stitching,
Bubbles, Lavender Happy, Derby fine-mane, Kiwi, Bessie,
Stinky, Red Digger, Tie-dyed Lizzy, Pink Inky,
Flutter and Sting

1996
Year in Review

1996 INTRODUCTIONS

l-r, top to bottom: Spooky, Fuchsia Patti, Light blue Peanut, Pinky, Ears, Garcia
Weenie, Twigs, Hoot, Tusk, Grunt, Seaweed
Inch with felt antennae, Derby coarse-mane, Chops, Nip with white paws, Zip with white paws, Flip
Coral, Tank 7-line, Bucky, Mystic coarse-mane, Ringo
Radar, Manny, Bumble and Lizzy blue/black

12

The Internet Brings Ty, Inc. to Life!

Not much was known about Ty, Inc. prior to their emergence on the Internet in 1996. In early January, 1996, the www.ty.com domain name was owned by a Mr. Philip Giacalone, who operated a business called Tech Yard. Giacalone used the web site, named after his son, for advertising his computer consulting business.

In late January 1996, Ty, Inc. offered to buy the domain name from Giacalone, but he refused to give it up. At that point Ty, Inc. sought suspension of the domain name under the Network Solutions, Inc. ("NSI" - the registrar of web site domain names) dispute resolution policy. Ty based their suspension request on the fact that they held the federal trademark registration of "TY", which appears in their red heart design.

This forced Giacalone to bring a legal action against Ty, Inc. and NSI, on May 30, 1996, to prevent the suspension of the domain name. This case, Giacalone vs. NSI and Ty, Inc., 1996 U.S. District LEXIS 20807 (N.D. Cal. 1996), was historic in the sense that it gave Ty, Inc. the right to the ty.com domain name and also opened up questions as to trademark and copyright rights on the Internet.

Giacalone argued that he used the ty.com domain for a web page, e-mail purposes, advertising and web site development. The court issued a preliminary injunction on June 13, 1996, preventing Ty, Inc. from interfering with Giacalone's use of the domain name ty.com. This case was later settled when Giacalone agreed to transfer the domain name to Ty, Inc. for an undisclosed amount.

Until the court case was legally settled, Ty, Inc. had to cover up the www.ty.com web page address on Beanie Baby heart tags. The web address was either cut off, whited out with liquid paper or a white sticker was placed over it. New tags were printed up with "Visit our web page!!!" or with no mention of the web site at all.

Summer 1996

Ty, Inc. introduces 13 new Beanie Babies: Congo, Freckles, Curly, Rover, Scoop, Sparky, Lefty, Righty, Libearty/Beanine, Scottie, Wrinkles, Sly brown-belly and Spike.

l-r, top to bottom: Congo, Freckles, Curly, Rover, Scoop Sparky, Lefty, Righty, Libearty Scottie, Wrinkles, Sly and Spike

Summer 1996

Beanie Babies appear with new 4th generation swing tags and 3rd generation tush tags.

4th generation swing tag

The Beanie Babies Collection™

ty®

Spot

HANDMADE IN KOREA © 1993 TY INC., OAKBROOK IL. U.S.A SURFACE WASHABLE ALL NEW MATERIAL POLYESTER FIBER & P.V.C. PELLETS **CE** REG. NO PA.1965 (KR)

3rd generation tush tag

July 1,1996

The first article written about H. Ty Warner appears in People magazine, written by Joni Blackman.

August, 1996

Ty emerges on the internet and provides information about Beanie Babies through the Ty "Guestbook." The "Guestbook," though simplistic, provides an opportunity for Beanie Baby collectors to exchange information and buy, sell and trade Beanie Babies.

October, 1996

The Ty Guestbook is shut down for a few days. Instead of being a source of information, it has become a teenage chat room, a source for foul language and a place for Ty retail stores to sell Ty products.

October, 1996

Ty Inc. issues a statement that sets the standards for posting information on the Guestbook.

October 21, 1996

An interview with H. Ty Warner appears in Forbes magazine.

December, 1996

The Ty Guestbook is not accessible during the last two weeks in December, because the web site is being upgraded. The only visible activity on the web site is the "countdown" clock that indicates the days left until the site will reopen - on January 1, 1997. On that date, Ty will make his first "official" Beanie Baby retirement and introduction announcement.

OTHER 1996 INTRODUCTIONS

These Beanie Babies were introduced throughout the year.

*l-r, top to bottom: Bongo brown tail r/w no name,
Bongo tan tail r/w no name,
Bongo tan tail r/w with name, Libearty/Beanie,
Tank with shell, Tank 9-line no shell,
Magic hot pink stitching, Stripes black and tan,
Sly white-belly, Tuck, Inch with yarn antennae,
Lucky 11 dots and Lucky 21 dots*

1997
Year in Review

1997

Year of the Beanie Baby Boom

1997 was an outstanding year for Ty, Inc. Their popular Beanie Babies line of stuffed toys became more than just popular – they became "The Collectible of the Year." 1997 saw an escalating interest in Beanie Babies by the general public, and a subsequent increase in the number of collectors. What follows are highlights of some of the more significant events that happened in 1997–The Year of the Beanie Baby Boom.

January 1 -
Through the use of a multi-media presentation on their Ty, Inc. web site (www.ty.com), Ty, Inc. makes the first public announcement of newly retired and newly released Beanie Babies.

Retired: Chops, Coral, Kiwi, Lefty, Libearty, Righty, Sting, Tabasco and Tusk/Tuck.

Introduced: Bernie, Crunch, Doby, Fleece, Floppity, Gracie, Hippity, Hoppity, Mel, Nuts, Pouch, Snip and Snort.

January 29 -
Ty, Inc. announces to reps. and dealers that Sparky and Radar are retired.

 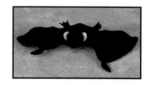

January 30 -
The next day Ty, Inc. rescinds the announcement of Sparky and Radar's retirement. From that day on, until their "official" retirement in May, Sparky and Radar become difficult to find.

February -
Ty, Inc. releases Maple the Bear, a Canadian exclusive. Maple is introduced to honor Canada's Independence Day, which is celebrated on July 1st. Maple was originally going to be called "Pride" but the name was changed after it was already in production. The first 3,000 Maples released have the name Pride on the tush tag.

March -
Ty, Inc. removes the listing of Beanie Baby poems from their web site.

March -
Roary, the lion, is introduced on the Today show. No information is given at the time as to the Beanie's name or poem.

March 20 -
Ty, Inc. changes their ordering policy. Initially, they require that a certain percentage of a retailer's order consist of Ty plush, but later rescind that decision.

March 22 -
Ty, Inc. introduces the "Info Beanie". A new Beanie is chosen each month to write in the Beanie Babies internet diary on Ty's web site. Quackers is chosen to be the first Info Beanie.

April 1 -
Ty, Inc. programs its computers to delete all Beanie Baby orders in the system except for the very first orders placed early in the year. As of April 1st, a retailer could only place one order per month with a maximum 36 pieces of each style Beanie. Any back orders are automatically deleted, making Beanies harder to come by, and causing some retailers to raise their prices. Retailers were also allowed to place a second order in May for only the new Beanies with a maximum of 36 of each one and with projected shipping to be 45-60 days.

April -
Ty, Inc. provides a service to help make it easier for people to locate stores in their area that carry Beanie Babies. They offer a toll-free Automated Consumer Information Line at 1-888-628-6111. After entering an area code, the service will give the names and phone numbers of 5 retailers that carry Beanie Babies in that area. The service is later discontinued after a few months.

April 11 -
McDonald's starts their first Teenie Beanie Babies promotion, planned to run for 5 weeks, introducing two new Teenie Beanies each week.

The Teenie Beanies in order of introduction are: Patti, Pinky, Chops, Chocolate, Goldie, Speedy, Seamore, Snort, Quacks and Lizz.

April 20 -
McDonald's issues a public announcement apologizing for running out of Beanie Babies and the need to stop the promotion 3 weeks earlier than the intended five-week run. Full-page ads appear around the country that also offer apologies to the public for running out of the toys.

Ad that was placed in Chicago area papers.

The ad states:

"We at McDonald's would like to thank all the folks who stopped by over the past few days to pick up a Ty Teenie Beanie Baby. In fact, there were so many of you, it has become the biggest Happy Meal in history (sort of a really Happy Meal). But, the Ty Teenie Beanie Babies have become so popular, we've run out of them. We'd like to thank our crew for making a great effort to fill the incredible demand, but unfortunately the Babies have flown the coop. We're sorry for any inconvenience this may cause, and thanks again for giving all our Ty Teenie Beanie Babies a home."

April -

Ty, Inc. revamps its computer and order entry system and introduces a long overdue new information system. Overwhelmed by thousands of calls per day from retailers, Ty, Inc. is forced to slash by two-thirds the amount of time it had planned to spend revamping its order entry system.

April 24 -

Blizzard makes an early appearance on the BeanieMom web site.

May -

Six of the yet to be announced Beanie Babies "escape" from the nursery and make an early public appearance. These include Blizzard, Echo, Jolly, Nanook, Pugsly and Waves.

May 11 -

On Mother's Day, Ty Inc. makes their second public announcement via their website, this time using their "Info Beanie" Garcia to provide clues leading up to the announcement starting at 12:01 a.m.

Retired: Bubbles, Digger, Flash, Garcia, Grunt, Manny, Radar, Sparky and Splash. Flash and Splash are the first of the "original nine" Beanie Babies to be retired.

Introduced: Baldy, Blizzard, Chip, Claude, Doodle, Dotty, Echo, Jolly, Nanook, Peace, Pugsly, Roary, Tuffy and Waves.

May 14 -

Dennis Berry, Associate General Counsel for the NFPA (National Fire Protection Association) sends the following letter to the BeanieMom web site:

Dear Beanie Mom,

We came across the article about you and your web site in last week's Washington Post. In particular we noted the "News Flash" about the replacement of the Sparky character with the dog Dotty. There is a story behind that change which we thought your readers might find interesting. The name Sparky™, as well as the title Sparky the Fire Dog™, are registered trademarks of the National Fire Protection Association. Sparky™ is, and for many years has been, the name of our Dalmatian character which serves as the mascot of the NFPA. In particular Sparky™ is associated with our fire safety education products and activities. The Sparky beanie baby did not look like the NFPA's Sparky but the name was the same.

When we heard about the name Sparky being the name of a Beanie Baby figure, we brought the fact of our long standing trademark in the name to the attention of the Ty, Inc. company. Without admitting any infringement, they agreed to cease manufacture of the doll with that name. I have not seen the dog "Dotty" and therefore don't know if this looks the same as the previous dog. So long as the name is changed, any confusion is avoided.

May 18 -

The Chicago Cubs sponsor their first Beanie Babies' Day at Wrigley Field. The first 10,000 children age 13 and under receive a free Cubbie Beanie Baby along with a commemorative card. Ty Warner throws out the first pitch of the game. The Cubs win the game in front of a sell-out crowd.

June 9 -

The Today Show presents a full-length segment on the Beanie Baby phenomenon.

June -

Beanie Babies start appearing with taped on red stars on their tush tags. These taped on stars are a "temporary" version of the new 4th generation tush tag with a red star located just to the upper left of the heart.

August 8 -

A full page color ad appears in the August 8, 1997 issue of USA Today. In it Ty writes:

Dear Friends:

Thank you. You've made TY a huge success! Because of your unparalleled enthusiasm, both consumers and retailers alike, Beanie Babies are the largest success story in the history of the toy and gift industries. Our other plush categories are experiencing similar growth and success as TY becomes the brand of choice. We are very grateful for your support.

However, unprecedented growth such as this brings tremendous challenges and we are doing our best to meet them...but it takes time. We are aware of the frustration that many of our loyal customers have felt recently when searching for TY products. We want you to know that we are doing all that we can to alleviate the delays and provide increased shipping in the next few weeks. Although we can not control the effect that the economics of supply and demand have on retail prices, we are making every effort to satisfy the supply in a timely manner so that the demand can be met.

Loyal customers are what makes a company strong. We thank all of you for your loyalty, support, determination, and patience, and we look forward to

Hang in there!

sharing our success with you for a long time to come.
Sincerely,
Ty Warner

August -

Doodle is officially renamed Strut on the Ty web site. Doodle was renamed due to a trademark infringement with the Chick-Fil-A fast food chain whose mascot is named Doodles™.

August -

The Canadian Special Olympics uses the Maple Beanie Baby to raise funds. An additional circular tag is attached to Maple that says "Special Olympics Celebrities Sports Festival" on it.

August -

Ziggy the zebra is appearing with wide stripes on his fabric.

September -

Ty UK and Ty Deutschland are consolidated into one company–Ty Europe. Ty Europe is headquartered in Fareham Hants, England.

September -

Word leaks out from England about the 5 newest Beanies - 1997 Teddy, Batty, Gobbles, Snowball and Spinner.

September 6 -

The Chicago Cubs sponsor their second Beanie Babies' Day with a "Cubbie Goes Back to School" event. The first 10,000 children age 13 and under receive a free Cubbie Beanie Baby along with a commemorative card. Once again, the Cubs win in front of a sell-out crowd.

September 23 -

Ty, Inc. receives Advertising Age's prestigious MARKETING 100 award. The awards, now in their sixth year, recognize 100 individuals for excellence in brand building–the geniuses behind today's marketing success stories.

October -

Two top executives from Enesco Corp. are brought over to the Ty Company, one as new acting president.

October 1 -

Eleven Beanies are retired, and five new "holiday" Beanies are introduced.

Retired: Ally, Bessie, Flip, Hoot, Legs, Seamore, Speedy, Spot, Tank, Teddy Brown and Velvet.

Introduced: 1997 Teddy, Batty, Gobbles, Snowball and Spinner.

October -

With the October introduction came some changes to Beanie Baby swing (heart) and tush (sewn-in) tags.

SWING TAG: The addresses of the Ty companies as listed on the inside of current Beanie Baby swing tags (4th version) have changed. Up to the middle of this year, the address for Ty UK Ltd. was Waterlooville, Hants, PO8 8HH. When Ty UK moved to new offices, the address changed to

Fareham, Hants, PO15 5TX. Then, mid-year, Ty UK and Ty Deutschland combined into Ty Europe Ltd. The addresses on swing tags now read: Ty Inc., Oakbrook, IL; Ty Europe Ltd., Fareham, Hants, PO15 5TX; and Ty Canada, Aurora Ontario.

Additionally, a registered ® mark appears after "Beanie Babies" and the trademark sign (TM) has been moved to include the entire phrase "The Beanie Babies Collection".

TUSH TAG: Changes made to the 4th version tush tags relate to the trademark (TM) and registered ® symbols. "Beanie Babies" now has registered ® after it, and the entire phrase "The Beanie Babies Collection" is trademarked (TM). There is also an additional trademark (TM) symbol after the Beanie's name on the tush tag.

October 7 -

An article appears in newspapers announcing the availability of Beanie Babies in Beijing's secondary market. This starts an influx of Beanie animals coming directly from China to the U.S. secondary market.

October 29 -

Ty, Inc. surprisingly announces the release of a new Beanie Baby:

"Welcome to the pre-introduction of the most unique and special Beanie Baby ever made...Princess. In loving memory of Diana, Princess of Wales, Ty is pleased to announce this special addition world wide to the 1997 Beanie Baby Collection. All of Ty's profits from this collectible will be donated to the Diana, Princess of Wales Memorial Fund. Princess will be available in December, 1997 at fine stores everywhere."

November -

Mystic starts appearing in stores with an iridescent horn.

November 1 -

Retailers are only allowed to place orders for the 5 new "Holiday" Beanies.

November 19 -

(PRNewswire) - The Children's Advertising Review Unit (CARU) of the Council of Better Business Bureaus, Inc. announces that Ty, Inc. ("Ty") has agreed to revise its web site for Beanie Babies. Ty will (1) obtain parental permission prior to a child's registration on the Beanie Babies web site, and (2) include a clear and prominent disclosure of Ty's privacy practices. Following CARU's recommendations, Ty will also more clearly indicate that its product information is advertising.

December 1 -

Retailers are allowed to order only Princess and the 5 new Holiday Beanies for the month of December. Ty releases a maximum of 12 Princess Beanie Babies to each account. Most retailers, in an effort to let everyone have an equal chance at Princess, either raffle or auction her off to their customers with proceeds usually going to charity.

December -

In an effort to control rumors, about possible changes to Princess, a memo was sent by Patricia A. Roche, Managing Director of Ty Europe to a select number of retailers. The letter read in part:

"The Committee for the Diana, Princess of Wales Foundation, authorized this bear just recently, and therefore, we were able to have only a small amount done before 1998... Just so you know, there will be one small shipment of PRINCESS this year in December, and in 1998 everyone should be able to get one. There will be no difference in the tags or anything else so there will be no reason for anyone to pay outrageous amounts for this Bear....!"

December 3 -

Maple is sold at the Special Olympics Celebrities Sports Festival to raise money for the Canadian Special Olympics.

December 15 -

The first museum exhibit of Beanie Babies takes place at the Collier County Museum in Naples, FL.

December -

New tags start appearing on Beanie Babies. The outside of the tag remains much the same except that the font used for the words "Original Beanie Baby" located inside the yellow star, and for the wording on the back, has changed to Comic Sans.

Inside the tag the font has also changed to Comic Sans. On the left-hand side of the tag the phrase "The Beanie Babies Collection" now has a registered mark ® after the entire phrase, and no registered mark ® after the word

Babies. The rest of the address information for Ty Inc., Ty Europe, and Ty Canada remain the same.

It is the right-hand side of the tag where the most noticeable changes have taken place. The Beanie's style number is no longer given (although it still appears in the UPC code on the back), and the Beanie's name is centered at the top. Double-spaced below the Beanie's name is the date of birth, but the month is now fully spelled out and the year written out completely instead of numerically with separating hyphens

Additionally, at the bottom of the tag where it previously said "Visit our web page!!!" http://www.ty.com, it now reads simply: "www.ty.com".

There has also been a slight change to the tush tag. Instead of just the phrase "Beanie Babies" being registered ®, the entire phrase "The Beanie Baby Collection®" is registered ®, and the trademark symbol (TM) has been removed. This information is now consistent with the information found inside the tag.

December 19 -

Ty, Inc. officially recognizes Doodle as a retired Beanie Baby and places it in the retired category on their web site.

December 19 -

Rosie O'Donnell, popular television talk show hostess, makes an eye-popping entrance at the beginning of her television show. She arrives on stage seated inside a large box filled with retired Beanies Babies. Inside the box are 1,000 Ty Beanie Babies consisting of Digger, Bubbles, Coral, Chops, Righty and Lefty.

Rosie tells her audience that she recently received a call from Ty Inc. asking if they could donate 1,000 retired Beanies to her Toys- for-Tots fund-raising efforts. Rosie, who knows about collectibles (she has a huge collection of

McDonald's Happy Meal toys), asked if these weren't the Beanies that were worth about $100 each. When told they were, she then asked if it would be possible to receive an additional 1,000 current Beanies to be given to the Toys-for-Tots children, and use the retired Beanies to auction off for charity. Ty Inc., who likes to support charities, readily agreed. Rosie ended up with 1,000 toys for the kids and $100,000 worth of Beanies to auction off for charity.

December 30 -

Chicago Cubs announce they will be having two more Beanie Baby days during the 1998 season - Gracie the Swan in honor of Cubs' first baseman Mark Grace, and Daisy the Cow in honor of the Cubs' announcer Harry Caray.

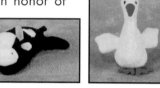

Introduced: Britannia, Bruno, Hissy, Iggy, Pounce, Prance, Puffer, Rainbow, Smoochy, Spunky and Stretch. ❋

December 30 -

By experimenting with numbers of existing URL codes for Beanie Baby pictures posted on the Ty web site, some-one discovers they can link to pictures of the yet to be announced Beanies. Website addresses are found for all ten of the soon to be released Beanie Babies and are post-ed on the Ty Guestbook. Pictures of all ten new Beanies (but no poems and birthdays) appear on a number of Beanie Baby web sites before the evening is over.

December 31 -

Ty, Inc. makes an early evening announcement of eleven new releases and nine retirements.

Retired: 1997 Teddy, Snowball, Spooky, Goldie, Nip, Lizzy, Magic, Bucky and Cubbie.

1998
Year in Review

1998
The Year of Expansion and Change

The Beanie Baby market continued to evolve in 1998, spurred on by many creative ideas coming out of Ty, Inc. headquarters along with various new promotional and licensing agreements. In 1998, Ty started the Beanie Baby Official Club, in association with Cyrk, Inc.; opened up new markets for Beanie Babies in the United Kingdom and Germany; participated with professional sports teams in Beanie Baby giveaways that proved to be a huge attendance booster for major league baseball; developed a line of licensed products, including tag protectors, calendars, trading cards and Beanie Baby display cases; and opened Ty-rrific, in Chicago, the first exclusive all-Ty product store.

January 1, 1998

Ty writes a letter to Ty dealers announcing the Beanie Babies Official Club. Only select retailers are chosen to carry Beanie Babies Official Club kits.

January, 1998

Derby, the horse, is introduced with a "star" on his forehead.

January, 1998

According to pictures found on the Ty web site and the retailer's catalog, Rainbow and Iggy's tags are switched with each other.

January, 1998

Valentino, Peace, Curly, Blackie, Hippity, Hoppity, Floppity, Squealer Tuffy and Roary start appearing with "ORIGIINAL" and "Suface" mistakes on the new 5th generation swing tags.

January 28, 1998

Kmart announces their intention of using Beanie Babies to help promote Valentine's Day jewelry.

January 29, 1998

Ty puts a disclaimer on their web site advising "consumers that it does not support, promote or condone the Valentine's Day promotion sponsored by the Kmart Corporation."

January 31, 1998

Ty introduces Erin, the green bear with the white shamrock.

February 8, 1998

Kmart and Service Merchandise start Beanie Baby/diamond promotions. As a result, Ty revises the disclaimer on their web site to include Service Merchandise along with Kmart.

Kmart promotion Beanie with diamond necklace

Service Merchandise promotion, Beanie with diamond earrings

February 13, 1998

It is announced that CYRK, Inc., in an agreement with Ty, Inc., will distribute the Beanie Babies Official Club Kits. Ty Warner invests 10 million in CYRK, Inc. based on his strong confidence in CYRK's growth.

February 13

Ty, Inc. sues Kmart for copyright violations in connection with their Valentine's Day Beanie/diamond promotion. Ty gets a court order halting Kmart from selling any more of the specially packaged Beanie Babies.

February 18, 1998

Erin arrives in the U.S.

February, 1998

In order to stop importation of commercial quantities of Beanie Babies into the U.S., Ty, Inc. registers their trademark with U.S. customs to restrict importation of Beanie Babies into the United States from Canada and Europe.

March 1, 1998

Ty accounts can only order the December 31, 1997 releases as well as Floppity, Hoppity, Hippity, Ears, Quackers, Erin and Princess. All other orders are put on hold. Also, retailers can order from a list of 7 previously retired Beanies on a first-come, first-serve basis: Nip, Cubbie, Lizzy, Spooky, '97 Teddy, Snowball, and Flip. The restriction on March orders is purportedly to allow Ty to catch up on all February orders not yet filled. As of 3:00 PM on Monday, March 2, 1998, Ty, Inc. is no longer accepting orders for these retired Beanies.

March 1, 1998

TY Canada sets new Beanie Baby Purchasing Policy:

Effective March 1, 1998 all orders placed for Beanie Babies that include Maple, Princess, and Peace will have to follow the 10:1 rule.

Example:

To Purchase 6 Maples you have to purchase 60 regular Beanie Babies.

To Purchase 12 Maples you have to purchase 120 regular Beanie Babies.

To Purchase 24 Maples you have to purchase 240 regular Beanie Babies

March 2, 1998

In remembrance of the Chicago Cubs announcer, Harry Caray, who passed away February 18, 1998, Ty Inc. announces it will produce a special one-time only, limited edition tag for Daisy, the cow, Harry's favorite Beanie Baby. The tag will be attached to Daisy for the Cubs' game on May 3, 1998 and will never be produced again.

March 13, 1998

Britannia hits the United States market.

March 13, 1998

Ty puts a link to CYRK, Inc. on the web site and redesigns the site.

March 16, 1998

Ty, Inc. sends letter to retailers:

Dear Valued Ty Customer:

This letter is in response to the concern that you expressed in your recent letter to Ty Inc. Please know that we fully understand the concerns that you addressed, as well as the frustration that you have experienced. We would like to take this opportunity to provide you with some information about our company and our policies, so that you have a clearer understanding of our position.

The ultimate goal of Ty, Inc. is to provide consumers with the highest product at the greatest value possible. We have never lost sight of this goal, even through our remarkable period of company growth. Everyone at Ty is very service oriented, and we have been working around the clock in our efforts to increase the production and distribution of our product.

Please understand that Ty has in no way manipulated the distribution or the marketing of our products, including the extremely successful Beanie Babies line. It is simply a situation where the demand for our product has greatly exceeded our production capacity, there by affecting the available supply. We are making every effort to increase our production, and look forward to coming closer to meeting customer demand.

We are also pleased to report that Ty has not had a price increase on the Beanie Babies product line since its introduction in 1994. Although our suggestion is that retailers sell this product for between $5 and $7, we can in no way demand or insist that they price items in this manner. However, we do encourage our consumers to shop at retail stores that they are comfortable with and that offer product at reasonable prices.

On behalf of Ty, thank you for taking the time to bring your concerns to our attention. Please know that we understand your issues, and we are doing everything possible to correct the situation.

Sincerely,
Ty, Inc.

March 19, 1998

Beanie Babies Official Club kits arrive in stores.

March, 1998

Ty, Inc. sets up a customs hotline 1-888-317-5488 for reporting Beanie Baby shipments that have been confiscated at the U.S. border.

April, 1998

Beanie Babies with the 5th generation misspelled tags have small stickers with "Surface Wash" printed on them, covering up the "Suface Wash" error.

April, 1998

Spinner, the spider is found in Europe with tush tags that have the name "Creepy" on them.

April 10, 1998

Ty Inc. publicly announces pricing policy on their web site:

Ty's philosophy has always been to create products of unique design, products of the highest quality, and to price these products so they can be easily affordable to children. This philosophy has never changed. Although we do not publish a suggested selling price, we have trusted our retail partners to remain true to the Ty pricing policy.

Situations we currently observe in the marketplace compel us to inform consumers of our position. BEANIE BABIES® plush styles are designed for children to collect and are priced to sell for about $5.00. This includes all current styles as well as new product introductions such as Princess and Erin. In addition, we expect retailers to place all Ty products out on the shelf so that each consumer has the opportunity to purchase every style that we produce and each style that they want.

Although we cannot control the secondary market, we decide who is a Ty customer. To this end, we will discontinue the sale of our products to accounts that knowingly sell to secondary market dealers, divert product, or sell on consignment. By not selling to the end consumer, the account becomes a distributor and our Company policy clearly states that we do not sell to distributors.

We take pride in creating and distributing a non-violent, creative toy for boys and girls that they can afford to collect. It is upsetting and intolerable to us when the "short-term greed" of some of our customers takes over.

Fortunately, there are loyal Ty retailers who share our philosophy and hold their prices at around $5.00. When we have determined that our pricing is not being followed, we will no longer support that retailer.

If we all work together, we can ensure that collecting BEANIE BABIES® plush is both fun and affordable for everyone!
Sincerely,
Ty, Inc.

April, 1998

Ty, Inc. sets up a counterfeit hotline 1-888-317-5489.

April 22, 1998

Ty, Inc. reiterates pricing philosophy with a personal letter to retailers that states:

A letter to all Ty Retailers:
The success of BEANIE BABIES® plush has always been predicated on style, quality, price, and customer niche. Our focus has not changed, and we count on you, our retail store partners, to support this direction. Our wholesale prices have not increased on any item in the Ty line since our inception in 1985. What other vendors in your store can say that?

Our vision has never been, and never will be, short term. We have discontinued opening new accounts for almost a year to better serve your needs. We've made a commitment to the specialty gift retailer and have avoided the mass market. We could have easily sold to Walmart, K-Mart, Target or Toys R Us, but we remained committed to you, the small independent retailer. We remained committed to you as you compete against the giant retailers with better service, better visual presentation of products, and consistent pricing integrity.

We firmly believe that the recommended $5.00 "magic" retail price point has contributed greatly to the success of the BEANIE BABIES® phenomenon. BEANIES® are cute, limited, well made, and affordable. Well, guess what, now

in far too many cases, they're not affordable. At least not for the children they were created for!

We receive letters from consumers daily complaining about exorbitant prices, stores that sell their shipments out the back door to secondary dealers, and product that never even makes it to the shelf for sale. We read criticism in the press for "gouging" customers when our prices haven't changed in 12 years. We're aware of retailers selling on the Internet at inflated prices. It's time for Ty to take a stand.

We expect you to mark up Ty products in line with all the other vendors in your store. We expect you to put BEANIE BABIES® on the shelf for keystone or around $5.00. In addition, we expect you to put all styles out on the shelves, so that each consumer has the opportunity to purchase every style that we produce and the styles they want the most! We believe retailers have a responsibility to treat their customers fairly. Our expectations are that you will be fair and just in the sale of BEANIE BABIES®.

Although we cannot control the secondary market, we decide who is a Ty customer. We will discontinue sale of our product to accounts that knowingly sell to secondary dealers. We will discontinue sales to those that divert product or sell on consignment. By not selling to the end consumer, you become a distributor, and our company policy clearly states that we do not sell to distributors.

Certainly, there are accounts that agree with our philosophy and retail BEANIES BABIES®, all BEANIE BABIES®for keystone or around $5.00. We applaud you! We will continue to support you with product as we work together to ensure that collecting BEANIE BABIES® plush is both fun and affordable, once again, for everyone...including children!

Sincerely,
Ty Warner

May 1, 1998

Ty Inc. announces at 3:00 a.m. CST the retirement of 28 Beanie Babies: Baldy, Blizzard, Bones, Ears, Echo, Floppity, Happy, Gracie, Hippity, Hoppity, Inch, Inky, Jolly, Lucky, Patti, Peanut, Pinchers, Quackers, Rover, Scottie, Squealer, Stripes, Twigs, Waddle, Waves, Weenie, Ziggy and Zip.

May 1, 1998

Clubby the bear, the first Beanie Babies Official Club member exclusive is announced.

May 3, 1998

Chicago Cubs have Daisy the Cow, "Harry Caray" Day. Daisy is given to the first 10,000 children age 13 and under. Supplies run out two hours before the gates open. The inside of Daisy's tag has a caricature of Harry Caray, a special poem, and is dated May 3, 1998. A commemorative card is also included with Daisy. An additional 400+ special Daisys are donated to Chicago's WGN Radio 720 who uses them to raise $107,250 for the Neediest Kid's Fund.

May 17, 1998

Beanie Babies Day is held at Yankee Stadium. David Wells, the New York Yankees pitcher, pitches a "Perfect Game." Several days later it is announced that Valentino, the Beanie Baby given out at the game, David Wells' hat, and the ticket stub from the May 17th game will be placed in the "Baseball Hall of Fame" in Cooperstown, N.Y.

May 22, 1998

McDonald's starts second Teenie Beanie Happy Meal promotion. Teenie Beanies include: Doby, Bongo, Twigs, Inch, Pinchers, Happy, Mel, Scoop, Bones, Waddle, Zip and Peanut. Many restaurants sell out within the first few days of the planned four-week promotion.

May 27, 1998

W.H. Smith opens Ty-rrific, a new, first-of-its-kind store/museum at Terminal 3 of O'Hare International Airport, Chicago, Illinois.

The store features not only the entire line of Ty products, but a display of Ty Warner's personal collection of prototypes and never-produced Ty products.

May 27, 1998

Ty sends a picture to major Beanie Baby web sites from a ceremony where Ty, Inc. presented the Diana, Princess of Wales memorial Fund a check for $2,004,850. This donation represents Ty's profits from the first quarter sales of Princess.

May 30, 1998

Ty, Inc. announces the release of 14 new Beanie Babies: Ants, Early, Fetch, Fortune, Gigi, Glory, Jabber, Jake, Kuku, Rocket, Stinger, Tracker, Whisper and Wise.

May 30, 1998

Ty, Inc. introduces 2 new Pillow Pals, Sherbet and Paddles. Poems started appearing on the inside of the heart tags instead of the previous to/from format.

May 30, 1998

Britannia with a sewn on Union Jack flag appears on the market. It is rumored that only 150 of the 500 experimental Beanies produced have escaped into the world at large.

June, 1998

The newly released Beanie Babies start appearing with a special production stamp mark on the inside of the tush tag. These marks then start appearing on all Beanies being produced in China.

June, 1998

Rainbow is redesigned to include a tongue, but still has Iggy's tags.

June, 1998

Smoochy is redesigned to include a felt mouth instead of the previous thread mouth.

July 9, 1998

Clubby, the bear, was unveiled on NBC's Today Show with Katie Couric and the president of CYRK Inc. Pat Brady.

July 9-12, 1998

At the Atlanta Gift Show, Ty introduces a new line of licensed products including calendars, tag protectors, collector cards, and storage cases. Cyrk, Inc. will wholesale these products, which are designed to capture the excitement of the brand and consumer demand for Beanie Baby merchandise.

July, 1998

U.S. customs eases their Beanie Baby importation requirements. People coming into the States from Canada, can now import as many as 30 Beanie Babies once every 30 days.

July, 1998

Peace and Rainbow undergo subtle color changes and start appearing with new tie-dyed pastel colors.

1998

July 31, 1998

Ty makes the first exclusive Attic Treasures retirement announcement. Amethyst, Christopher, Dickens, Ebony, Fraser, Gloria, Morgan, Nicholas, Scotch, and Sidney are retired.

August 2, 1998

The first UK Beanie Baby Fair takes place at the Royal Ascot Racecourse. Jayne Connelly-Bloom and her sister Janice were the fair organizers.

August 12, 1998

Ty, Inc. adds a "Consumer Survey" to their web site (www.ty.com). The purpose of this survey is to help with Ty's efforts to make sure consumers are provided the quality goods and services they deserve, but also to determine which authorized dealers provide Ty products at fair prices and in a comfortable shopping environment.

August 19, 1998

Ty Inc. posts a warning on their web site to beware of unauthorized sports promotions.

August 1998

Ty Inc. discontinues the Consumer Survey due to the high volume of responses.

August, 1998

Iggy and Rainbow undergo fabric and design changes.

Rainbow & Iggy "Year in Review"

January 1998

Iggy, the blue tie-dyed iguana with RAINBOW hang and tush tags.

January 1998

Rainbow, the multi-colored chameleon with IGGY hang and tush tags.

June, 1998

Rainbow, the multi-colored chameleon with IGGY hang and tush tags is redesigned to include a tongue.

July, 1998

Rainbow, the multi-colored chameleon with IGGY hang and tush tags and tongue starts appearing with new pastel tie-dyed colors.

August, 1998

Rainbow, the multi-colored chameleon now has a collar and tongue and correct RAINBOW hang and tush tags.

August, 1998

Iggy, the blue tie-dyed iguana now has avocado felt green spikes along his back and correct IGGY hang and tush tags.

September, 1998

Retailers can now order 36 each of Princess, Erin, and the 14 new releases. All other Beanies are now being classified as "Classic Beanies" and can only be ordered in quantities of 12 for September.

September, 1998

Retailers can place orders for Ty calendars, trading cards, and tag protectors.

September 1, 1998

Info Beanie, Wise, peaks interest when he writes in his diary that there is a lot of excitement at Ty Inc. He indicates that surprises will be coming soon. Clues are posted up to September 14, 1998.

September 3, 1998

Ty puts newsflash on web site that Clubby has arrived and orders are being filled.

September 4, 1998

New Britannias appear on the UK market. These Britannias are now produced in China and do not have a red ribbon. The last line of the poem now reads: "And wear the Union Jack with pride".

1998

September 15, 1998
Beanie Baby sand prints of Snort, Blackie and Daisy appear to indicate the first three Beanie Babies to be retired.

September 16, 1998
Ty retires Ringo, the raccoon.

September 17, 1998
A sign is posted "Beach Closed Today". No Beanie Baby is retired today.

September 18, 1998
Ty retires Puffer and Bruno.

September 19, 1998
Ty retires Spinner and Seaweed.

September 20, 1998
Ty retires eight Attic Treasures: Bearington, Chelsea, Grace, Montgomery, Precious, Prince, Sire and Squeaky.

September 21, 1998
A sign is posted "Beach Closed Today".

September 22, 1998
Ty retires Bernie, Sly white-belly and Wrinkles.

September 23, 1998
A sign is posted "Beach Closed Today".

September 24, 1998
Ty retires Crunch, the Shark.

September 25, 1998
A sign is posted "Beach Closed Today".

September 26, 1998
Ty retires six Pillow Pals: Clover, Moo, Oink, Red, Ribbit and Tubby.

September 27, 1998
A sign is posted "Beach Closed Today".

September 28, 1998
Ty retires Stinky, the skunk. Also posted is, "That's All Folks! We think?"

September 29, 1998
A sign is posted "Beach Closed Today".

September 30, 1998
Ty introduces a whole new line of Ty Products called Beanies Buddies. The 9 new introductions are: Beak, the kiwi, Humphrey, the camel, Jake, the mallard duck, Peanut, the royal blue elephant, Quackers, the duck, Rover, the red dog, Stretch, the ostrich, Teddy, the cranberry teddy bear and Twigs, the giraffe. These buddies are approximately 3 times bigger than the Beanie Babies.

September 30, 1998
Ty introduces 10 new Beanie Babies: Beak, the kiwi, Canyon, the cougar, Halo, the white angel bear, Loosy, the goose, Pumkin, the jack-o-lantern, Roam, the buffalo, Santa, the Santa Claus, Scorch, the dragon, 1998 Holiday Teddy, and Zero, the holiday penguin.

September 30, 1998
Ty introduces a new Pillow Pal: Antlers, the moose.

September 30, 1998
Ty introduces 8 new Attic Treasures: Esmerelda, the witch, Gem, the white teddy bear, Isabella, the cream teddy bear, Jangle, the cream bear with Santa hat and scarf, Laurel, the bear, Peter, the pumpkin bear, Sterling, the white angel bear, and Tyrone, the brown bear.

BEANIE BABY PROTOTYPES

Bronty - Prototype

Rex - Prototype

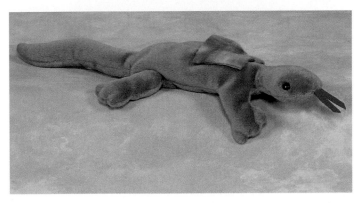

Lizzy - Prototype

Steg - Prototype

Bronty, Rex, Steg and Lizzy Prototypes – The patch of fabric that is sewn on the prototype indicates the final material chosen for that Beanie Baby.

During the production process, a Beanie Baby goes through many changes before its final approval. This process can take years of preparation. The design, colors, features, and accessories, as well as the name, poem and type of tags, require a monumental amount of thought, time and effort.

When Ty Warner designs a Beanie Baby, he makes several prototypes of the same Beanie Baby. He designs them in different shapes and colors, and uses a variety of features and accessories. He then calls upon his friends and employees to help make the final selection. He is extremely interested in their opinions and even has them help with the name selection.

Because of Ty Warner's strong desire for perfection, Beanie Babies are in a constant state of change. The most noticeable changes are color variations and redesigns. There are changes made during the photo shoot, after the catalogs and mid-year "New Introduction" sheets are distributed, and for some, during the years that followed.

BEANIE BABY PROTOTYPES

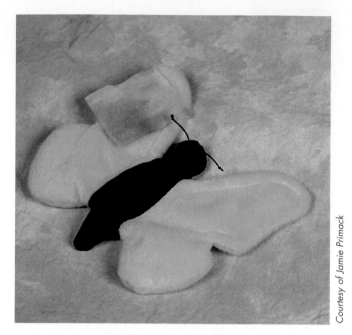

Courtesy of Jamie Primack

Flutter – Prototype

Courtesy of Jamie Primack

Coral – Prototype

The Beanie Babies that are pictured in the catalogs and mid-year "New Introduction" sheets are prototypes. The majority of the prototypes pictured were produced as Beanie Babies, but there are several prototypes pictured that did not make the "final cut."

One of the more unusual prototypes pictured was Nana, the red monkey. In the 1995 mid-year "New Introduction" sheet, Nana is a red-colored monkey with a cream face, hands and feet. Before Nana was introduced in 1995, its color was changed to medium-brown. Also pictured is Stripes, the tiger, with stripes only visible on his face; Sting, the ray, with a white belly and Lizzy, the tie-dyed lizard, with a white belly.*

*See page 250.

BEANIE BABIES FROM A TO Z

Collectors love to look at pictures of Beanie Babies, but they also want key information about that Beanie Baby. This Beanie Baby section has the current and retired Beanie Babies pictured alphabetically. The style number, poem, date introduced and retired, birthdate, gender and description of each Beanie Baby are included. If the Beanie Baby was retired prior to mid-1996, when the 4th generation hang tags with the poems were introduced, there is no poem for that Beanie Baby.

Ally, the alligator, is an olive-green reptile with a distinctive brown and green mottled back. He has a long snout, black eyes and black thread nostrils.

ALLY
the alligator

Style #4032
Date Introduced: Mid–1994
Date Retired: October 1, 1997
Birthday: March 14, 1994
Gender: Male

Poem:
When Ally gets out of classes
He wears a hat and dark glasses
He plays bass in a street band
He's the coolest gator in the land!

Ants, the anteater, has a long gray snout, a gray tail and distinctive white and black markings across his back and forelegs. He has black eyes and small gray felt ears.

ANTS
the anteater

Style #4195
Date Introduced: May 30,1998
Date Retired: Current
Birthday: November 7, 1997
Gender: Male

Poem:
Most anteaters love to eat bugs
But this little fellow gives big hugs
He'd rather dine on apple pie
Than eat an ant or harm a fly!

Baldy, the eagle is black and white with a large yellow bill. He has yellow webbed feet, black eyes with a yellow outer rim and black thread nostrils.

BALDY
the eagle

Style #4074
Date Introduced: May 11, 1997
Date Retired: May 1, 1998
Birthday: February 17, 1996
Gender: Male

Poem:
   Hair on his head is quite scant
   We suggest Baldy get a transplant
   Watching over the land of the free
   Hair in his eyes would make it hard to see!

B

Batty, the bat, has soft light brown fur and black eyes. She has a triangular, flesh-colored nose and a black stitched mouth. Her webbed feet are made of light brown felt and a felt thumb projects from the topside of each wing. She is the first Beanie to be produced with velcro on her body so that she can open and close her wings.

BATTY
the bat

Style #4035
Date Introduced: October 1, 1997
Date Retired: Current
Birthday: October 29, 1996
Gender: Unknown

Poem:
   Bats may make some people jitter
   Please don't be scared of this critter
   If you're lonely or have nothing to do
   This Beanie Baby would love to hug you!

Bernie, the dog, is a brown and cream-colored St. Bernard with black eye patches and floppy, dark brown ears. He has brown-rimmed black eyes, a black nose and a black thread mouth.

BERNIE
the St. Bernard

Style #4109
Date Introduced: January 1, 1997
Date Retired: September 22,1998
Birthday: October 3, 1996
Gender: Male

Poem:
This little dog can't wait to grow
To rescue people lost in the snow
Don't let him out – keep him on your shelf
He doesn't know how to rescue himself!

Bessie, the cow, is medium-brown and white with beige-colored "horns" and white and brown ears. She has black eyes, white hooves and a large white snout with black thread nostrils.

BESSIE
the brown and white cow

Style #4009
Date Introduced: Mid–1995
Date Retired: October 1, 1997
Birthday: June 27, 1995
Gender: Female

Poem:
Bessie the cow likes to dance and sing
Because music is her favorite thing
Every night when you are counting sheep
She'll sing you a song to help you sleep.

Blackie, the bear, is black with a medium-brown snout. He has black eyes and a black triangular nose.

BLACKIE
the black bear

Style #4011
Date Introduced: Mid–1994
Date Retired: September 15, 1998
Birthday: July 15, 1994
Gender: Male

Poem:
Living in a national park
He only played after dark
Then he met his friend Cubbie
Now they play when it's sunny!

B

Blizzard, the tiger, has black and white stripes. Her eyes are black with a blue outer rim. She has a velvety flesh-tone nose and two black string whiskers droop from each side of her mouth.

BLIZZARD
the black and white tiger

Style #4163
Date Introduced: May 11, 1997
Date Retired: May 1, 1998
Birthday: December 12, 1996
Gender: Female

Poem:
In the mountains where it's snowy and cold
Lives a beautiful tiger, I've been told
Black and white, she's hard to compare
Of all the tigers, she is most rare.

Bones, the dog, is light brown with dark brown ears and tail. He has black oval eyes, black thread eyebrows and a large black oval nose. He has a delightful "hangdog" expression on his long face.

BONES
the brown dog

Style #4001
Date Introduced: Mid–1994
Date Retired: May 1, 1998
Birthday: January 18, 1994
Gender: Male

Poem:
Bones is a dog that loves to chew
Chairs and a table and a smelly old shoe
"You're so destructive" all would shout
But that all stopped, when his teeth fell out!

Also found:
That stopped, when his teeth fell out!

Bongo, the brown tail monkey, is a medium-brown monkey with a tan face, ears, hands and feet. He has black eyes and a "V" stitched thread nose.

BONGO
the monkey with brown tail

Style #4067
Version #1: 3rd gen. swing tag–
  red and white tush tag
  Date Introduced: 1996
  Date Retired: 1996
Version #2: 4th gen. swing tag–
  red and white tush tag
  Date Introduced: 1997
  Date Retired: 1997
Gender: Male
Birthday: August 17, 1995

Poem:
Bongo the monkey lives in a tree
The happiest monkey you'll ever see
In his spare time he plays the guitar
One of these days he will be a big star!

Bongo, the tan tail monkey, is medium-brown with a tan face, ears, hands and feet. He has black eyes and a "V" stitched thread nose.

BONGO
the monkey with tan tail

Style #4067
Version #1: 3rd gen. swing tag—black and white tush tag
  Date Introduced: 1995
  Date Retired: 1996
Version #2: 3rd gen. swing tag—red and white tush tag
  Date Introduced: 1996
  Date Retired: 1996
Version #3: 4th gen. swing tag—red
          and white tush tag
  Date Introduced: 1996
  Date Retired: Current
Birthday: August 17, 1995
Gender: Male

Poem:
  Bongo the monkey lives in a tree
  The happiest monkey you'll ever see
  In his spare time he plays the guitar
  One of these days he will be a big star!

B

Britannia, the bear, is a Ty Europe exclusive. She resembles the retired new face Brown Teddy, with black eyes, a black nose and a red ribbon around her neck. She proudly wears an embroidered Union Jack Flag on her chest.

BRITANNIA
the brown bear
with the Union Jack Flag

Style #4601
Date Introduced: December 31, 1997
Date Retired: Current
Birthday: December 15, 1997
Gender: Female

Poem:
  Britannia the bear will sail the sea
  So she can be with you and me
  She's always sure to catch the tide
  And wear the Union Flag with pride

Bronty, the brontosaurus, is a bluish tie-dyed dinosaur with shades of gray and aqua. He walks on all fours and his black eyes peer up. Because of his scarcity, he is the most sought after of the three dinosaurs. Bronty was only produced with a third generation heart tag.

BRONTY
the brontosaurus

Style #4085
Date Introduced: Mid–1995
Date Retired: 1996
Birthday: Unknown
Gender: Unknown

Poem:
  None available

Brownie, the bear, was the original name for Cubbie. He is a medium-brown colored bear with a lighter colored snout. He has black eyes and a brown triangular nose. He was produced only in Korea, and only with a first generation heart tag.

BROWNIE
the brown bear

Style #4010
Date Introduced: 1993
Date Retired: 1993
Birthday: Unknown
Gender: Male

Poem:
  None available

The Beanie Babies Collection
Brownie ™: Style 4010
TY (UK) LTD. P.O. BOX 18 WATERLOOVILLE
HANTS PO8 9RF
REMOVE TAG/RIBBON BEFORE
GIVING TO A CHILD.
FOR AGES 3 & UP.
RETAIN TAG FOR
REFERENCE.
CE

Beanie Mania II

Bruno, the terrier, is a brown and white dog. He has brown-rimmed black eyes, a black nose, a long snout and a black stitched mouth. He has white paws and a white tipped tail.

BRUNO
the terrier

Style #4183
Date Introduced: December 31, 1997
Date Retired: September 18, 1998
Birthday: September 9, 1997
Gender: Male

Poem:
  Bruno the dog thinks he's a brute
  But all the other Beanies think he's cute
  He growls at his tail and runs in a ring
  And everyone says, "Oh, how darling!"

Bubbles, the fish, is black and yellow striped with an oval shaped body. She has black eyes, a yellow dorsal fin and a yellow tail. Two large yellow pectoral fins protrude from the sides of her body.

BUBBLES
the black and yellow fish

Style #4078
Date Introduced: Mid–1995
Date Retired: May 11, 1997
Birthday: July 2, 1995
Gender: Female

Poem:
  All day long Bubbles likes to swim
  She never gets tired of flapping her fins
  Bubbles lived in a sea of blue
  Now she is ready to come home with you!

Bucky, the beaver, is brown with a dark brown paddle shaped tail. He has black eyes, a black nose, black thread whiskers and tiny dark brown ears. His name comes from the two white felt "buck" teeth that protrude from his mouth.

BUCKY
the beaver

Style #4016
Date Introduced: 1996
Date Retired: December 31, 1997
Birthday: June 8, 1995
Gender: Male

Poem:
His teeth are as shiny as he can be
Often used for cutting trees
He hides in his dam night and day
Maybe for you he will come out and play!

Bumble, the bee, has black and yellow stripes. He has two black yarn antennae that are knotted at the top, and little black eyes. He rests on six tiny legs and is ready to take flight with his oversized black wings. Bumble was produced with a third and fourth generation heart tag with the fourth being the more rare of the two.

BUMBLE
the bee

Style #4045
Date Introduced: 1996
Date Retired: 1996
Birthday: October 16, 1995
Gender: Unknown
Version #1: 3rd gen. swing tag
Version #2: 4th gen. swing tag

Poem:
Bumble the bee will not sting you
It is only love that this bee will bring you
So don't be afraid to give this bee a hug
Because Bumble the bee is a love-bug!

Caw, the crow, is velvety black and is perched on orange feet. He has black eyes and an orange beak. His black wings blend in with the rest of his body, making them look inconspicuous. Caw was produced with a third generation heart tag only.

CAW
the crow
Style #4071
Date Introduced: Mid–1995
Date Retired: 1996
Birthday: Unknown
Gender: Unknown

Poem:
None available

C

Chilly, the polar bear, is smooth velvety-white with black eyes and a black triangular nose.

CHILLY
the polar bear

Style #4012
Date Introduced: Mid–1994
Date Retired: 1995
Birthday: Unknown
Gender: Unknown

Poem:
None available

Chip, the calico cat, is brown, black and white with white "fur" inside her ears, a white belly and white paws. She has gold-rimmed black eyes, a pink nose, white whiskers and a white thread mouth.

Poem:
Black and gold, brown and white
The shades of her coat are quite a sight
At mixing her colors she was a master
On anyone else it would be a disaster!

CHIP
the calico cat

Style #4121
Date Introduced: May 11, 1997
Date Retired: Current
Birthday: January 26, 1996
Gender: Female

Chocolate, the moose, is chocolate-brown with a long snout and dark brown rimmed eyes. One of his distinguishing features is his oversized orange antlers.

Poem:
Licorice, gum and peppermint candy
This moose always has these handy
There is one more thing he likes to eat
Can you guess his favorite sweet?

CHOCOLATE
the moose

Style #4015
Date Introduced: 1994
Date Retired: Current
Birthday: April 27, 1993
Gender: Male

Chops, the lamb, is cream-colored
with a black face and two-tone ears.
He has black eyes, a triangular pink
nose and a pink mouth.

Poem:
Chops is a little lamb
This lamb you'll surely know
Because every path that you may take
This lamb is sure to go!

CHOPS
the lamb

Style #4019
Date Introduced: 1996
Date Retired: January 1, 1997
Birthday: May 3, 1996
Gender: Unknown

Clubby, the bear, is available exclusively to
members of the Beanie Babies Official Club.
He is a royal blue bear with a club pin on his
chest and a rainbow-colored ribbon around
his neck. He has black eyes and
a black oval nose.

CLUBBY
the bear

Style#: Not available
Date Introduced: May 1, 1998
Date Retired: Current
Birthday: July 7, 1998
Gender: Male

Poem:
Wearing his club pin for all to see
He's a proud member like you and me
Made especially with you in mind
Clubby the bear is one of a kind!

Claude, the tie-dyed crab, has eight legs and two pincer claws. His black eyes are set close together and two black string feelers protrude from his face. Claude's tie-dyed colors consist primarily of earth tones such as orange, rust, burgundy, green, blue and brown, and he rests on his solid beige belly.

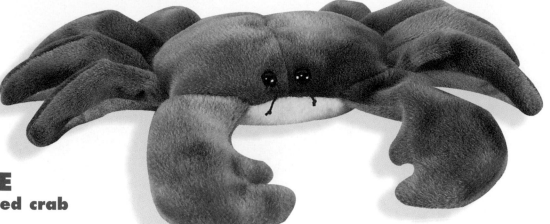

CLAUDE
the tie-dyed crab

Style #4083
Date Introduced: May 11, 1997
Date Retired: Current
Birthday: September 3, 1996
Gender: Male

Poem:
Claude the crab paints by the sea
A famous artist he hopes to be
But the tide came in and his paints fell
Now his art is on his shell!

Congo, the gorilla, is black with black eyes and a black nose. He sits upright with his arms extended. Congo has a brown face, brown hands, feet and ears.

CONGO
the gorilla

Style #4160
Date Introduced: Mid–1996
Date Retired: Current
Birthday: November 9, 1996
Gender: Male

Poem:
Black as night and fierce is he
On the ground or in a tree
Strong and mighty as the Congo
He's related to our Bongo!

Coral, the fish, is a multi-colored tie-dyed fish. He has black eyes, a dorsal fin and a tail. Two over-sized pectoral fins protrude from the sides of his body.

CORAL
the tie-dyed fish

Style #4079
Date Introduced: 1996
Date Retired: January 1, 1997
Birthday: March 2, 1995
Gender: Unknown

Poem:
Coral is beautiful, as you know
Made of colors in the rainbow
Whether it's pink, yellow, or blue
These colors were chosen just for you!

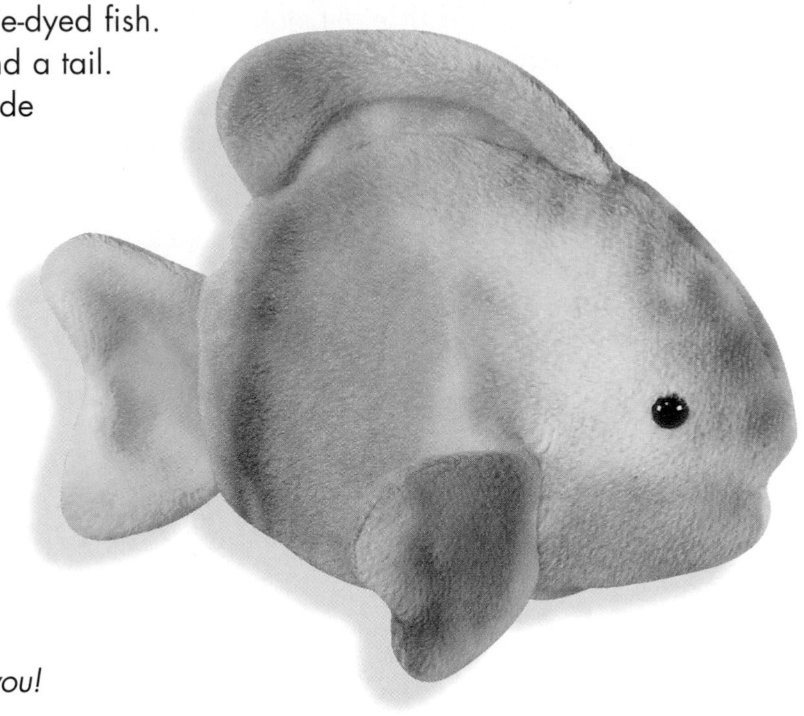

C

Crunch, the shark, is bluish-gray with a white belly and black eyes. He has a sleek, streamlined appearance with two pectoral fins, a large dorsal fin and tail. Crunch has a red mouth and two rows of felt white teeth.

Poem:
What's for breakfast? What's for lunch?
Yum! Delicious! Munch, munch, munch!
He's eating everything by the bunch
That's the reason we named him Crunch!

CRUNCH
the shark

Style #4130
Date Introduced: January 1, 1997
Date Retired: September 24, 1998
Birthday: January 13, 1996
Gender: Male

Cubbie, the brown bear has honey-colored brown fur, and a lighter brown snout. He has black eyes and a brown nose. Cubbie was introduced in 1994, taking the place of Brownie the bear.

CUBBIE
the brown bear

Style #4010
Date Introduced: 1994
Date Retired: December 31, 1997
Birthday: November 14, 1993
Gender: Male

Poem:
Cubbie used to eat crackers and honey
And what happened to him was funny
He was stung by fourteen bees
Now Cubbie eats broccoli and cheese!

Curly, the light brown-napped teddy, has black eyes, a brown oval nose and a burgundy ribbon tied around his neck.

CURLY
the brown napped teddy

Style #4052
Date Introduced: Mid–1996
Date Retired: Current
Birthday: April 12, 1996
Gender: Male

Poem:
A bear so cute with hair that's curly
You will love and want him surely
To this bear always be true
He will be a friend to you!

Daisy, the cow, is black and white with beige-colored "horns" and two-tone ears. She has black eyes, a large white snout with black thread nostrils and a white spot on her back.

Poem:
Daisy drinks milk each night
So her coat is shiny and bright
Milk is good for your hair and skin
What a way for your day to begin!

DAISY
the black cow

Style #4006
Date Introduced: Mid–1994
Date Retired: September 15, 1998
Birthday: May 10, 1994
Gender: Female

Derby, the coarse-mane horse with a star, is light brown with a darker brown mane and tail. He has two-tone ears, and his eyes and thread nostrils are black. He has approximately 8 thick pieces of yarn for a tail. A white "star" in the middle of his forehead is his most prominent feature.

DERBY
the coarse-mane horse with a star

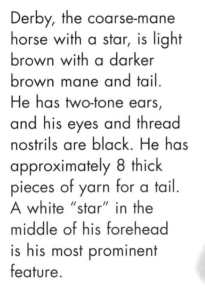

Style #4008
Date Introduced: January 1998
Date Retired: Current
Birthday: September 16, 1995
Gender: Male

Poem:
All the other horses used to tattle
Because Derby never wore his saddle
He left the stables, and the horses too
Just so Derby can be with you!

Derby, the coarse-mane horse, is light brown with a darker brown mane and tail. He has two-tone ears, and his eyes and thread nostrils are black. He has approximately 8 thick pieces of yarn for a tail.

DERBY
the coarse-mane horse without a star

Style #4008
Date Introduced: 1996
Date Retired: 1998
Birthday: September 16, 1995
Gender: Male

Poem:
All the other horses used to tattle
Because Derby never wore his saddle
He left the stables, and the horses too
Just so Derby can be with you!

Derby, the fine-mane horse, is light brown with a darker brown mane and tail. He has two-tone ears, and his eyes and thread nostrils are black. He has approximately 20 pieces of yarn for a tail, and was only produced with a third generation heart tag.

DERBY
the fine-mane horse

Style #4008
Date Introduced: Mid–1995
Date Retired: 1995
Birthday: Unknown
Gender: Male

Poem:
None available

Digger, the orange crab, has
eight legs and two pincer
claws. Her black eyes
are set close together
and two black string
feelers protrude from
her face.

DIGGER
the orange crab

Style #4027
Date Introduced: Mid–1994
Date Retired: 1995
Birthday: Unknown
Gender: Female

Poem:
   None available

Digger, the red crab, has eight legs and
two pincer claws. She has black eyes
and two black string feelers protrude from
her face.

DIGGER
the red crab

Style #4027
Date Introduced: Mid–1995
Date Retired: May 11, 1997
Birthday: August 23, 1995
Gender: Female

Poem:
   Digging in the sand and walking sideways
   That's how Digger spends her days
   Hard on the outside but sweet deep inside
   Basking in the sun and riding the tide!

Also found:
   Basking in the sun, riding the tide!

Doby, the Doberman, is a black and brown dog with two-tone ears, brown paws and the characteristic "markings" of a Doberman. He has brown-rimmed black eyes, a black nose and a black thread mouth.

DOBY
the doberman

Style #4110
Date Introduced: January 1, 1997
Date Retired: Current
Birthday: October 9, 1996
Gender: Male

Poem:
This dog is little but he has might
Keep him close when you sleep at night
He lays around with nothing to do
Until he sees it's time to protect you!

Doodle, the rooster, is tie-dyed with shades of red, pink and yellow. He has dangling yellow feet, a yellow beak and gold-rimmed black eyes. A red felt crest, and a wattle under his chin, complement Doodle's red wings. Doodle was officially renamed Strut in August 1997.

DOODLE
the rooster

Style #4171
Date Introduced: May 11, 1997
Date Retired: December 1997
Birthday: March 8, 1996
Gender: Male

Poem:
Listen closely to "Cock-a-doodle-doo"
What's the rooster saying to you?
Hurry, wake up sleepy head
We have lots to do, get out of bed!

Dotty, the dalmatian, is a white dog with black spots splattered from head to tail. She has black eyes, a black triangular nose and a black thread mouth. She is distinguished from Sparky, the dalmatian, by her black ears and tail.

DOTTY
the dalmatian
with black ears

Style #4100
Date Introduced: May 11, 1997
Date Retired: Current
Birthday: October 17, 1996
Gender: Female

Poem:
The Beanies all thought it was a big joke
While writing her tag, the ink pen broke
She got in the way, and got all spotty
So now the Beanies call her Dotty!

D

Early, the robin, has a dark gold beak, webbed medium-brown feet and a bright red breast. He is a brown tie-dyed bird with cream colored fabric under his tail, feathers and rump.

EARLY
the robin

Style #4190
Date Introduced: May 30, 1998
Date Retired: Current
Birthday: March 20, 1997
Gender: Male

Poem:
Early is a red breasted robin
For a worm he'll soon be bobbin'
Always known as a sign of spring
This happy robin loves to sing!

Ears, the brown rabbit, has long, floppy brown and white ears, a white snout and black eyes. Pink whiskers, a pink nose and a white "cottontail" add to this bunny's charm.

EARS
the brown rabbit

Style #4018
Date Introduced: 1996
Date Retired: May 1, 1998
Birthday: April 18, 1995
Gender: Male

Poem:
He's been eating carrots so long
Didn't understand what was wrong
Couldn't see the board during classes
Until the doctor gave him glasses.

E

Echo, the dolphin, has black eyes, a bluish-gray topside and a white belly. She has black eyes, a beak-like snout, horizontal tail flukes, flippers, and a dorsal fin.

ECHO
the dolphin

Style #4180
Date Introduced: May 11, 1997
Date Retired: May 1, 1998
Birthday: December 21, 1996
Gender: Female

Poem:
Echo the dolphin lives in the sea
Playing with her friends, like you and me
Through the waves she echos the sound
"I'm so glad to have you around!"

Erin, the bear, is emerald-colored with black eyes and a black oval nose. For the "luck of the Irish," she wears a white embroidered shamrock on her chest.

ERIN
the green bear
with white shamrock

Style #4186
Date Introduced: January 31, 1998
Date Retired: Current
Birthday: March 17, 1997
Gender: Female

Poem:
Named after the beautiful Emerald Isle
This Beanie Baby will make you smile,
A bit of luck, a pot of gold,
Light up the faces, both young and old!

Fetch, the golden retriever, has a soft tan coat, black eyes, a black nose and a black stitched thread mouth.

FETCH
the golden retriever

Style #4189
Date Introduced: May 30, 1998
Date Retired: Current
Birthday: February 4, 1997
Gender: Unknown

Poem:
Fetch is alert at the crack of dawn
Walking through dew drops on the lawn
Always golden, loyal and true
This little puppy is the one for you!

Flash, the dolphin, is gray with a white belly. She has black eyes, a beak-like snout, horizontal tail flukes, flippers and a dorsal fin.

Poem:
You know dolphins are a smart breed
Our friend Flash knows how to read
Splash the whale is the one who taught her
Although reading is difficult under the water!

FLASH
the dolphin

Style #4021
Date Introduced: 1994
Date Retired: May 11, 1997
Birthday: May 13, 1993
Gender: Female

Fleece, the lamb is made up entirely of ivory-colored nappy fabric, except for her smooth, beige-colored face and ears. She has black eyes, a pink nose and a pink thread mouth.

FLEECE
the napped lamb

Style #4125
Date Introduced: January 1, 1997
Date Retired: Current
Birthday: March 21, 1996
Gender: Female

Poem:
Fleece would like to sing a lullaby
Please be patient, she's rather shy
When you sleep, keep her by your ear
Her song will leave you nothing to fear.

Flip, the white cat, has blue eyes which create a striking contrast to her all-white body and head. Her nose, whiskers and mouth are pink. Her pink ears curve inward, and have rounded tips.

Poem:
Flip the cat is an acrobat
She loves playing on her mat
This cat flips with such grace and flair
She can somersault in mid-air!

FLIP
the white cat

Style #4012
Date Introduced: 1996
Date Retired: October 1, 1997
Birthday: February 28, 1995
Gender: Female

Floppity, the lavender bunny, wears a matching lavender ribbon around his neck. He has "floppity" pink and lavender ears, black eyes, pink nose and whiskers and a small white tail.

FLOPPITY
the lavender bunny

Style #4118
Date Introduced: January 1, 1997
Date Retired: May 1, 1998
Birthday: May 28, 1996
Gender: Unknown

Poem:
Floppity hops from here to there
Searching for eggs without a care
Lavender coat from head to toe
All dressed up and nowhere to go!

Flutter, the butterfly, has a black body and tie-dyed wings. He has
two black antennae, and two knotted pieces of string for eyes.
Varying in color from dazzling to drab, Flutter was
produced with a third generation
heart tag only.

FLUTTER
the tie-dyed butterfly

Style #4043
Date Introduced: Mid–1995
Date Retired: 1996
Birthday: Unknown
Gender: Unknown

Poem:
  None available

Fortune, the panda bear, sits upright and
wears a red ribbon around his neck. He
has black ears, a small triangular black
nose and characteristic black markings
under his black eyes.

FORTUNE
the panda

Style #4196
Date Introduced: May 30, 1998
Date Retired: Current
Birthday: December 6, 1997
Gender: Unknown

Poem:
  Nibbling on a bamboo tree
  This little panda is hard to see
  You're so lucky with this one you found
  Only a few are still around!

Freckles, the leopard, has an ivory-colored body that is covered from head to tail with dark brown spots with gold centers. He has a flesh colored nose, black whiskers and black eyes with a gold outer rim.

Poem:
From the tree he hunts his prey
In the night and in the day
He's the king of camouflage
Look real close, he's no mirage!

FRECKLES
the leopard

Style #4066
Date Introduced: Mid–1996
Date Retired: Current
Birthday: June 3, 1996
            July 28, 1996
Gender: Male

F

Garcia, the bear, is tie-dyed with black eyes and a large black oval nose.

GARCIA
the tie-dyed bear

Style #4051
Date Introduced: 1996
Date Retired: May 11, 1997
Birthday: August 1, 1995
Gender: Male

Poem:
The Beanies used to follow him around
Because Garcia traveled from town to town
He's pretty popular as you can see
Some even say he's legendary.

Note: Most have "use to" in the first line, but some were printed correctly with "used to".

Gigi, the French poodle, resembles Scottie, the retired terrier, except that her nappy fur is smooth along her back and snout. Her ears are larger and floppy. She has black eyes, a black nose and sports bright red ribbons on each ear.

GIGI
the poodle

Style #4191
Date Introduced: May 30, 1998
Date Retired: Current
Birthday: April 7, 1997
Gender: Female

Poem:
Prancing and dancing all down the street
Thinking her hairdo is oh so neat
Always so careful in the wind and rain
She's a dog that is anything but plain!

Glory, the bear, has black eyes and a black oval nose. He shares his July 4th birthday with Lefty and Righty. Red and blue stars adorn his white body and he proudly wears a U.S. flag on his chest.

GLORY
the bear

Style #4188
Date Introduced: May 30, 1998
Date Retired: Current
Birthday: July 4, 1997
Gender: Unknown

Poem:
Wearing the flag for all to see
Symbol of freedom for you and me
Red white and blue – Independence Day
Happy Birthday USA!

Gobbles, the turkey, has a brown body and a red head. She has black eyes, yellow feet, and black thread nostrils are sewn onto her yellow beak. Her two-tone wings are lined with yellow fabric, and her brown, red and white tail feathers are sewn in nine separate sections. She has a red felt wattle that extends from her beak to her chest.

GOBBLES
the turkey

Style #4034
Date Introduced: October 1, 1997
Date Retired: Current
Birthday: November 27, 1996
Gender: Female

Poem:
Gobbles the turkey loves to eat
Once a year she has a feast
I have a secret I'd like to divulge
If she eats too much her tummy will bulge!

G

Goldie, the goldfish, has black eyes, a puckered mouth, and two over-sized pectoral fins protrude from the sides of her body. She has a large dorsal fin, and a tail.

GOLDIE
the goldfish

Style #4023
Date Introduced: Mid–1994
Date Retired: December 31, 1997
Birthday: November 14, 1994
Gender: Female

Poem:
She's got rhythm, she's got soul
What more to like in a fishbowl?
Through sound waves Goldie swam
Because this goldfish likes to jam.

Gracie, the swan, has a completely white body and wings. She has small black eyes, an orange beak and webbed orange feet.

GRACIE
the swan

Style #4126
Date Introduced: January 1, 1997
Date Retired: May 1, 1998
Birthday: June 17, 1996
Gender: Female

Poem:
As a duckling, she was confused
Birds on the lake were quite amused
Poking fun until she would cry,
Now the most beautiful swan at Ty!

Grunt, the razorback, is a red hog with black eyes, thread eyebrows, and thread nostrils sewn onto his red snout. Thick, white felt tusks flare up from each side of his mouth. He has small, pointed red ears, and razor-like felt spikes protrude from his back and extend the length of his body.

Poem:
Some Beanies think Grunt is tough
No surprise, he's scary enough
But if you take him home you'll see
Grunt is the sweetest Beanie Baby!

GRUNT
the razorback

Style #4092
Date Introduced: 1996
Date Retired: May 11, 1997
Birthday: July 19, 1995
Gender: Male

Happy, the gray hippo, has tiny black eyes, small rounded ears and soft velvety gray fur.

HAPPY
the gray hippo

Style #4061
Date Introduced:
Mid–1994
Date Retired: 1995
Birthday: Unknown
Gender: Male

Poem:
   None available

Happy, the lavender hippo, has tiny black eyes, small rounded ears and lavender fur.

HAPPY
the lavender hippo

Style #4061
Date Introduced: Mid–1995
Date Retired: May 1, 1998
Birthday: February 25, 1994
Gender: Male

Poem:
   Happy the hippo loves to wade
   In the river and in the shade
   When Happy shoots water out of his snout
   You know he's happy without a doubt!

Hippity, the mint green bunny, has pink and green ears, black eyes, a pink nose, pink whiskers and a white tail. He wears a green ribbon around his neck.

HIPPITY
the mint green bunny

Style #4119
Date Introduced: January 1, 1997
Date Retired: May 1, 1998
Birthday: June 1, 1996
Gender: Male

Poem:
Hippity is a cute little bunny
Dressed in green, he looks quite funny
Twitching his nose in the air
Sniffing a flower here and there!

Hissy, the snake, is bluish-green tie-dyed, with a lime green belly, large black eyes and a forked red tongue. Elastic inside the length of his body creates the coiled affect.

HISSY
the snake

Style #4185
Date Introduced: December 31, 1997
Date Retired: Current
Birthday: April 4, 1997
Gender: Male

Poem:
Curled and coiled and ready to play
He waits for you patiently every day
He'll keep his best friend, but not his skin
And stay with you through thick and thin!

Hoot, the owl, is brown and tan. He has black eyes, two-tone brown and tan wings and a small orange felt beak.

HOOT
the owl

Style #4073
Date Introduced: 1996
Date Retired: October 1, 1997
Birthday: August 9, 1995
Gender: Unknown

Poem:
Late to bed, late to rise
Nevertheless, Hoot's quite wise
Studies by candlelight, nothing new
Like a president, do you know whooo?

Also found:
Nevertheless, Hoot's "qutie" wise
Nevertheless, Hoot is quite wise

Hoppity, the rose bunny, has black eyes, a pink nose and pink whiskers. The ribbon around her neck matches her soft pink color, and she has a fluffy white tail.

HOPPITY
the rose bunny

Style #4117
Date Introduced: January 1, 1997
Date Retired: May 1, 1998
Birthday: April 3, 1996
Gender: Female

Poem:
Hopscotch is what she likes to play
If you don't join in, she'll hop away
So play a game if you have the time,
She likes to play, rain or shine!

Humphrey, the camel, is a deep-tan color with black eyes and thread nostrils. He has one hump that protrudes from the top of his back and a long knotted tail.

HUMPHREY
the camel

Style #4060
Date Introduced: Mid–1994
Date Retired: 1995
Birthday: Unknown
Gender: Unknown

Poem:
   None available

Iggy, the iguana, is a bluish-green tie-dyed lizard. He has yellow eyes, a lime-green thread mouth, a long curled tail and felt avacado spikes down his back. Iggy was originally issued with a collar and "Rainbow" heart and tush tags.

IGGY
the iguana

Style #4038
Date Introduced: August, 1998
Date Retired: Current
Birthday: August 12, 1997
Gender: Male

Poem:
   Sitting on a rock, basking in the sun
   Is this iguana's idea of fun
   Towel and glasses, book and beach chair
   His life is so perfect without a care!

Iggy with collar and
"Rainbow" heart & tush tags.
Intro: December 31, 1997
Retired: August 1998

Inch, the inchworm, has five multi-colored segments: yellow, orange, green, blue, and fuchsia. He has black eyes and rounded felt antennae.

INCH
the inchworm
with felt antennas

Style #4044
Date Introduced: 1996
Date Retired: 1996
Birthday: Unknown
Gender: Male

Poem:
None available

Inch, the inchworm, has five multi-colored segments: yellow, orange, green, blue, and fuchsia. He has black eyes and black yarn antennae that are knotted at the end.

INCH
the inchworm
with yarn antennas

Style #4044
Date Introduced: 1996
Date Retired: May 1, 1998
Birthday: September 3, 1995
Gender: Male

Poem:
Inch the worm is a friend of mine
He goes so slow all the time
Inching around from here to there
Traveling the world without a care!

Inky, the pink octopus, has black and white oval eyes. His large head is filled with pellets and stuffing, and eight tentacles swoop below his body. Even though Inky was designed to have eight tentacles, it is not unusual to find Inky with nine or ten tentacles.

INKY
the pink octopus

Style #4028
Date Introduced: Mid–1995
Date Retired: May 1, 1998
Birthday: November 29, 1994
Gender: Male

Poem:
*Inky's head is big and round
As he swims he makes no sound
If you need a hand, don't hesitate
Inky can help because he has eight!*

Inky, the tan octopus, has black and white oval eyes. His large head is filled with pellets and stuffing and eight tentacles swoop below his body. He appeared with a "V" shaped mouth in 1995. The majority of these Inkys have the third generation heart tag.

INKY
the tan octopus
with a mouth

Style #4028
Date Introduced: 1995
Date Retired: 1995
Birthday: Unknown
Gender: Male

Poem:
None available

Inky, the tan octopus with a mouth, has black and white oval eyes. His large head is filled with pellets and stuffing and eight tentacles swoop below his body. He was first produced without a mouth. The majority of these Inkys have the first and second generation heart tags.

INKY
the tan octopus without a mouth

Style #4028
Date Introduced: Mid–1994
Date Retired: 1994
Birthday: Unknown
Gender: Male

Poem:
  None available

Jabber, the parrot, is a multi-colored parrot. His bright red body is accented with wings of blue, green and yellow. The top of his head is blue, and there are characteristic black and white "stripes" on his face. He has a hooked yellow bill, big yellow feet, and yellow rimmed black eyes.

JABBER
the parrot

Style #4197
Date Introduced: May 30, 1998
Date Retired: Current
Birthday: October 10, 1997
Gender: Male

Poem:
  Teaching Jabber to move his beak
  A large vocabulary he now can speak
  Jabber will repeat what you say
  Teach him a new word everyday!

Jake, the mallard duck, has a dark teal head, gold beak with black thread nostrils, black eyes and a beige "collar." He has a tie-dyed brown and gray body and the underside of his dark gray wings is beige. He has teal and beige tail feathers, and gold webbed feet.

JAKE
the mallard duck

Style #4199
Date Introduced: May 30, 1998
Date Retired: Current
Birthday: April 16, 1997
Gender: Male

Poem:
Jake the drake likes to splash in a puddle
Take him home and give him a cuddle
Quack, Quack, Quack, he will say
He's so glad you're here to play!

Jolly, the walrus, is brown with black eyes and a large black oval nose. He has a thick, light brown, fur moustache and two cream colored tusks protrude from his mouth.

JOLLY
the walrus

Style #4082
Date Introduced: May 11, 1997
Date Retired: May 1, 1998
Birthday: December 2, 1996
Gender: Male

Poem:
Jolly the walrus is not very serious
He laughs and laughs until he's delirious
He often reminds me of my dad
Always happy, never sad!

Kiwi, the toucan, is a brightly colored black, red, yellow and blue bird. He has black eyes and his oversized royal blue bill droops down toward his body. He perches majestically on royal blue feet.

KIWI
the toucan

Style #4070
Date Introduced: Mid–1995
Date Retired: January 1, 1997
Birthday: September 16, 1995
Gender: Male

Poem:
Kiwi waits for April showers
Watching a garden bloom with flowers
Their trees grow with fruit that's sweet
I'm sure you'll guess his favorite treat!

Kuku, the cockatoo, is a fancy white bird with fluffy pink "hair," yellow rimmed eyes and pink fabric under his tail and feathers. He has a gray beak and matching gray webbed feet.

KUKU
the cockatoo

Style #4192
Date Introduced: May 30, 1998
Date Retired: Current
Birthday: January 5, 1997
Gender: Male

Poem:
This fancy bird loves to converse
He talks in poems, rhythms and verse
So take him home and give him some time
You'll be surprised how he can rhyme!

K

Lefty, the donkey, is grayish blue with a black muzzle and black hooves. He has black eyes, two-tone ears and a black mane and tail made out of yarn. He was introduced in 1996, the same year as the presidential election and was given the name Lefty to honor the Democratic Party.

Poem:
Donkeys to the left, elephants to the right
Often seems like a crazy sight
This whole game seems very funny
Until you realize they're spending your money!

LEFTY
the American flag donkey

Style #4085
Date Introduced: Mid–1996
Date Retired: January 1, 1997
Birthday: July 4, 1996
Gender: Unknown

Legs, the frog, is solid green. His eyes are black with a green outer rim.

Poem:
Legs lives in a hollow log
Legs likes to play leap frog
If you like to hang out at the lake
Legs will be the new friend you'll make!

LEGS
the frog

Style #4020
Date Introduced: 1994
Date Retired: October 1, 1997
Birthday: April 25, 1993
Gender: Unknown

Libearty, the bear, is white with a red and blue ribbon tied around his neck. He has a brown oval nose and black eyes. He wears the American flag proudly on his chest.

LIBEARTY
the white bear with American flag

Style #4057
Date Introduced: Mid–1996
Date Retired: January 1, 1997
Birthday: Summer 1996
Gender: Unknown

Poem:
I am called libearty
I wear the flag for all to see
Hope and freedom is my way
That's why I wear flag USA

Note: Libearty is capitalized only on the very first tags to come out where the swing tag said, "Summer Olympics 1996, Atlanta, GA," but the word Olympics was whited-out. Subsequent tags all have Libearty uncapitalized.

L

Lizzy, the lizard, is blue and black with a yellow and orange belly. She has an elongated body with black eyes, four appendages, and a long tail. Protruding from her mouth is a forked tongue made of thick red felt.

Poem:
Lizzy loves Legs the frog
She hides with him under logs
Both of them search for flies
Underneath the clear blue skies.

LIZZY
the blue/black lizard

Style #4033
Date Introduced: 1996
Date Retired: December 31, 1997
Birthday: May 11, 1995
Gender: Female

Lizzy, the tie-dyed lizard, is made up of a wide range of vibrant colors. She has a thin, elongated body with black eyes, four appendages and a long tail. Protruding from her mouth is a forked tongue made of thick red felt. The tie-dyed version of Lizzy was issued with a third generation heart tag only.

LIZZY
the tie-dyed lizard

Style #4033
Date Introduced: Mid–1995
Date Retired: 1995
Birthday: Unknown
Gender: Female

Poem:
   None available

L

Lucky, the ladybug, was first produced with seven "Lucky" felt, glued-on dots. Her head, eyes and knotted thread antennae are black. She rests on her black belly with six black felt legs protruding from her sides.

LUCKY
the ladybug
with 7 felt dots

Style #4040
Date Introduced: Mid–1994
Date Retired: 1996
Birthday: Unknown
Gender: Female

Poem:
   None available

Lucky, the ladybug, has approximately 11 "Lucky" dots printed on the fabric. Depending on how the fabric was cut, many of them appear with partial dots.

LUCKY
the ladybug with 11 dots

Style #4040
Date Introduced: 1996
Date Retired: May 1, 1998
Birthday: May 1, 1995
Gender: Female

Poem:
Lucky the ladybug loves the lotto
"Someone must win" that's her motto
But save your dimes and even a penny
Don't spend on the lotto and you'll have many!

Lucky, the ladybug, has approximately 21 small dots printed on the fabric. This ladybug is very scarce, because it was only available for a few months in 1996.

LUCKY
the ladybug with 21 dots

Style #4040
Date Introduced: 1996
Date Retired: 1997
Birthday: May 1, 1995
Gender: Female

Poem:
Lucky the ladybug loves the lotto
"Someone must win" that's her motto
But save your dimes and even a penny
Don't spend on the lotto and you'll have many!

Magic, the dragon with light pink stitching, has black eyes, tiny pink thread nostrils and a long curved tail. She has iridescent scales running down the back of her all-white body, and a large pair of iridescent wings top-stitched with light pink thread.

MAGIC
the dragon with light pink stitching

Style #4088
Date Introduced: Mid–1995
Date Retired: December 31, 1997
Birthday: September 5, 1995
Gender: Female

Poem:
   Magic the dragon lives in a dream
   The most beautiful that you have ever seen
   Through magic lands she likes to fly
   Look up and watch her, way up high!

Magic, the dragon with hot pink stitching, has black eyes, tiny pink thread nostrils and a long curved tail. She has iridescent scales running down the back of her all-white body, and a large pair of iridescent wings top-stitched with hot pink thread.

MAGIC
the dragon with hot pink stitching

Style #4088
Date Introduced: 1996
Date Retired: 1996
Birthday: September 5, 1995
Gender: Female

Poem:
   Magic the dragon lives in a dream
   The most beautiful that you have ever seen
   Through magic lands she likes to fly
   Look up and watch her, way up high!

Manny, the manatee, is gray with black eyes and black thread nostrils. Her body tapers to a horizontal, flattened tail. The forelimbs are flippers set close to the head. Her head is small with a straight snout and a cleft upper lip.

MANNY
the manatee

Style #4081
Date Introduced: 1996
Date Retired: May 11, 1997
Birthday: June 8, 1995
Gender: Female

Poem:
Manny is sometimes called a sea cow
She likes to twirl and likes to bow
Manny sure is glad you bought her
Because it's so lonely under water!

Maple, the bear, is white with a red ribbon tied around his neck. He has a brown oval nose and black eyes. He wears the Canadian flag proudly on his chest. Maple was originally named Pride, but the name was changed before being introduced to the public.

MAPLE
the white bear
with Canadian flag

Style #4600
Date Introduced: February 1997
Date Retired: Current
Birthday: July 1, 1996
Gender: Male
Version #1: 4th gen. swing tag
  Pride tush tag
Version #2: 4th gen. swing tag
  Maple tush tag

Poem:
Maple the bear likes to ski
With his friends, he plays hockey
He loves his pancakes and eats every crumb,
Can you guess which country he's from?

Special Olympics Maple - Ty Canada donated 5,000 Maples to the Canadian Special Olympics. At the Special Olympics Sports Celebrities Festival, these Maples were sold with an additional circular tag that says "Special Olympics Sports Festival" on the front, and the Special Olympics oath on the back.

MAPLE
the white bear with Canadian flag and Special Olympics tag

Style #4600
Date Introduced: August 1997
Date Retired: December 1997
Birthday: July 1, 1996
Gender: Male

Poem:
  Maple the bear likes to ski
  With his friends, he plays hockey
  He loves his pancakes and eats every crumb,
  Can you guess which country he's from?

Mel, the koala is gray and white with large, rounded white and gray ears, small black eyes and a black thread mouth that curves into a smile. He has a white belly, and his black oval-shaped nose is his most prominent feature.

MEL
the koala bear

Style #4162
Date Introduced: January 1, 1997
Date Retired: Current
Birthday: January 15, 1996
Gender: Male

Poem:
  How do you name a Koala bear?
  It's rather tough, I do declare!
  It confuses me, I get in a funk
  I'll name him Mel, my favorite hunk!

Mystic, the iridescent horn unicorn, is white with black nostrils and blue rimmed eyes. Her silvery horn is accented with a spiral of pink thread. She has approximately 8 thick pieces of yarn for a tail.

MYSTIC
the coarse-mane unicorn with iridescent horn

Style #4007
Date Introduced: November 1997
Date Retired: Current
Birthday: May 21, 1994
Gender: Female

Poem:
Once upon a time so far away
A unicorn was born one day in May
Keep Mystic with you, she's a prize
You'll see the magic in her blue eyes!

Mystic, the coarse-mane unicorn, is white with black nostrils, blue eyes and a tan horn that protrudes from the top of her head. She has approximately 8 thick pieces of yarn for a tail.

MYSTIC
the coarse-mane unicorn with tan horn

Style #4007
Date Introduced: 1996
Date Retired: November 1997
Birthday: May 21, 1994
Gender: Female

Poem:
Once upon a time so far away
A unicorn was born one day in May
Keep Mystic with you, she's a prize
You'll see the magic in her blue eyes!

Mystic, the fine-mane unicorn, is white with black nostrils, blue eyes and a tan horn that protrudes from the top of her head. She has approximately 20 pieces of fine yarn for a tail.

MYSTIC
the fine-mane unicorn

Style #4007
Date Introduced: Mid–1994
Date Retired: 1995
Birthday: Unknown
Gender: Female

Poem:
None available

Nana was the original name for Bongo. She is a medium-brown monkey with a tan face, ears, hands and feet. She has black eyes, a "V" stitched thread nose, a tan tail and a black and white 1995 tush tag. Nana, which carries only a third generation heart tag, was produced with either the name "Nana" on her heart tag, or with a white "Bongo" sticker covering up her name.

NANA
the monkey with tan tail

Style #4067
Date Introduced: 1995
Date Retired: 1995
Birthday: Unknown
Gender: Female

Poem:
None available

The Beanie Babies ™ Collection
© Ty Inc.
Oakbrook IL. U.S.A.
© Ty UK Ltd.
Waterlooville, Hants
PO8 8HH
© Ty Deutschland
90008 Nürnberg
Handmade in China

Nana™ style 4067
to _____
from _____
with
love

Nanook, the husky, is a charcoal gray and white dog with rounded two-tone ears and bright blue eyes. He has a black nose and a black thread mouth.

Poem:
  Nanook is a dog that loves cold weather
  To him a sled is light as a feather
  Over the snow and through the slush
  He runs at hearing the cry of "mush"!

NANOOK
the husky

Style #4104
Date Introduced: May 11, 1997
Date Retired: Current
Birthday: November 21, 1996
Gender: Male

Nip, the all gold cat, has a pink mouth, nose and whiskers. His pink ears curve inward and the tips are rounded. His body and head are completely gold, and his eyes are black with a gold outer rim. This version of Nip was only produced with a third generation heart tag.

NIP
the all gold cat
with pink ears
(no white on paws)

Style #4003
Date Introduced: 1995
Date Retired: 1995
Birthday: Unknown
Gender: Male

Poem:
  None available

Nip, the gold cat, has a larger face and body than the later Nips. His belly and the triangular shape on his face are white. He has a pink triangular nose and solid black eyes. His triangular pink ears stick straight up and are not curved like the later Nips. His mouth and whiskers are a light pink, as compared to the first Nips that were produced with a brighter pink color.

NIP
the gold cat with white face and belly

Style #4003
Date Introduced: 1995
Date Retired: 1995
Birthday: Unknown
Gender: Male

Poem:
  None available

Nip, the gold cat, has a white mouth, white whiskers, ears and paws. He has a pink nose and black eyes with a gold outer rim.

NIP
the gold cat with white paws

Style #4003
Date Introduced: 1996
Date Retired: December 31, 1997
Birthday: March 6, 1994
Gender: Male

Poem:
  His name is Nipper, but we call him Nip
  His best friend is a black cat named Zip
  Nip likes to run in races for fun
  He runs so fast he's always number one!

Nuts, the squirrel, is medium-brown and beige with a large bushy tail. He has beige and brown ears, black eyes, a black nose and brown whiskers.

NUTS
the squirrel

Style #4114
Date Introduced: January 1, 1997
Date Retired: Current
Birthday: January 21, 1996
Gender: Male

Poem:
*With his bushy tail, he'll scamper up a tree
The most cheerful critter you'll ever see,
He's nuts about nuts, and he loves to chat
Have you ever seen a squirrel like that?*

Patti, the deep fuchsia platypus, lays flat on her belly and four yellowish-gold webbed feet, full of stuffing, protrude from the sides of her body. Her black eyes peer up, and her yellowish-gold bill juts out waiting for a squeeze. She was the first platypus produced. She has the original black and white tush tag and the first generation hang tag.

PATTI
the deep fuchsia platypus

Style #4025
Date Introduced: 1993
Date Retired: 1993
Birthday: Unknown
Gender: Female

Poem:
None available

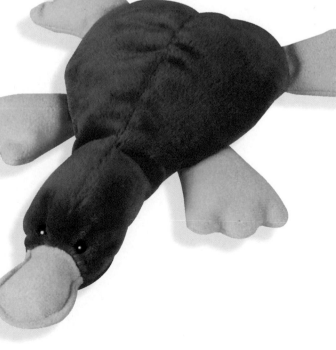

Patti, the fuchsia platypus, was the fourth Patti produced. She is the same color as the fuchsia segment found on Inch's tail.

PATTI
the fuchsia platypus

Style #4025
Date Introduced: 1996
Date Retired: May 1, 1998
Birthday: January 6, 1993
Gender: Female

Poem:
  Ran into Patti one day while walking
  Believe me she wouldn't stop talking!
  Listened and listened to her speak
  That would explain her extra large beak!

Patti, magenta, was the third Patti produced. She has a red overtone. The majority of these have the third generation tag.

PATTI
the magenta platypus

Style #4025
Date Introduced: 1995
Date Retired: 1995
Birthday: Unknown
Gender: Female

Poem:
  None available

Patti, the raspberry platypus, was the second Patti produced. She has a burgundy overtone. The majority of these have the first and second generation hang tag

PATTI
the raspberry platypus

Style #4025
Date Introduced: 1994
Date Retired: 1994
Birthday: Unknown
Gender: Female

Poem:
None available

Peace, the pastel tie-dyed bear has black eyes, a large black oval nose and wears a multi-colored peace sign on the left side of his chest.

PEACE
the pastel tie-dyed bear

Style #4053
Date Introduced: July 1998
Date Retired: Current
Birthday: February 1, 1996
Gender: Unknown

Poem:
All races, all colors, under the sun
Join hands together and have some fun
Dance to the music, rock and roll is the sound
Symbols of peace and love abound!

Peace, the tie-dyed bear
Intro: May 11, 1997
Retired: July 1998

Peanut, the light blue elephant, has black eyes and oversized pink and blue ears.

PEANUT
the light blue elephant

Style #4062
Date Introduced: 1996
Date Retired: May 1, 1998
Birthday: January 25, 1995
Gender: Female

Poem:
Peanut the elephant walks on tip-toes
Quietly sneaking wherever she goes
She'll sneak up on you and a hug you will get
Peanut is a friend you won't soon forget!

Peanut, the royal blue elephant, has black eyes and oversized pink and blue ears. Originally, Peanut was supposed to be a light-blue color, but because of a communication error, she was produced with a royal blue color instead. This version of Peanut was only produced with a third generation heart tag.

PEANUT
the royal blue elephant

Style #4062
Date Introduced: Mid–1995
Date Retired: 1995
Birthday: Unknown
Gender: Female

Poem:
None available

Peking, the panda bear, has a white body with black legs, shoulders, arms, and tail. He has a black triangular nose. Black felt patches attached underneath his eyes complete his panda look.

PEKING
the panda

Style #4013
Date Introduced: Mid–1994
Date Retired: 1995
Birthday: Unknown
Gender: Unknown

Poem:
  None available

Pinchers, the red lobster, has two large pincer claws, black eyes and black string whiskers. Originally his tail segments were evenly spaced, and he was produced with a first generation heart tag. Eventually the three lines of stitching were placed closer together. The only way to tell which lobster you've "caught" is by the name on the heart tag.

PINCHERS
the lobster

Style #4026
Date Introduced: 1994
Date Retired: May 1, 1998
Birthday: June 19, 1993
Gender: Male

Poem:
  This lobster loves to pinch
  Eating his food inch by inch
  Balancing carefully with his tail
  Moving forward slow as a snail!

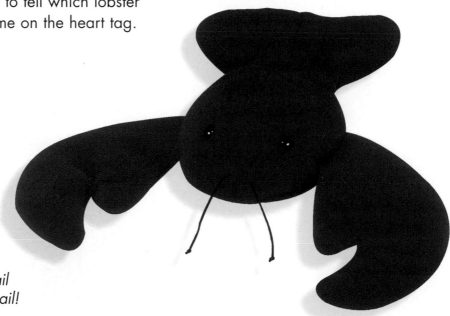

Pinky, the flamingo, is hot pink with lighter pink legs that dangle from her body and two-tone pink wings. She has black eyes and a large, slightly hooked orange beak.

PINKY
the flamingo

Style #4072
Date Introduced: 1996
Date Retired: Current
Birthday: February 13, 1995
Gender: Female

Poem:
Pinky loves the everglades
From the hottest pink she's made
With floppy legs and big orange beak
She's the Beanie that you seek!

Pouch, the kangaroo, is medium-brown and beige. She has black eyes, a black triangular nose and large two-tone ears. In her pouch, she carries a baby kangaroo.

POUCH
the kangaroo

Style #4161
Date Introduced: January 1, 1997
Date Retired: Current
Birthday: November 6, 1996
Gender: Female

Poem:
My little pouch is handy I've found
It helps me carry my baby around
I hop up and down without any fear
Knowing my baby is safe and near.

P

Pounce, the brown tie-dyed cat, has two-tone ears, a beige muzzle with a pink nose, beige paws and brown whiskers. He has black eyes with a gold outer rim.

POUNCE
the brown tie-dyed cat

Style #4122
Date Introduced: December 31, 1997
Date Retired: Current
Birthday: August 28, 1997
Gender: Unknown

Poem:
Sneaking and slinking down the hall
To pounce upon a fluffy yarn ball
Under the tables, around the chairs
Through the rooms and down the stairs!

P

Prance, the gray-striped cat, has a light gray body with evenly spaced charcoal gray stripes. She has two-tone ears, white paws, and blue rimmed eyes. Her nose, mouth, and whiskers are pink and she has a distinctive white spot on her forehead.

PRANCE
the gray striped cat

Style #4123
Date Introduced:
        December 31, 1997
Date Retired: Current
Birthday: November 20, 1997
Gender: Female

Poem:
She darts around and swats the air
Then looks confused when nothing's there
Pick her up and pet her soft fur
Listen closely, and you'll hear her purr!

Princess, the bear, is deep purple and was issued to honor the late Princess Diana. She has black eyes, a black oval nose and wears a purple ribbon around her neck. On her chest is an embroidered white rose with a long green stem.

PRINCESS
the Princess Diana Bear

Style #4300
Date Introduced: October 29, 1997
Date Retired: Current
Birthday: Unknown
Gender: Female

Poem:
> Like an angel she came from heaven above
> She shared her compassion, her pain, her love
> She only stayed with us long enough to teach
> The world to share, to give, to reach.

Puffer, the puffin, is a black and white marine bird with a large red and yellow bill. She has black triangular felt patches under her gold rimmed black eyes, white and black tail feathers and red webbed feet. Her velvety black wings blend in perfectly with her body.

PUFFER
the puffin

Style #4181
Date Introduced: December 31, 1997
Date Retired: September 18, 1998
Birthday: November 3, 1997
Gender: Female

Poem:
> What in the world does a puffin do?
> We're sure that you would like to know too
> We asked Puffer how she spends her days
> Before she answered, she flew away!

Pugsly, the pug dog, is tan-colored with short black ears, a black nose, large black muzzle and black eyes with a brown outer rim. He has a wrinkled forehead and a short upturned tail.

PUGSLY
the pug dog

Style#4106
Date Introduced: May 11, 1997
Date Retired: Current
Birthday: May 2, 1996
Gender: Male

Poem:
Pugsly is picky about what he will wear
Never a spot, a stain or a tear
Image is something of which he'll gloat
Until he noticed his wrinkled coat!

Punchers, the red lobster, has black eyes and black string whiskers. His tail segments are evenly spaced. He was made in Korea, and has a 1993 black and white tush tag. The only way you can distinguish Punchers from the original Pinchers is by the name on the first generation heart tag.

PUNCHERS
the lobster

Style#4026
Date Introduced: 1994
Date Retired: 1994
Birthday: Unknown
Gender: Male

Poem:
None available

The Beanie Babies Collection
Punchers ™· Style 4026
TY (UK) LTD. P.O. BOX 18 WATERLOOVILLE
HANTS. PO8 9RF
REMOVE TAG/RIBBON BEFORE
GIVING TO A CHILD.
FOR AGES 3 & UP.
RETAIN TAG FOR
REFERENCE.
CE

Quacker(s), the duck with wings, has a bright yellow body, oversized orange webbed feet and an orange bill. He has black eyes and black string eyebrows. The addition of wings allows him to stand upright, instead of leaning to one side as his wingless predecessor often did.

QUACKER(S)
the duck with wings

Style #4024
Date Introduced: 1995
Date Retired: May 1, 1998
Birthday: April 19, 1994
Gender: Male

Poem:
There is a duck by the name of Quackers
Every night he eats animal crackers
He swims in a lake that's clear and blue
But he'll come to the shore to be with you!

Quacker(s), the duck without wings, has a yellow body, orange, oversized webbed feet and an orange bill. He has black eyes and black string eyebrows. He was only produced with a first generation "Quackers" tag and a second generation "Quacker" tag.

The Beanie Babies Collection
Quackers ™ Style 4024
© 1993 Ty Inc. Oakbrook, IL. USA
All Rights Reserved. Caution
Remove this tag before giving
toy to a child. For ages 5 and up
Handmade in China
Surface
Wash

CE Distributeur
TylUKJLtd.
P.O.Box 18
Waterlooville
Hampshire PO8 8HG

The Beanie Babies Collection
Quacker ™ style 4024
© 1993 Ty Inc. Oakbrook, IL. USA
All Rights Reserved. Caution
Remove this tag before giving
toy to a child. For ages 3 and up
Handmade in China
Surface
Wash

QUACKER(S)
the duck without wings

Style #4024
Date Introduced: Mid–1994
Date Retired: 1995
Birthday: Unknown
Gender: Male

Poem:
None available

Radar, the bat, is black with two-tone ears, red eyes and a black triangular shaped nose. He has webbed feet that are made of black felt and a thumb that projects from the top of each wing.

RADAR
the bat

Style #4091
Date Introduced: 1996
Date Retired: May 11, 1997
Birthday: October 30, 1995
Gender: Male

Poem:
Radar the bat flies late at night
He can soar to an amazing height
If you see something as high as a star
Take a good look, it might be Radar!

Rainbow, the chameleon, is a pastel tie-dyed lizard. He has red eyes, a red thread mouth, a solid beige belly and a collar.

RAINBOW
the chameleon

Style #4037
Date Introduced: August, 1998
Date Retired: Current
Birthday: October 14, 1997
Gender: Male

Poem:
Red, green, blue and yellow
This chameleon is a colorful fellow
A blend of colors, his own unique hue
Rainbow was made especially for you!

Rainbow with spikes & "Iggy" heart and tush tags.
Intro: December 31, 1997
Retired: June 1998

Pastel Rainbow with tongue
Intro: July 1998
Retired: August 1998

Rainbow with tongue
Intro: June 1998
Retired: July 1998

Rex, the tyrannosaurus, is a pinkish tie-dyed dinosaur with shades of blue, green, burgundy, violet, gray and brown. His black eyes appear smaller because they are set deep in his face. The only dinosaur sold in the UK, Rex was produced in both China and Korea, with a third generation heart tag only.

REX
the tyrannosaurus

Style #4086
Date Introduced: Mid–1995
Date Retired: 1996
Birthday: Unknown
Gender: Unknown

Poem:
None available

Righty, the elephant, is gray with black eyes and oversized pink and gray ears. He was introduced the same year as the 1996 presidential election and was given the name Righty to represent the Republican Party. He proudly wears the American flag on the left side of his body.

RIGHTY
the American flag elephant

Style #4086
Date Introduced: Mid–1996
Date Retired: January 1, 1997
Birthday: July 4, 1996
Gender: Unknown

Poem:
Donkeys to the left, elephants to the right
Often seems like a crazy sight
This whole game seems very funny
Until you realize they're spending your money!

Ringo, the raccoon, is grayish-brown with two-tone black and white ears, a black triangular nose and black stripes on his tail. Two black thread whiskers hang from each side of his white snout, and he wears a black "mask" over his black eyes.

Poem:
Ringo hides behind his mask
He will come out, if you should ask
He loves to chitter, He loves to chatter
Just about anything, it doesn't matter!

RINGO
the raccoon

Style #4014
Date Introduced: 1996
Date Retired: September 16, 1998
Birthday: July 14, 1995
Gender: Male

R

Roary, the lion, is honey-colored with a medium-brown mane and bushy tail. He has white and brown ears, black eyes with a gold outer rim, a flesh colored nose, white chin and a brown thread mouth and whiskers.

Poem:
Deep in the jungle they crowned him king
But being brave is not his thing
A cowardly lion some may say
He hears his roar and runs away!

ROARY
the lion

Style #4069
Date Introduced: May 11, 1997
Date Retired: Current
Birthday: February 20, 1996
Gender: Male

Rocket, the blue jay, is a striking bright blue and white bird with a blue crested head. His wings and tail feathers are blue and white. He has black eyes, a black beak and black webbed feet.

ROCKET
the blue jay

Style #4202
Date Introduced: May 30, 1998
Date Retired: Current
Birthday: March 12, 1997
Gender: Male

Poem:
  Rocket is the fastest blue jay ever
  He flies in all sorts of weather
  Aerial tricks are his specialty
  He's so entertaining for you and me!

Rover, the dog, is a short red puppy with a long snout and long floppy ears. He has black eyes and a large black oval nose. Many collectors think he resembles "Clifford" the dog.

Poem:
  This dog is red and his name is Rover
  If you call him he is sure to come over
  He barks and plays with all his might
  But worry not, he won't bite!

ROVER
the red dog

Style #4101
Date Introduced: Mid–1996
Date Retired: May 1, 1998
Birthday: May 30, 1996
Gender: Male

Scoop, the pelican, is a large, bluish-gray bird with an enormous orange bill and large orange webbed feet. He has black eyes and black thread nostrils. His large wings stand off to the sides, as if he's about to take flight.

SCOOP
the pelican

Style #4107
Date Introduced: Mid–1996
Date Retired: Current
Birthday: July 1, 1996
Gender: Male

Poem:
  All day long he scoops up fish
  To fill his bill, is his wish
  Diving fast and diving low
  Hoping those fish are very slow!

S

Scottie, the Scottish terrier, is a short black dog with a black nappy coat. He has small black eyes, a black nose and small perky ears.

SCOTTIE
the Scottish terrier

Style #4102
Date Introduced: Mid–1996
Date Retired: May 1, 1998
Birthday: June 15, 1996
          June 3, 1996
Gender: Male

Poem:
  Scottie is a friendly sort
  Even though his legs are short
  He is always happy as can be
  His best friends are you and me!

Seamore, the seal, is white with paddle-like flippers. She has black eyes, a black triangular nose, black thread whiskers and tiny black eyebrows.

Poem:
Seamore is a little white seal
Fish and clams are her favorite meal
Playing and laughing in the sand
She's the happiest seal in the land!

SEAMORE
the seal

Style #4029
Date Introduced: Mid–1994
Date Retired: October 1, 1997
Birthday: December 14, 1996
Gender: Female

S

Seaweed, the otter, is dark brown with black eyes, a black nose and a lighter brown snout. Often posed reclining on her back, she holds a piece of green felt "seaweed" between her flippers.

SEAWEED
the otter

Style #4080
Date Introduced: 1996
Date Retired: September 19, 1998
Birthday: March 19, 1996
Gender: Female

Poem:
Seaweed is what she likes to eat
It's supposed to be a delicious treat
Have you tried a treat from the water
If you haven't, maybe you "otter"!

Slither, the snake, is green on top, with brown spots splattered from head to tail. He has a long elegant body that measures 23 inches in length. His bright yellow belly adds to his striking appearance. He has black eyes and protruding from his mouth is a red forked tongue.

SLITHER
the snake

Style #4031
Date Introduced: Mid–1994
Date Retired: 1995
Birthday: Unknown
Gender: Unknown

Poem:
   None available

S

Sly, the fox, is medium brown with a brown belly, a white chin, and two-tone ears. He has black eyes, a triangular nose, and two string whiskers project from each side of his mouth.

SLY
the brown-belly fox

Style #4115
Date Introduced: Mid–1996
Date Retired: 1996
Birthday: September 12, 1996
Gender: Male

Poem:
   Sly is a fox and tricky is he
   Please don't chase him, let him be
   If you want him, just say when
   He'll peek out from his den!

Sly, the fox, is medium brown with a white belly, chin, and
two-tone ears. He has black eyes, a triangular nose,
and two string whiskers project
from each side of his mouth.

SLY
the white-belly fox

Style #4115
Date Introduced: 1996
Date Retired: September 22, 1998
Birthday: September 12, 1996
Gender: Male

Poem:
Sly is a fox and tricky is he
Please don't chase him, let him be
If you want him, just say when
He'll peek out from his den!

Smoochy, the frog is bright green and orangish-yellow, with
bulging green-rimmed black eyes. He has orangish-yellow
"hands" and "feet," and has been spotted with three different
mouths: a single red thread, a double red thread and a
felt mouth.

SMOOCHY
the frog with
a felt mouth

Style #4039
Date Introduced: June 1998
Date Retired: Current
Birthday: October 1, 1997
Gender: Male

Poem:
Is he a frog or maybe a prince?
This confusion makes him wince
Find the answer, help him with this
Be the one to give him a kiss!

Smoochy with thread mouth
Intro: December 31, 1997
Retired: June 1998

Snip, the cat, is ivory-colored with the characteristic "markings" of a Siamese cat. She has brown paws, brown ears, a brown-tipped tail and a brown patch on her forehead. Snip has blue eyes, a black nose, brown whiskers and a brown thread mouth.

SNIP
the Siamese cat

Style #4120
Date Introduced: January 1, 1997
Date Retired: Current
Birthday: October 22, 1996
Gender: Female

Poem:
Snip the cat is Siamese
She'll be your friend if you please
So toss her a toy or a piece of string
Playing with you is her favorite thing!

S

Snort, the bull, is red with cream colored horns, paws and two-tone ears. He has black eyes, and black nostrils are sewn onto his cream colored snout.

SNORT
the red bull
with cream paws

Style #4002
Date Introduced: January 1, 1997
Date Retired: September 15, 1998
Birthday: May 15, 1995
Gender: Male

Poem:
Although Snort is not so tall
He loves to play basketball
He is a star player in his dreams
Can you guess his favorite team?

Note: Snort has also been found with the word Tabasco in the first line of the poem instead of Snort.

Snowball, the snowman, is a jolly white fellow with black oval eyes, an orange "carrot" nose and a large black "V" shaped thread mouth. He wears a felt black hat with a red band, and a red scarf with white fringe is tied around his neck. Two black "buttons" grace the front of his "snowsuit."

SNOWBALL
the snowman

Style #4201
Date Introduced: October 1, 1997
Date Retired: December 31, 1997
Birthday: December 22, 1996
Gender: Male

Poem:
There is a snowman, I've been told
That plays with Beanies out in the cold
What is better in a winter wonderland
Than a Beanie Snowman in your hand!

Sparky, the dalmatian, is white with black spots splattered from head to tail. He has black eyes, a black triangular nose, and a black sewn on mouth.

SPARKY
the dalmatian

Style #4100
Date Introduced: Mid–1996
Date Retired: May 11, 1997
Birthday: February 27, 1996
Gender: Male

Poem:
Sparky rides proud on the fire truck
Ringing the bell and pushing his luck
Gets underfoot when trying to help
Step on him and he'll let out a yelp!

Also found:
He often gets stepped on crying yelp!
Step on him and he'll let out a yelp!

Speedy, the turtle, is green with a distinctive brown-and-green dappled shell. He has small black eyes and a small green tail.

SPEEDY
the turtle

Style #4030
Date Introduced: Mid–1994
Date Retired: October 1, 1997
Birthday: August 14, 1994
Gender: Male

Poem:
Speedy ran marathons in the past
Such a shame, always last
Now Speedy is a big star
After he bought a racing car!

Spike, the rhinoceros, is a sturdy looking jungle beast with brown and gray ears, black eyes, a short gray tail and a brown horn.

SPIKE
the rhinoceros

Style #4060
Date Introduced: Mid–1996
Date Retired: Current
Birthday: August 13, 1996
Gender: Male

Poem:
Spike the rhino likes to stampede
He's the bruiser that you need
Gentle to birds on his back and spike
You can be his friend if you like!

Spinner, the spider, is orange and black with eight spindly black legs and knotted pieces of red string for eyes. His body fabric resembles that of the black and orange Stripes.

Gender: Unknown
Poem:
Does this spider make you scared?
Among many people that feeling is shared
Remember spiders have feelings too
In fact, this spider really likes you!

SPINNER
the spider

Style #4036
Date Introduced: October 1, 1997
Date Retired: September 19, 1998
Birthday: October 28, 1996

Splash, the whale, has black eyes, a black topside, and a white belly. He has black paddle-shaped flippers, horizontal tail flukes and a dorsal fin.

Poem:
Splash loves to jump and dive
He's the fastest whale alive
He always wins the 100 yard dash
With a victory jump he'll make a splash!

SPLASH
the orca whale

Style #4022
Date Introduced: 1994
Date Retired: May 11, 1997
Birthday: July 8, 1993
Gender: Male

Spook, the ghost, is white with black oval eyes. He has a red crescent mouth and his black grin comes in different shapes depending on how it was sewn on. Around his neck, is a bright orange ribbon tied in a bow. Spook was designed by Jenna Boldebuck. Spook only comes with a third generation hang tag.

SPOOK
the ghost

Style #4090
Date Introduced: 1995
Date Retired: 1995
Birthday: Unknown
Gender: Unknown

Poem:
  None available

S

Spooky, the ghost, is white with black oval eyes. He has a red crescent mouth and his black grin comes in different shapes depending on how it was sewn on. Around his neck, is a bright orange ribbon tied in a bow. Spooky was designed by Jenna Boldebuck.

SPOOKY
the ghost

Style #4090
Date Introduced: 1996
Date Retired: December 31, 1997
Birthday: October 31, 1995
Gender: Unknown

Poem:
  Ghosts can be a scary sight
  But don't let Spooky bring you any fright
  Because when you're alone, you will see
  The best friend that Spooky can be!

Spot, with a spot, is a black and white dog. He has a black tail, ears and a patch that extends from his left eye to his neck. He has black eyes and a small black nose. To complement his name, a black spot was sewn onto the left side of his back.

SPOT
the dog with a spot

Style #4000
Date Introduced: 1994
Date Retired: October 1, 1997
Birthday: January 3, 1993
Gender: Male

S

Poem:
  See Spot sprint, see Spot run
  You and Spot will have lots of fun
  Watch out now, because he's not slow
  Just stand back and watch him go!

Spot, without a spot, is a black and white dog. He has a black tail, ears and a patch that extends from his left eye to his neck. He has black eyes and a small black nose. This valuable version of Spot was only produced with first and second generation hang tags.

SPOT
the dog without a spot

Style #4000
Date Introduced: 1994
Date Retired: 1994
Birthday: Unknown
Gender: Male

Poem:
  None available

Spunky, the cocker spaniel, is a beige dog with black eyes, a black nose and a black thread mouth. He has curly napped fabric on his long floppy ears, which stand out straight to each side.

SPUNKY
the cocker spaniel

Style #4184
Date Introduced: December 31, 1997
Date Retired: Current
Birthday: January 14, 1997
Gender: Male

Poem:
Bouncing around without much grace
To jump on your lap and lick your face
But watch him closely, he has no fears
He'll run so fast, he'll trip over his ears!

Squealer, the pig, is light pink with a darker pink snout, ears and knotted tail. He has black eyes and prominent nostrils that are sewn with barely visible, mauve-colored thread.

SQUEALER
the pig

Style #4005
Date Introduced: 1994
Date Retired: May 1, 1998
Birthday: April 23, 1993
Gender: Male

Poem:
Squealer likes to joke around
He is known as class clown
Listen to his stories a while
There is no doubt he will make you smile!

Also found:
There is no doubt he'll will make you smile!

Steg, the stegosaurus, is a brownish-green tie-dyed dinosaur with shades of yellow. He has the most consistent full-form of all the dinosaurs. He has black eyes and rounded spikes that run the length of his back and tail. Produced only with a third generation heart tag, he was never sold in the UK.

STEG
the stegosaurus

Style #4087
Date Introduced: Mid–1995
Date Retired: 1996
Birthday: Unknown
Gender: Unknown

Poem:
   None available

Sting, the ray, is a bluish tie-dyed manta ray with shades of green. His black eyes peer up from the top of his head. His body cavity and long tail are filled with pellets and stuffing.

STING
the stingray

Style #4077
Date Introduced: Mid–1995
Date Retired: January 1, 1997
Birthday: August 27, 1995
Gender: Unknown

Poem:
   I'm a manta ray and my name is Sting
   I'm quite unusual and this is the thing
   Under the water I glide like a bird
   Have you ever seen something so absurd?

Stinger, the scorpion, is shimmery grayish-brown with black eyes and a black thread mouth. He has two pincer claws, eight legs and a long elasticized tail with a stinger at the tip.

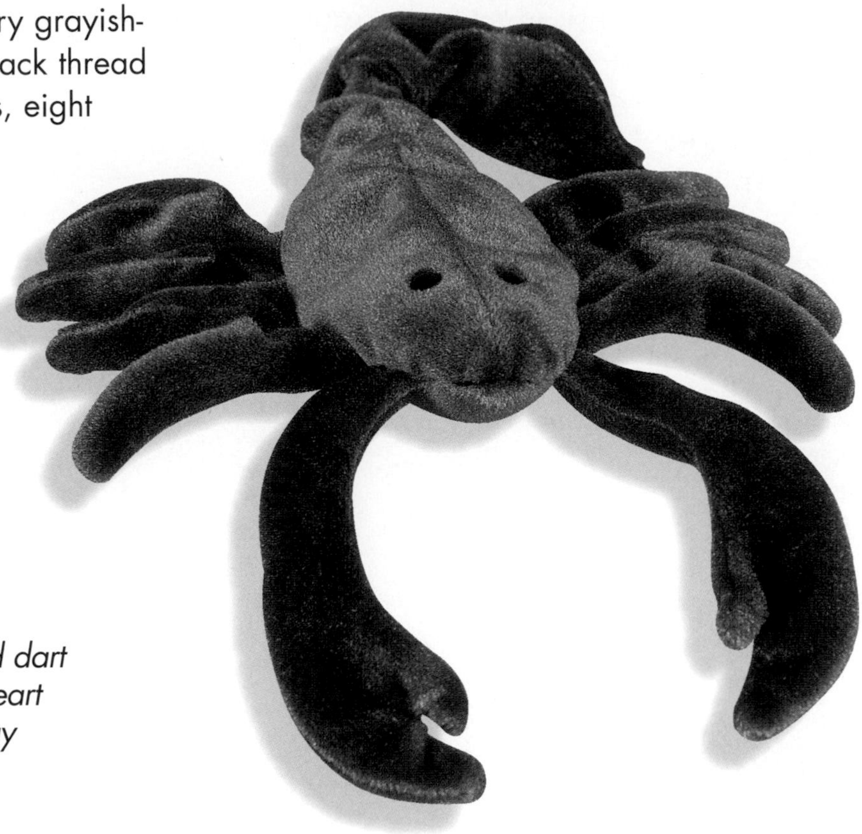

STINGER
the scorpion

Style #4193
Date Introduced: May 30, 1998
Date Retired: Current
Birthday: September 29, 1997
Gender: Male

Poem:
  Stinger the scorpion will run and dart
  But this little fellow is really all heart
  So if you see him don't run away
  Say hello and ask him to play!

Stinky, the skunk, is black and white with a characteristic large band of white that extends from head to tail. He has a large, paddle-shaped tail, black eyes, a black nose and two-tone ears.

STINKY
the skunk

Style #4017
Date Introduced: Mid–1995
Date Retired: September 28, 1998
Birthday: February 13, 1995
Gender: Male

Poem:
  Deep in the woods he lived in a cave
  Perfume and mints were the gifts they gave
  He showered every night in the kitchen sink
  Hoping one day he wouldn't stink!

Stretch, the ostrich, is a brown and white bird with a long beige neck, long dangling legs and beige feet. She has gold rimmed black eyes, a beige bill with two black thread nostrils and a ring of fluffy white "feathers" around her neck.

STRETCH
the ostrich

Style #4182
Date Introduced: December 31, 1997
Date Retired: Current
Birthday: September 21, 1997
Gender: Female

Poem:
*She thinks when her head is underground
The rest of her body can't be found
The Beanie Babies think it's absurd
To play hide and seek with this bird!*

S

Stripes, the orange and black tiger, has closely aligned black stripes. His eyes are black with a gold outer rim. He has a velvety flesh tone nose, and string whiskers droop from each side of his mouth. This version of Stripes was only produced with a third generation hang tag.

STRIPES
the black and orange tiger

Style #4065
Date Introduced: Mid–1995
Date Retired: 1996
Birthday: Unknown
Gender: Male

Poem:
None available

Stripes, the tiger, is tan and black. His eyes are black with a gold outer rim. He has a velvety flesh tone nose, and string whiskers droop from each side of his mouth.

STRIPES
the black and tan tiger

Style #4065
Date Introduced: 1996
Date Retired: May 1, 1998
Birthday: June 11, 1995
Gender: Male

Poem:
  Stripes was never fierce nor strong
  So with tigers, he didn't get along
  Jungle life was hard to get by
  So he came to his friends at Ty!

Also found:
  Jungle life was hard getting by

Strut, the rooster, is identical to Doodle except in name. His tie-dyed fabric consists mainly of pink, yellow and red, and he has gold rimmed black eyes. Strut has a red felt wattle under his neck, a red felt crest, red wings and tail. He has a bright yellow beak and yellow feet.

STRUT
the rooster

Style #4171
Date Introduced: August 1997
Date Retired: Current
Birthday: March 8, 1996
Gender: Male

Poem:
  Listen closely to "Cock-a-doodle-doo"
  What's the rooster saying to you?
  Hurry, wake up sleepy head
  We have lots to do, get out of bed!

Tabasco, the bull, is red with cream colored horns, paws and two-tone ears. He has black eyes, and black nostrils are sewn onto his cream colored snout. Rumor has it he was retired because of a lawsuit filed by the company that owns the Tabasco trademark.

TABASCO
the red bull

Style #4002
Date Introduced: Mid–1995
Date Retired: January 1, 1997
Birthday: May 15, 1995
Gender: Male

Poem:
   Although Tabasco is not so tall
   He loves to play basketball
   He is a star player in his dreams
   Can you guess his favorite team?

Tank, the gray armadillo, has black eyes and black thread nostrils. He has 7-lines of stitching on his back to represent a shell. His ears are placed on the side of his head outside the "V" stitching on his face.

TANK
the 7-line armadillo with no shell

Style #4031
Date Introduced: 1996
Date Retired: 1996
Birthday: Unknown
Gender: Male

Poem:
   None available

Tank, the gray armadillo, has black eyes and black thread nostrils. He has 9-lines of stitching on his back to represent a shell. His ears are placed on the side of his head outside the "V" stitching on his face.

TANK
the 9-line armadillo with no shell

Style #4031
Date Introduced: 1996
Date Retired: 1996
Birthday: February 22, 1995
Gender: Male

Poem:
This armadillo lives in the South
Shoving Tex-Mex in his mouth
He sure loves it south of the boarder
Keeping his friends in good order!

Also found:
He sure loves it south of the border

Tank, the gray armadillo, has black eyes. He has lines of stitching on his back and an additional line of stitching is sewn on each side of his body to make the shell look more realistic. His ears are placed on top of his head, and he does not have nostrils like the earlier armadillos.

TANK
the armadillo with shell

Style #4031
Date Introduced: 1996
Date Retired: October 1, 1997
Birthday: February 22, 1995
Gender: Male

Poem:
This armadillo lives in the South
Shoving Tex-Mex in his mouth
He sure loves it south of the boarder
Keeping his friends in good order!

Also found:
He sure loves it south of the border

1997 Teddy is a light brown Christmas bear with black eyes and a brown oval nose. This festive Teddy wears a red and white "Santa hat" over one ear, and a red scarf with white ends is tied around his neck.

1997 TEDDY
the holiday bear

Style #4200
Date Introduced: October 1, 1997
Date Retired: December 31, 1997
Birthday: December 25, 1996
Gender: Male

Poem:

Beanie Babies are special no doubt
All filled with love – inside and out
Wishes for fun times filled with joy
Ty's holiday teddy is a magical toy!

TEDDY-EMPLOYEE
the employee bears

During December of 1996, new-face violet Teddy bears were given to employees and representatives of Ty, Inc. These violet bears have red or green colored ribbons around their necks. These Teddies do not have swing tags and were produced with a 1993 or 1995 red and white tush tag. Approximately 300 employee Teddies were produced.

Note: The original new-face violet Teddy had a green ribbon and a 1993 black and white tush tag.

Date Introduced: November 1996
Date Retired: December 1996
Birthday: Unknown
Gender: Male

NEW FACE TEDDYS

In 1995, six "new face" colored bears were introduced. There was a transformation from the "old world" bears to the "new world" bears. The body is fuller and the head is larger and more rounded. The new face bears have black eyes set close together inside the "V" seam on the face, and a large black oval nose that is situated on the top of the "V" seam. Different colored ribbons tied in a bow add an accent to the uniform color. The ears have increased in size and protrude from the top of the head. Teddy cranberry, jade, magenta, teal and violet retired in 1995, and Teddy brown on October 1, 1997. Except for the brown Teddy, the new face bears were produced with second and third generation heart tags only.

TEDDY
the new face brown bear

Style #4050
Date Introduced: 1995
Date Retired: October 1, 1997
Birthday: November 28, 1995
Gender: Male

Poem:
Teddy wanted to go out today
All of his friends went out to play
But he'd rather help whatever you do
After all, his best friend is you!

Teddy, new face cranberry, has a green ribbon around its neck.

TEDDY
the new face cranberry bear

Style #4052
Date Introduced: 1995
Date Retired: 1995
Birthday: Unknown
Gender: Male

Poem:
None available

Teddy, new face jade, has a magenta colored ribbon around its neck.

TEDDY
the new face jade bear

Style #4057
Date Introduced: 1995
Date Retired: 1995
Birthday: Unknown
Gender: Male

Poem:
  None available

Teddy, new face magenta, comes in different shade variations. He has a pink ribbon tied around his neck.

TEDDY
the new face magenta bear

Style #4056
Date Introduced: 1995
Date Retired: 1995
Birthday: Unknown
Gender: Male

Poem:
  None available

Teddy, new face teal, is one of the rarest of the new face bears. He has a blue ribbon around his neck.

TEDDY
the new face teal bear

Style #4051
Date Introduced: 1995
Date Retired: 1995
Birthday: Unknown
Gender: Male

Poem:
  None available

Teddy, new face violet, is one of the most sought after new face bears. He has a green ribbon around his neck.

TEDDY
the new face violet bear

Style #4055
Date Introduced: 1995
Date Retired: 1995
Birthday: Unknown
Gender: Male

Poem:
  None available

OLD FACE TEDDYS

In mid-1994, six "old face" bears were introduced. These bears have thin faces and elongated bodies. They have black eyes set outside the "V" seam on the face, and a small black triangular nose that is situated on the top of the "V" seam. The old face bears do not have ribbons around their necks. They come in the following colors: brown, cranberry, jade, magenta, teal and violet. There are shade variations between the same color bears. Produced with only first or second generation heart tags, the old face bears were retired in 1994.

Teddy, old face brown, is the rarest of the six old face colored bears that were produced.

TEDDY
the old face brown bear

Style #4050
Date Introduced: Mid–1994
Date Retired: 1995
Birthday: Unknown
Gender: Male

Poem:
  None available

Teddy, old face cranberry, is one of the rarer old face bears.

TEDDY
the old face cranberry bear

Style #4052
Date Introduced: Mid–1994
Date Retired: 1995
Birthday: Unknown
Gender: Male

Poem:
  None available

Teddy, old face jade, is a dark forest green color. He comes in different shade variations.

TEDDY
the old face jade bear

Style #4057
Date Introduced: Mid–1994
Date Retired: 1995
Birthday: Unknown
Gender: Male

Poem:
   None available

Teddy, old face magenta, comes in different shade variations.

TEDDY
the old face magenta bear

Style #4056
Date Introduced: Mid–1994
Date Retired: 1995
Birthday: Unknown
Gender: Male

Poem:
   None available

Teddy, old face teal, comes in different shade variations.

TEDDY
the old face teal bear

Style #4051
Date Introduced: Mid–1994
Date Retired: 1995
Birthday: Unknown
Gender: Male

Poem:
   None available

Teddy, old face violet, is highly sought after because of its rich looking violet color.

TEDDY
the old face violet bear

Style #4055
Date Introduced: Mid–1994
Date Retired: 1995
Birthday: Unknown
Gender: Male

Poem:
   None available

Tracker, the basset hound, is a brown and beige dog with a black nose and black thread mouth. His adorable, upward-glancing black eyes are set in white felt "sockets," and he has long floppy brown ears.

TRACKER
the basset hound

Style #4198
Date Introduced: May 30, 1998
Date Retired: Current
Birthday: June 5, 1997
Gender: Male

Poem:
Sniffing and tracking and following trails
Tracker the basset always wags his tail
It doesn't matter what you do
He's always happy when he's with you!

Trap, the mouse, is small and gray with pink ears, legs, nose and knotted tail. His black thread whiskers are in constant need of straightening.

TRAP
the mouse

Style #4042
Date Introduced: Mid–1994
Date Retired: 1995
Birthday: Unknown
Gender: Unknown

Poem:
None available

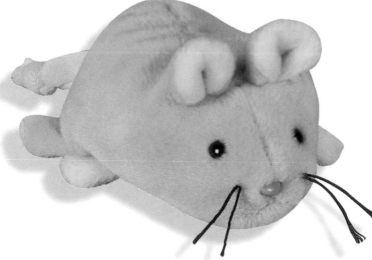

Tuffy, the terrier, is two-tone brown with nappy fur. He has perky little ears. He has black eyes, a black nose, a black thread mouth and a short dark brown tail.

TUFFY
the terrier

Style #4108
Date Introduced: May 11, 1997
Date Retired: Current
Birthday: October 12, 1996
Gender: Male

Poem:
Taking off with a thunderous blast
Tuffy rides his motorcycle fast
The Beanies roll with laughs & squeals
He never took off his training wheels!

Tusk/Tuck, the walrus, is a medium-brown walrus with black eyes and a large black oval nose. Protruding from his mouth are white felt tusks. During the latter part of 1996, Tusk was misspelled "Tuck" on the heart tag. Tuck was only produced with a fourth generation heart tag.

TUSK/TUCK
the walrus

Style #4076
Date Introduced: 1996
Date Retired: January 1, 1997
Birthday: September 18, 1995
Gender: Male

Poem:
Tusk brushes his teeth everyday
To keep them shiny, it's the only way
Teeth are special, so you must try
To sparkle when you say "Hi"!

Also found:
So they will sparkle when you say "Hi"!
So they sparkle when you say "Hi"!
And they will sparkle when you say "Hi"!

Twigs, the giraffe, has bright yellow and orange fabric. He has black eyes, and his elongated neck tends to flop to one side. He has a brown mane, brown hoofs and brown-tipped ears.

TWIGS
the giraffe

Style #4068
Date Introduced: 1996
Date Retired: May 1, 1998
Birthday: May 19, 1995
Gender: Male

Poem:
Twigs has his head in the clouds
He stands tall, he stands proud
With legs so skinny they wobble and shake
What an unusual friend he will make!

T

Valentino, the bear, is white with a red heart sewn on his chest. He has black eyes, an oval brown nose and wears a red ribbon around his neck.

VALENTINO
the white bear with red heart

Style #4058
Date Introduced: 1995
Date Retired: Current
Birthday: February 14, 1994
Gender: Male

Poem:
His heart is red and full of love
He cares for you so give him a hug
Keep him close when feeling blue
Feel the love he has for you!

1998 Special
Olympics Valentino

Velvet, the panther, is a "velvety" all-black jungle cat with gold-rimmed black eyes, black whiskers and a flesh-colored nose.

VELVET
the panther

Style #4064
Date Introduced: Mid–1995
Date Retired: October 1, 1997
Birthday: December 16, 1995
Gender: Female

Poem:
Velvet loves to sleep in the trees
Lulled to dreams by the buzz of the bees
She snoozes all day and plays all night
Running and jumping in the moonlight!

Waddle, the penguin, is a black and white bird who looks as though he's dressed in a tuxedo. He has an orange bill and feet, a bright yellow "collar" around his neck and black eyes.

WADDLE
the penguin

Style #4075
Date Introduced: Mid–1995
Date Retired: May 1, 1998
Birthday: December 19, 1995
Gender: Male

Poem:
Waddle the penguin likes to dress up
Every night he wears his tux
When Waddle walks, it never fails
He always trips over his tails!

Waves, the whale, has black eyes, a black topside, and a white belly. He has black flippers, horizontal tail flukes and a dorsal fin.

WAVES
the whale

Style #4084
Date Introduced: May 11, 1997
Date Retired: May 1, 1998
Birthday: December 8, 1996
Gender: Male

Poem:
 Join him today on the Internet
 Don't be afraid to get your feet wet
 He taught all the Beanies how to surf
 Our web page is his home turf!

W

Web, the spider, is a soft velvety black spider with black eyes. He rests on his red belly and eight black elongated legs.

WEB
the spider

Style #4041
Date Introduced: Mid–1994
Date Retired: 1995
Birthday: Unknown
Gender: Unknown

Poem:
 None available

Weenie, the dachshund, is a brown dog who resembles the "hot dog" for which he was named. He has a long body and short legs. Weenie has black eyes with a brown rim and a black nose.

WEENIE
the dachshund

Style #4013
Date Introduced: 1996
Date Retired: May 1, 1998
Birthday: July 20, 1995
Gender: Male

W

Poem:
Weenie the dog is quite a sight
Long of body and short of height
He perches himself high on a log
And considers himself to be top dog!

Whisper, the deer, is a light brown fawn with the characteristic white markings of a young deer. She has a beige belly, two-tone ears, black eyes, a brown oval nose and dark brown hoofs.

WHISPER
the deer

Style #4194
Date Introduced: May 30, 1998
Date Retired: Current
Birthday: April 5, 1997
Gender: Female

Poem:
She's very shy as you can see
When she hides behind a tree
With big brown eyes and soft to touch
This little fawn will love you so much!

Wise, the owl, is a large brown tie-dyed and beige owl "who" wears a black "Class of '98" graduation cap, complete with an orange tassel. He has brown and beige wings and tail feathers. He has large gold rimmed black eyes, a felt orange nose and webbed taupe-colored feet.

WISE
the graduation owl

Style #4187
Date Introduced: May 30, 1998
Date Retired: Current
Birthday: May 31, 1997
Gender: Male

Poem:
  Wise is the head of the class
  With A's and B's he'll always pass
  He's got his diploma and feels really great
  Meet the newest graduate: Class of '98!

Wrinkles, the dog, is light brown and white with a decidedly "wrinkled" appearance to his fur. He has black eyes with a brown outer rim, a black nose, white and brown ears and a large white muzzle.

WRINKLES
the dog

Style #4103
Date Introduced: Mid–1996
Date Retired: September 22, 1998
Birthday: May 1, 1996
Gender: Male

Poem:
  This little dog is named Wrinkles
  His nose is soft and often crinkles
  Likes to climb up on your lap
  He's a cheery sort of chap!

Ziggy, the zebra with thin stripes, has closely spaced black
and white horizontal stripes often ending in a "Y"
formation. He has black eyes, a coarse
black mane and eight pieces
of black yarn for a tail.

ZIGGY
**the zebra with
thin stripes**

Style #4063
Date Introduced: Mid–1995
Date Retired: 1997
Birthday: December 24, 1995
Gender: Male

Poem:
  *Ziggy likes soccer–he's a referee
  That way he watches the games for free
  The other Beanies don't think it's fair
  But Ziggy the Zebra doesn't care.*

Ziggy, the zebra with wide stripes, was introduced in 1997. This variation
has black and white horizontal stripes that are set farther apart. He has
black eyes, a coarse black mane and eight pieces of black yarn for a tail.

ZIGGY
the zebra with wide stripes

Style #4063
Date Introduced: August 1997
Date Retired: May 1, 1998
Birthday: December 24, 1995
Gender: Male

Poem:
  *Ziggy likes soccer–he's a referee
  That way he watches the games for free
  The other Beanies don't think it's fair
  But Ziggy the Zebra doesn't care.*

Zip, the all black cat, has a pink mouth, nose and whiskers. His pink ears curve inward and the tips are rounded. His body and head are completely black, and his eyes are black with a green outer rim. This rarest version of Zip was only produced with a third generation heart tag.

ZIP
the all black cat

Style #4004
Date Introduced: 1995
Date Retired: 1995
Birthday: Unknown
Gender: Unknown

Poem:
  None available

Zip, the black cat, has a larger face and body than the later Zips. His belly and the triangular shape on his face are white. He has a pink triangular nose and solid black eyes. His triangular pink ears stick straight up and are not curved like the later Zips. His mouth and whiskers are a light pink, as compared to the first Zips that were produced with a brighter pink color.

ZIP
the black cat with
the white face and belly

Style #4004
Date Introduced: 1995
Date Retired: 1995
Birthday: Unknown
Gender: Unknown

Poem:
  None available

Zip, the black cat, has a white mouth, white whiskers, ears and paws. He has a pink nose and black eyes with a green outer rim.

ZIP
the black cat
with white paws

Style #4004
Date Introduced: 1996
Date Retired: May 1, 1998
Birthday: March 28, 1994
Gender: Unknown

Poem:
    Keep Zip by your side all day through
    Zip is good luck, you'll see it's true
    When you have something you need to do
    Zip will always believe in you!

Z

INFORMATION GUIDE

Style No.	Beanie Name	Date Introduced	Date Retired	Birthday
4032	Ally, the alligator	Mid-1994	Oct. 1, 1997	Mar. 14, 1994
4195	Ants, the anteater	May 30, 1998		Nov. 7, 1997
4074	Baldy, the eagle	May 11, 1997	May 1, 1998	Feb. 17, 1996
4035	Batty, the brown bat	Oct. 1, 1997		Oct. 29, 1996
4109	Bernie, the St. Bernard	Jan. 1, 1997	Sept. 22, 1998	Oct. 3, 1996
4009	Bessie, the brown and white cow	Mid-1995	Oct. 1, 1997	June 27, 1995
4011	Blackie, the black bear	Mid-1994	Sept. 15, 1998	July 15, 1994
4163	Blizzard, the black and white tiger	May 11, 1997	May 1, 1998	Dec. 12, 1996
4001	Bones, the brown dog	Mid-1994	May 1, 1998	Jan. 18, 1994
4067	Bongo, the monkey with brown tail - r/w tush tag/no name	1996	1996	
4067	Bongo, the monkey with brown tail - r/w tush tag/with name	1997	1997	Aug. 17, 1995
4067	Bongo, the monkey with tan tail - b/w tush tag	1995	1996	
4067	Bongo, the monkey with tan tail - r/w tush tag/no name	1996	1996	
4067	Bongo, the monkey with tan tail - r/w tush tag/with name	1996		Aug. 17, 1995
4601	Britannia, the brown bear with the Union Jack Flag-sewn on	May 1998	May 1998	
4601	Britannia, the brown bear with the Union Jack Flag-embroidered	Dec. 31, 1997		Dec. 15, 1997
4085	Bronty, the brontosaurus	Mid-1995	1996	
4010	Brownie, the brown bear	1993	1993	
4183	Bruno, the terrier	Dec. 31, 1997	Sept. 18, 1998	Sept. 9, 1997
4078	Bubbles, the black and yellow fish	Mid-1995	May 11, 1997	July 2, 1995
4016	Bucky, the beaver	1996	Dec. 31, 1997	June 8, 1995
4045	Bumble, the bumble bee	1996	1996	Oct. 16, 1995
4071	Caw, the crow	Mid-1995	1996	
4012	Chilly, the white polar bear	Mid-1994	1995	
4121	Chip, the calico cat	May 11, 1997		Jan. 26, 1996
4015	Chocolate, the moose	1994		Apr. 27, 1993
4019	Chops, the lamb	1996	Jan. 1, 1997	May 3, 1996
4083	Claude, the tie-dyed crab	May 11, 1997		Sept. 3, 1997
n/a	Clubby, the BBOC royal blue bear	May 1, 1998		July 7, 1998
4160	Congo, the gorilla	Mid-1996		Nov. 9, 1996
4079	Coral, the tie-dyed fish	1996	Jan. 1, 1997	Mar. 2, 1995
4130	Crunch, the shark	Jan. 1, 1997	Sept. 24,1998	Jan. 13, 1996
4010	Cubbie, the brown bear	1994	Dec. 31, 1997	Nov. 14, 1993
4052	Curly, the brown napped bear	Mid-1996		Apr. 12, 1996
4006	Daisy, the black and white cow	Mid-1994	Sept. 15, 1998	May 10, 1994
4008	Derby, the coarse-mane horse	1996	1998	Sept. 16, 1995
4008	Derby, the coarse-mane horse with star on forehead	Jan. 1998		Sept. 16, 1995
4008	Derby, the fine-mane horse	Mid-1995	1995	
4027	Digger, the orange crab	Mid-1994	1995	
4027	Digger, the red crab	Mid-1995	May 11, 1997	Aug. 23, 1995
4110	Doby, the Doberman	Jan. 1, 1997		Oct. 9, 1996
4171	Doodle, the rooster	May 11, 1997	Dec. 1997	Mar. 8, 1996
4100	Dotty, the dalmatian with black ears	May 11, 1997		Oct. 17, 1996
4190	Early, the robin	May 30, 1998		Mar. 20, 1997
4018	Ears, the brown rabbit	1996	May 1, 1998	Apr. 18, 1995
4180	Echo, the dolphin	May 11, 1997	May 1, 1998	Dec. 21, 1996
4186	Erin, the green bear with white shamrock	Jan. 31, 1998		Mar. 17, 1997
4189	Fetch, the golden retriever	May 30, 1998		Feb. 4, 1997
4021	Flash, the dolphin	1994	May 11, 1997	May 13, 1993
4125	Fleece, the napped lamb	Jan. 1, 1997		Mar. 21, 1996
4012	Flip, the white cat	1996	Oct. 1, 1997	Feb. 28, 1995

INFORMATION GUIDE

Style No.	Beanie Name	Date Introduced	Date Retired	Birthday
4118	Floppity, the lavender bunny	Jan. 1, 1997	May 1, 1998	May 28, 1996
4043	Flutter, the tie-dyed butterfly	Mid-1995	1996	
4196	Fortune, the panda-sitting	May 30, 1998		Dec. 6, 1997
4066	Freckles, the leopard	Mid-1996		June 3, 1996
4051	Garcia, the tie-dyed bear	1996	May 11, 1997	Aug. 1, 1995
4191	GiGi, the poodle	May 30, 1998		Apr. 7, 1997
4188	Glory, the white bear with red/blue stars	May 30, 1998		July 4, 1997
4034	Gobbles, the turkey	Oct. 1, 1997		Nov. 27, 1996
4023	Goldie, the goldfish	Mid-1994	Dec. 31, 1997	Nov. 14, 1994
4126	Gracie, the swan	Jan. 1, 1997	May 1, 1998	June 17, 1996
4092	Grunt, the razorback hog	1996	May 11, 1997	July 19, 1995
4061	Happy, the gray hippo	Mid-1994	1995	
4061	Happy, the lavender hippo	Mid-1995	May 1, 1998	Feb. 25, 1994
4119	Hippity, the mint green bunny	Jan. 1, 1997	May 1, 1998	June 1, 1996
4185	Hissy, the snake	Dec. 31, 1997		Apr. 4, 1997
4073	Hoot, the owl	1996	Oct. 1, 1997	Aug. 9, 1995
4117	Hoppity, the rose bunny	Jan. 1, 1997	May 1, 1998	Apr. 3, 1996
4060	Humphrey, the camel	Mid-1994	1995	
4038	Iggy, the iguana-Rainbow tags-collar	Dec. 31, 1997	Aug. 1998	Aug. 12, 1997
4038	Iggy, the iguana-Rainbow tags-spikes	Aug. 1998		Aug. 12, 1997
4044	Inch, the inchworm with felt antennae	1996	1996	
4044	Inch, the inchworm with yarn antennae	1996	May 1, 1998	Sept. 3, 1995
4028	Inky, the pink octopus	Mid-1995	May 1, 1998	Nov. 29, 1994
4028	Inky, the tan octopus with a mouth	1995	1995	
4028	Inky, the tan octopus without a mouth	Mid-1994	1994	
4197	Jabber, the parrot	May 30, 1998		Oct. 10, 1997
4199	Jake, the mallard duck	May 30, 1998		Apr. 16, 1997
4082	Jolly, the walrus	May 11, 1997	May 1, 1998	Dec. 2, 1996
4070	Kiwi, the toucan	Mid-1995	Jan. 1, 1997	Sept. 16, 1995
4192	Kuku, the cockatoo	May 30, 1998		Jan. 5, 1997
4085	Lefty, the donkey with American flag	Mid-1996	Jan. 1, 1997	July 4, 1996
4020	Legs, the frog	1994	Oct. 1, 1997	Apr. 25, 1993
4057	Libearty, the white bear with American flag	1996	Jan. 1, 1997	Summer 1996
4057	Libearty/Beanine, the white bear with American flag	Mid-1996	Jan. 1, 1997	Summer 1996
4033	Lizzy, the blue lizard with black spots	1996	Dec. 31, 1997	May 11, 1995
4033	Lizzy, the tie-dyed lizard	Mid-1995	1995	
4040	Lucky, the ladybug with 7 felt dots	Mid-1994	1996	
4040	Lucky, the ladybug with approx. 11 dots	1996	May 1, 1998	May 1, 1995
4040	Lucky, the ladybug with approx. 21 dots	1996	1997	May 1, 1995
4088	Magic, the white dragon-hot pink stitching	1996	1996	Sept. 5, 1995
4088	Magic, the white dragon-light pink stitching	Mid-1995	Dec. 31, 1997	Sept. 5, 1995
4081	Manny, the manatee	1996	May 11, 1997	June 8, 1995
4600	Maple/Maple, the white bear with Canadian flag	1997		July 1, 1996
4600	Maple/Pride, the white bear with Canadian flag	Feb. 1997	Feb. 1997	July 1, 1996
4600	Maple/Special Olympics, the white bear with Canadian flag	Aug. 1997	Dec. 1997	July 1, 1996
4162	Mel, the Koala	Jan. 1, 1997		Jan. 15, 1996
4007	Mystic, the unicorn with iridescent horn	Nov. 1997		May 21, 1994
4007	Mystic, the unicorn with tan horn	1996	Nov. 1997	May 21, 1994
4007	Mystic, the unicorn with tan horn/fine-mane	Mid-1994	1995	
4067	Nana, the monkey with tan tail - b/w tush tag	1995	1995	
4104	Nanook, the Siberian Husky	May 11, 1997		Nov. 21, 1996

INFORMATION GUIDE

Style No.	Beanie Name	Date Introduced	Date Retired	Birthday
4003	Nip, the all gold cat with pink ears (no white)	1995	1995	
4003	Nip, the gold cat with white face and belly	1995	1995	
4003	Nip, the gold cat with white paws	1996	Dec. 31, 1997	Mar. 6, 1994
4114	Nuts, the squirrel	Jan. 1, 1997		Jan. 21, 1996
4025	Patti, the deep fuchsia platypus	1993	1993	
4025	Patti, the fuchsia platypus	1996	May 1, 1998	Jan. 6, 1993
4025	Patti, the magenta platypus	1995	1995	
4025	Patti, the raspberry platypus	1994	1994	
4053	Peace, the tie-dyed bear	May 11, 1997		Feb. 1, 1996
4053	Peace, the tie-dyed pastel bear	July 1998		Feb. 1, 1996
4062	Peanut, the light blue elephant	1996	May 1, 1998	Jan. 25, 1995
4062	Peanut, the royal blue elephant	Mid-1995	1995	
4013	Peking, the panda bear	Mid-1994	1995	
4026	Pinchers, the red lobster	1994	May 1, 1998	June 19, 1993
4072	Pinky, the pink flamingo	1996		Feb. 13, 1995
4161	Pouch, the kangaroo	Jan. 1, 1997		Nov. 6, 1996
4122	Pounce, the brown tie-dyed cat	Dec. 31, 1997		Aug. 28, 1997
4123	Prance, the gray striped cat	Dec. 31, 1997		Nov. 20, 1997
4300	Princess, the purple bear with white rose	Oct. 29, 1997		
4181	Puffer, the puffin	Dec. 31, 1997	Sept. 18, 1998	Nov. 3, 1997
4106	Pugsly, the Pug dog	May 11, 1997		May 2, 1996
4026	Punchers, the red lobster	1994	1994	
4024	Quacker, the duck with wings	1995	1995	
4024	Quacker, the duck with no wings	1994	1995	
4024	Quackers, the duck with wings	1995	May 1, 1998	Apr. 19, 1994
4024	Quackers, the duck with no wings	Mid-1994	1995	
4091	Radar, the bat	1996	May 11, 1997	Oct. 30, 1995
4037	Rainbow, the chameleon-Iggy tags-spikes	Dec. 31, 1997	June 1998	Oct. 14, 1997
4037	Rainbow, the chameleon with tongue-Iggy tags-spikes	June 1998	July 1998	Oct. 14, 1997
4037	Rainbow, the pastel chameleon with tongue-Iggy tags-spikes	July 1998	Aug. 1998	Oct. 14, 1997
4037	Rainbow, the pastel chameleon w/tongue-Rainbow tags-collar	Aug. 1998		Oct. 14, 1997
4086	Rex, the tyrannosaurus	Mid-1995	1996	
4086	Righty, the elephant with American flag	Mid-1996	Jan. 1, 1997	July 4, 1996
4014	Ringo, the raccoon	1996	Sept. 16, 1998	July 14, 1995
4069	Roary, the lion	May 11, 1997		Feb. 20, 1996
4202	Rocket, the bluejay	May 30, 1998		Mar. 12, 1997
4101	Rover, the red dog	Mid-1996	May 1, 1998	May 30, 1996
4107	Scoop, the pelican	Mid-1996		July 1, 1996
4102	Scottie, the Scottish terrier	Mid-1996	May 1, 1998	June 15, 1996
4029	Seamore, the seal	Mid-1994	Oct. 1, 1997	Dec. 14, 1996
4080	Seaweed, the otter	1996	Sept. 19, 1998	Mar. 19, 1996
4031	Slither, the snake	Mid-1994	1995	
4115	Sly, the brown-belly fox	Mid-1996	1996	Sept. 12, 1996
4115	Sly, the white-belly fox	1996	Sept. 22, 1998	Sept. 12, 1996
4039	Smoochy, the frog with single thread mouth	Dec. 31, 1997		Oct. 1, 1997
4039	Smoochy, the frog with double thread mouth	May 1998		Oct. 1, 1997
4039	Smoochy, the frog with felt mouth	June 1998		Oct. 1, 1997
4120	Snip, the Siamese cat	Jan. 1, 1997		Oct. 22, 1996
4002	Snort, the red bull with cream paws	Jan. 1, 1997	Sept. 15, 1998	May 15, 1995
4201	Snowball, the snowman	Oct. 1, 1997	Dec. 31, 1997	Dec. 22, 1996
4100	Sparky, the Dalmatian	Mid-1996	May 11, 1997	Feb. 27, 1996

INFORMATION GUIDE

Style No.	Beanie Name	Date Introduced	Date Retired	Birthday
4030	Speedy, the turtle	Mid-1994	Oct. 1, 1997	Aug. 14, 1994
4060	Spike, the rhino	Mid-1996		Aug. 13, 1996
4036	Spinner, the spider	Oct. 1, 1997	Sept. 19, 1998	Oct. 28, 1996
4022	Splash, the orca whale	1994	May 11, 1997	July 8, 1993
4090	Spook, the ghost	1995	1995	
4090	Spooky, the ghost	1996	Dec. 31, 1997	Oct. 31, 1995
4000	Spot, the black and white dog with a spot	1994	Oct. 1, 1997	Jan. 3, 1993
4000	Spot, the black and white dog without a spot	1994	1994	
4184	Spunky, the cocker spaniel	Dec. 31, 1997		Jan. 14, 1997
4005	Squealer, the pig	1994	May 1, 1998	Apr. 23, 1993
4087	Steg, the stegosaurus	Mid-1995	1996	
4077	Sting, the ray	Mid-1995	Jan. 1, 1997	Aug. 27, 1995
4193	Stinger, the scorpion	May 30, 1998		Sept. 29, 1997
4017	Stinky, the skunk	Mid-1995	Sept. 28, 1998	Feb. 13, 1995
4182	Stretch, the ostrich	Dec. 31, 1997		Sept. 21, 1997
4065	Stripes, the black and orange tiger	Mid-1995	1996	
4065	Stripes, the black and tan tiger	1996	May 1, 1998	June 11, 1995
4171	Strut, the rooster	Aug. 1997		Mar. 8, 1996
4002	Tabasco, the red bull	Mid-1995	Jan. 1, 1997	May 15, 1995
4031	Tank, the 7-line armadillo	1996	1996	
4031	Tank, the 9-line armadillo	1996	1996	Feb. 22, 1995
4031	Tank, the armadillo with shell	1996	Oct. 1, 1997	Feb. 22, 1995
4200	Teddy, 1997 light brown holiday bear	Oct. 1, 1997	Dec. 31, 1997	Dec. 25, 1996
N/A	Teddy, the employee bear-green ribbon	Nov/Dec. 1996	Dec. 1996	
N/A	Teddy, the employee bear-red ribbon	Nov/Dec. 1996	Dec. 1996	
4050	Teddy, the new face-brown bear	1995	Oct. 1, 1997	Nov. 28, 1995
4052	Teddy, the new face-cranberry bear	1995	1995	
4057	Teddy, the new face-jade bear	1995	1995	
4056	Teddy, the new face-magenta bear	1995	1995	
4051	Teddy, the new face-teal bear	1995	1995	
4055	Teddy, the new face-violet bear	1995	1995	
4050	Teddy, the old face-brown bear	Mid-1994	1995	
4052	Teddy, the old face-cranberry bear	Mid-1994	1995	
4057	Teddy, the old face-jade bear	Mid-1994	1995	
4056	Teddy, the old face-magenta bear	Mid-1994	1995	
4051	Teddy, the old face-teal bear	Mid-1994	1995	
4055	Teddy, the old face-violet bear	Mid-1994	1995	
4198	Tracker, the basset hound	May 30, 1998		June 5, 1997
4042	Trap, the mouse	Mid-1994	1995	
4076	Tuck, the walrus	1996	Jan. 1, 1997	Sept. 18, 1995
4108	Tuffy, the terrier	May 11, 1997		Oct. 12, 1997
4076	Tusk, the walrus	1996	Jan. 1, 1997	Sept. 18, 1995
4068	Twigs, the giraffe	1996	May 1, 1998	May 19, 1995
4058	Valentino, the white bear with red heart	1995		Feb. 14, 1994
4058	Valentino/Special Olympics, the white bear with red heart	July 1998		Feb. 14, 1994
4064	Velvet, the panther	Mid-1995	Oct. 1, 1997	Dec. 16, 1995
4075	Waddle, the penguin	Mid-1995	May 1, 1998	Dec. 19, 1995
4084	Waves, the orca whale	May 11, 1997	May 1, 1998	Dec. 8, 1996
4041	Web, the spider	Mid-1994	1995	
4013	Weenie, the dachshund dog	1996	May 1, 1998	July 20, 1995

INFORMATION GUIDE

Style No.	Beanie Name	Date Introduced	Date Retired	Birthday
4194	Whisper, the deer	May 30, 1998		Apr. 5, 1997
4187	Wise, the graduation owl	May 30, 1998		May 31, 1997
4103	Wrinkles, the bulldog	Mid-1996	Sept. 22, 1998	May 1, 1996
4063	Ziggy, the zebra with thin stripes	Mid-1995	May 1, 1998	Dec. 24, 1995
4063	Ziggy, the zebra with wide stripes	Aug. 1997	May 1, 1998	Dec. 24, 1995
4004	Zip, the all black cat with pink ears (no white)	1995	1995	
4004	Zip, the black cat with white face and belly	1995	1995	
4004	Zip, the black cat with white paws	1996	May 1, 1998	Mar. 28, 1994

BEANIE BABY BIRTHDAYS!

JANUARY
Jan. 3, 1993 – Spot
Jan. 5, 1997 – Kuku
Jan. 6, 1993 – Patti
Jan. 13, 1996 – Crunch
Jan. 14, 1996 – Spunky
Jan. 15, 1996 – Mel
Jan. 18, 1994 – Bones
Jan. 21, 1996 – Nuts
Jan. 25, 1995 – Peanut
Jan. 26, 1996 – Chip

FEBRUARY
Feb. 1, 1996 – Peace
Feb. 4, 1997 – Fetch
Feb. 13, 1995 – Stinky
Feb. 13, 1995 – Pinky
Feb. 14, 1994 – Valentino
Feb. 17, 1996 – Baldy
Feb. 20, 1996 – Roary
Feb. 22, 1995 – Tank
Feb. 25, 1994 – Happy
Feb. 27, 1996 – Sparky

MARCH
Mar. 2, 1995 – Coral
Mar. 6, 1994 – Nip
Mar. 8, 1996 – Doodle
Mar. 8, 1996 – Strut
Mar. 12, 1997 – Rocket
Mar. 14, 1994 – Ally
Mar. 17, 1997 – Erin
Mar. 19, 1996 – Seaweed
Mar. 20, 1997 – Early
Mar. 21, 1996 – Fleece
Mar. 28, 1994 – Zip

APRIL
Apr. 3, 1996 – Hoppity
Apr. 4, 1997 – Hissy
Apr. 5, 1997 – Whisper
Apr. 7, 1997 – GiGi
Apr. 12, 1996 – Curly
Apr. 16, 1997 – Jake
Apr. 18, 1995 – Ears
Apr. 19, 1994 – Quackers
Apr. 23, 1993 – Squealer
Apr. 25, 1993 – Legs
Apr. 27, 1993 – Chocolate

MAY
May 1, 1995 – Lucky
May 1, 1996 – Wrinkles
May 2, 1996 – Pugsly
May 3, 1996 – Chops
May 10, 1994 – Daisy
May 11, 1995 – Lizzy
May 13, 1993 – Flash
May 15, 1995 – Tabasco
May 15, 1995 – Snort
May 19, 1995 – Twigs
May 21, 1994 – Mystic
May 28, 1996 – Floppity
May 30, 1996 – Rover
May 31, 1997 – Wise

JUNE
June 1, 1996 – Hippity
June 3, 1996 – Freckles
June 5, 1997 – Tracker
June 8, 1995 – Bucky
June 8, 1995 – Manny
June 11, 1995 – Stripes
June 15, 1996 – Scottie
June 17, 1996 – Gracie
June 19, 1993 – Pinchers
June 27, 1995 – Bessie

JULY
July 1, 1996 – Scoop
July 1, 1996 – Maple
July 2, 1995 – Bubbles
July 4, 1996 – Lefty
July 4, 1997 – Glory
July 4, 1996 – Righty
July 7, 1998 – Clubby
July 8, 1993 – Splash
July 14, 1995 – Ringo
July 15, 1994 – Blackie
July 19, 1995 – Grunt
July 20, 1995 – Weenie

AUGUST
Aug. 1, 1995 – Garcia
Aug. 9, 1995 – Hoot
Aug. 12, 1997 – Iggy
Aug. 13, 1996 – Spike
Aug. 14, 1994 – Speedy
Aug. 17, 1995 – Bongo
Aug. 23, 1995 – Digger
Aug. 27, 1995 – Sting
Aug. 28, 1997 – Pounce

SEPTEMBER
Sept. 3, 1995 – Inch
Sept. 3, 1996 – Claude
Sept. 5, 1995 – Magic
Sept. 9, 1997 – Bruno
Sept. 12, 1996 – Sly
Sept. 16, 1995 – Kiwi
Sept. 16, 1995 – Derby
Sept. 18, 1995 – Tusk
Sept. 21, 1997 – Stretch
Sept. 29, 1997 – Stinger

OCTOBER
Oct. 1, 1997 – Smoochy
Oct. 3, 1996 – Bernie
Oct. 9, 1996 – Doby
Oct. 10, 1997 – Jabber
Oct. 12, 1996 – Tuffy
Oct. 14, 1997 – Rainbow
Oct. 16, 1995 – Bumble
Oct. 17, 1996 – Dotty
Oct. 22, 1996 – Snip
Oct. 28, 1996 – Spinner
Oct. 29, 1996 – Batty
Oct. 30, 1995 – Radar
Oct. 31, 1995 – Spooky

NOVEMBER
Nov. 3, 1997 – Puffer
Nov. 6, 1996 – Pouch
Nov. 7, 1997 – Ants
Nov. 9, 1996 – Congo
Nov. 14, 1993 – Cubbie
Nov. 14, 1994 – Goldie
Nov. 20, 1997 – Prance
Nov. 21, 1996 – Nanook
Nov. 27, 1996 – Gobbles
Nov. 28, 1995 – Teddy Brown
Nov. 29, 1994 – Inky

DECEMBER
Dec. 2, 1996 – Jolly
Dec. 6, 1997 – Fortune
Dec. 8, 1996 – Waves
Dec. 12, 1996 – Blizzard
Dec. 14, 1996 – Seamore
Dec. 15, 1997 – Britannia
Dec. 16, 1995 – Velvet
Dec. 19, 1995 – Waddle
Dec. 21, 1996 – Echo
Dec. 22, 1996 – Snowball
Dec. 24, 1995 – Ziggy
Dec. 25, 1996 – Teddy 1997

- Freckles is also found with a July 28, 1996 birthday and Scottie with a June 3, 1996 birthday.
- Princess does not have a birthday.
- Libearty's birthday is Summer 1996.

HEART TAG CHRONOLOGY

There are five versions of the Ty heart tag that are attached to Beanie Babies.

The first version is a single heart tag with a skinny "Ty" printed on it. It does not open like a book. The style number, name and Ty information is printed on the back of these tags.

The second version heart tag has the same skinny "Ty" printed on it as the first version, but now the tag opens like a book. It is also referred to as a double tag.

The third version heart tag still opens like a book, but the "Ty" has a different look. The "Ty" is now larger and more rounded. It is also referred to as a bubble Ty.

The fourth version heart tag is the same size and shape as the third version heart tag, but a yellow star that says "BEANIE ORIGINAL BABY" was added. The "TY" was downsized and the gold trim is removed from the "TY."

The fifth version heart tag is the same size and shape as the fourth version heart tag, but the font has been changed to Comic Sans.

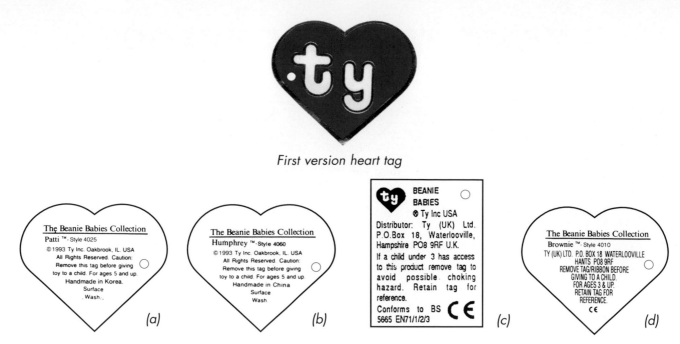

First version heart tag

NOTE: This was the first version Ty (UK) hang tag that was attached to Beanie Babies (c). The identifying marking "CE" was added. The Brownie tag (d) indicates that the age requirement for a child given this toy changed from "ages 5 and up" to "ages 3 and up."

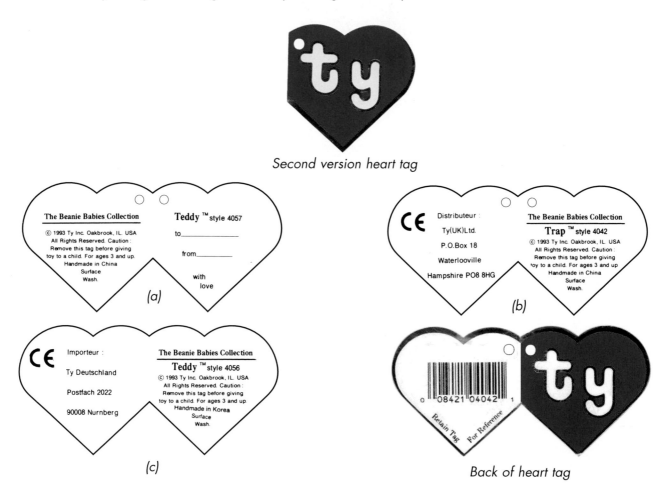

Second version heart tag

Note: Example (c) has the words "Handmade in China" covered up with "Handmade in Korea."

Third version heart tag

The Beanie Babies Collection

All Rights Reserved. Caution :
Remove this tag before giving
toy to a child.

Handmade in China
Surface
Wash.

Peking ™ style 4013
© Ty Inc. Oakbrook, IL. USA

to_____

from_____

*with
love*

(a)

The Beanie Babies Collection

© 1993 Ty Inc. Oakbrook, IL. USA
All Rights Reserved. Caution :
Remove this tag before giving
toy to a child. For ages 3 and up.
Handmade in China
Surface
Wash.

Trap ™ style 4042

to_____

from_____

with
love

(b)

Importeur Ty Deutschland
Postfach 2022 90008 Nürnberg

CE

0 08421 04013 1

Please remove all
tags and accessories
before giving this
item to a
child

Back of tag (a)

0 08421 04042 1

Retain Tag For Reference

Back of tag (b)

The Beanie Babies ™ Collection

© Ty Inc.
Oakbrook IL. U.S.A.

Ty UK Ltd.
Waterlooville, Hants
PO8 8HH

Ty Deutschland
90008 Nürnberg

Handmade in Korea

Bumble ™ style 4045

to _____

from _____

with

love

(c)

The Beanie Babies ™ Collection

© Ty Inc.
Oakbrook IL. U.S.A.

© Ty UK Ltd.
Waterlooville, Hants
PO8 8HH

© Ty Deutschland
90008 Nürnberg

Handmade in China

Tusk ™ style 4076

to _____

from _____

with

love

(d)

Please remove all swing tags before giving
this item to a child under 36 months.

CE

0 08421 04045 2

Retain Tag For Reference
Surface
Wash

Back of tag (c)

Please remove all swing tags
before giving this item to a child

CE

0 08421 04076 6

Retain Tag For Reference
Surface
Wash

Back of tag (d)

NOTE: This rare tag (a) has been found on several Beanie Babies including: Peking, Chilly, Trap, and Web.
When all three Ty locations were listed (c and d) on this third version heart tag, the child safety
regulations were transferred to the back.

Fourth version heart tag

The Beanie Babies™ Collection
© Ty Inc.
Oakbrook IL. U.S.A.
© Ty UK Ltd.
Waterlooville, Hants
PO8 8HH
© Ty Deutschland
90008 Nürnberg
Handmade in Korea

Tabasco™ style 4002
DATE OF BIRTH : 5-15-95

Although Tabasco is not so tall
He loves to play basketball
He is a star player in his dreams
Can you guess his favorite team?

Visit our web page!!!
http://www.ty.com

(a)

The Beanie Babies™ Collection
© Ty Inc.
Oakbrook IL. U.S.A.
© Ty UK Ltd.
Waterlooville, Hants
PO8 8HH
© Ty Deutschland
90008 Nürnberg
Handmade in China

CLAUDE™ style 4083
DATE OF BIRTH : 9-3-96

Claude the crab paints by the sea
A famous artist he hopes to be
But the tide came in and his paints fell
Now his art is on his shell!

Visit our web page!!!
http://www.ty.com

(b)

The Beanie Babies™ Collection
© Ty Inc.
Oakbrook IL. U.S.A.
© Ty UK Ltd.
Waterlooville, Hants
PO8 8HH
© Ty Deutschland
90008 Nürnberg
Made in Korea

Legs™ style 4020
DATE OF BIRTH : 4-25-93

Legs lives in a hollow log
Legs likes to play leap frog
If you like to hang out at the lake
Legs will be the new friend you'll make!

(c)

Please remove all swing tags
re giving this item to a child

0 08421 04020 9

Retain Tag For Reference
For ages 3 and up
Surface
Wash

(d)

The Beanie Babies™ Collection
© Ty Inc.
Oakbrook IL. U.S.A.
© Ty UK Ltd.
Fareham, Hants
PO15 5TX
© Ty Deutschland
90008 Nürnberg
Handmade in China

Blizzard™ style 4163
DATE OF BIRTH : 12-12-96

In the mountains, where it's snowy and cold
Lives a beautiful tiger, I've been told
Black and white, she's hard to compare
Of all the tigers, she is most rare!

Visit our web page!!!
http://www.ty.com

(e)

Please remove all swing tags
before giving this item to a child

0 08421 04163 3

Retain Tag For Reference
For ages 3 and up
Surface
Wash

(f)

The Beanie Babies® Collection™
© Ty Inc.
Oakbrook IL. U.S.A.
© Ty Europe Ltd.
Fareham, Hants
PO15 5TX
© Ty Canada
Aurora, Ontario
Handmade in China

Strut™ style 4171
DATE OF BIRTH : 3-8-96

Listen closely to "cock-a-doodle-doo"
What's the rooster saying to you?
Hurry, wake up sleepy head
We have lots to do, get out of bed!

Visit our web page!!!
http://www.ty.com

(g)

The name of the country where the Beanie Baby was produced (Korea and China) is printed on the heart tag (a and b), as well as the tush tag.

Some of the Beanie Babies' names are printed in all capital letters (b).

A circular sticker with "CE" printed on it (d) has also been found on the back of the heart tag.

The Ty UK address has changed from Waterlooville, Hants to Fareham, Hants (e).

Mid-1997, Ty UK Ltd. and Ty Deutschland consolidated to form Ty Europe Ltd. Ty Canada is now listed on the tag (g).

Fifth version heart tag

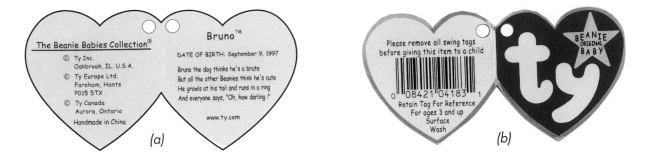

(a)   (b)

A new font, called Comic Sans, is used for the 5th generation heart tags.

Inside the heart tag, the phrase "Beanie Babies" is no longer trademarked. Instead, the whole phrase "The Beanie Babies Collection" is now registered so the trademark symbol was removed. The style number has been eliminated, and the Beanie Baby's name is centered at the top of the tag. The month and year of the Beanie Baby's birthdate are completely written out; not abbreviated as in the past. The phrase "Visit our web page!!!" is now eliminated as well as "http://" before the Ty web page address (a).

On the back of the tag, the font has also been changed to Comic Sans. The style number, which has been eliminated from the inside of the tag, still appears in the UPC code (b).

HEART TAG FASTENERS

These plastic strips attach the heart tag to the Beanie Baby. They come in two colors, red and clear. The majority of the heart tags are attached with the red strip. Both of these colors have been used to attach the heart tag to the Beanie Baby as far back as the 1994 introductions. These strips are approximately 1/2" and 3/4" in size.

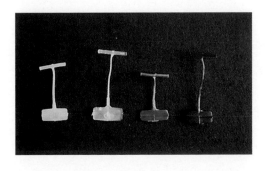

SPECIAL HEART TAGS

Princess heart tag

On October 29, 1997, Ty Inc. announced the release of Princess in memory of Diana, Princess of Wales. During December of 1997, Princess arrived at the stores with a special swing tag. Inside the swing tag is a poem dedicated to Princess Diana. There is no birthday listed for Princess. This is the first time that a special heart tag was designed for a person instead of a Beanie Baby.

*Heart tag with caricature of Harry Caray
and a special poem dedicated to him.*

For the first time in the history of Ty Inc., a limited edition swing tag was attached to a Beanie Baby and offered at a sports event. On May 3, 1998, the Chicago Cubs and Ty Inc. presented Daisy, the cow, in memory of Harry Caray, the legendary Chicago Cubs sportscaster. Attached to Daisy, the cow, is a special heart tag. Inside the swing tag is a caricature of Harry Caray and a special poem dedicated to him.

Clubby - front and back of Clubby heart tag

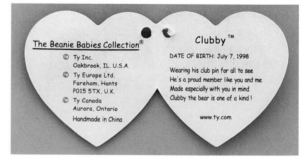

Clubby - inside of heart tag

Clubby is the limited edition Beanie Baby that can only be ordered by members of the Beanie Babies Official Club. He is a royal blue bear with a tie-dyed ribbon. On his chest is the BBOC club pin. Inside the Clubby swing tag there is no style number listed. The back of the heart tag does not have a UPC code.

TUSH TAG CHRONOLOGY
FIRST VERSION TUSH TAGS

The first tush tag (body tag) was black and white and was created in 1993. In the majority of cases, the type of tush tag that your Beanie Baby has indicates the age of your Beanie Baby, but there are exceptions. There is no 1994 tush tag. The Beanie Babies produced in 1994 have the 1993 black and white tush tag. The name of the country where the Beanie Babies were produced, Korea or China, is printed on the tush tag. The first version tush tag was black and white. It was produced in 1993 and 1995.

© 1993 TY INC., OAKBROOK IL. U.S.A. ALL RIGHTS RESERVED HAND MADE IN KOREA	ALL NEW MATERIAL POLYESTER FIBER & P.V.C. PELLETS PA. REG #1965

© 1993 TY INC., OAKBROOK IL. U.S.A. ALL RIGHTS RESERVED HAND MADE IN KOREA SURFACE WASHABLE	ALL NEW MATERIAL POLYESTER FIBER & P.V.C. PELLETS PA. REG #1965 FOR AGES 3 AND UP

© 1995 TY INC., OAKBROOK IL. U.S.A. ALL RIGHTS RESERVED HAND MADE IN KOREA SURFACE WASHABLE	ALL NEW MATERIAL POLYESTER FIBER & P.V.C. PELLETS **CE** PA. REG #1965 FOR AGES 3 AND UP

© 1993 TY INC., OAKBROOK IL. U.S.A. ALL RIGHTS RESERVED HAND MADE IN CHINA SURFACE WASHABLE	ALL NEW MATERIAL POLYESTER FIBER & P.V.C. PELLETS PA. REG #1965 **CE** FOR AGES 3 AND UP

© 1995 TY INC., OAKBROOK IL. U.S.A. ALL RIGHTS RESERVED HAND MADE IN CHINA SURFACE WASHABLE	ALL NEW MATERIAL POLYESTER FIBER & P.V.C. PELLETS PA. REG #1965 FOR AGES 3 AND UP

© 1993 TY INC., OAKBROOK IL. U.S.A. ALL RIGHTS RESERVED HAND MADE IN CHINA SURFACE WASHABLE	ALL NEW MATERIAL POLYESTER FIBER & P.V.C. PELLETS **CE** PA. REG #1965

The identifying marking "CE" is also printed on some of these first version tush tags. When the identifying marking "CE" was added to some of these tush tags, "FOR AGES 3 AND UP" was eliminated. It has 1993 or 1995 printed on it.

CE: "CE" stands for "Conformite Europeene". This identifying marking indicates that the product complies with the essential requirements for health, safety, environment and consumer protection for the European market; however, it is not a guarantee of quality. This mark is required for products to enter European customs, and move freely from country to country.

SECOND VERSION TUSH TAGS

The second version tush tag was red and white. It has 1993 or 1995 printed on it.
The name of the Beanie Baby does not appear on the tag.

HAND MADE IN KOREA
© 1993 TY INC.,
OAKBROOK IL. U.S.A.
SURFACE WASHABLE
ALL NEW MATERIAL
POLYESTER FIBER &
P.V.C. PELLETS
REG. NO PA-1965(KR)
FOR AGES 3 AND UP
CE

HAND MADE IN CHINA
© 1993 TY INC.,
OAKBROOK IL. U.S.A.
SURFACE WASHABLE
ALL NEW MATERIAL
POLYESTER FIBER &
P.V.C. PELLETS
REG. NO PA-1965(KR)
FOR AGES 3 AND UP
CE

HAND MADE IN KOREA
© 1995 TY INC.,
OAKBROOK IL. U.S.A.
SURFACE WASHABLE
ALL NEW MATERIAL
POLYESTER FIBER &
P.V.C. PELLETS
REG. NO PA-1965(KR)
FOR AGES 3 AND UP
CE

HAND MADE IN CHINA
© 1995 TY INC.,
OAKBROOK IL. U.S.A.
SURFACE WASHABLE
ALL NEW MATERIAL
POLYESTER FIBER &
P.V.C. PELLETS
REG. NO PA-1965(KR)
FOR AGES 3 AND UP
CE

On some of these later second version tush tags, "FOR AGES 3 AND UP" was eliminated.

HAND MADE IN KOREA
© 1993 TY INC.,
OAKBROOK IL. U.S.A.
SURFACE WASHABLE
ALL NEW MATERIAL
POLYESTER FIBER &
P.V.C. PELLETS
REG. NO PA-1965(KR)
CE

HAND MADE IN CHINA
© 1993 TY INC.,
OAKBROOK IL. U.S.A.
SURFACE WASHABLE
ALL NEW MATERIAL
POLYESTER FIBER &
P.V.C. PELLETS
REG. NO PA-1965(KR)
CE

HAND MADE IN KOREA
© 1995 TY INC.,
OAKBROOK IL. U.S.A.
SURFACE WASHABLE
ALL NEW MATERIAL
POLYESTER FIBER &
P.V.C. PELLETS
REG. NO PA-1965(KR)
CE

HAND MADE IN CHINA
© 1995 TY INC.,
OAKBROOK IL. U.S.A.
SURFACE WASHABLE
ALL NEW MATERIAL
POLYESTER FIBER &
P.V.C. PELLETS
REG. NO PA-1965(KR)
CE

THIRD VERSION TUSH TAGS

The third version is also red and white, but now the name of the Beanie Baby appears on the tag. It has 1993, 1995 or 1996 printed on it.

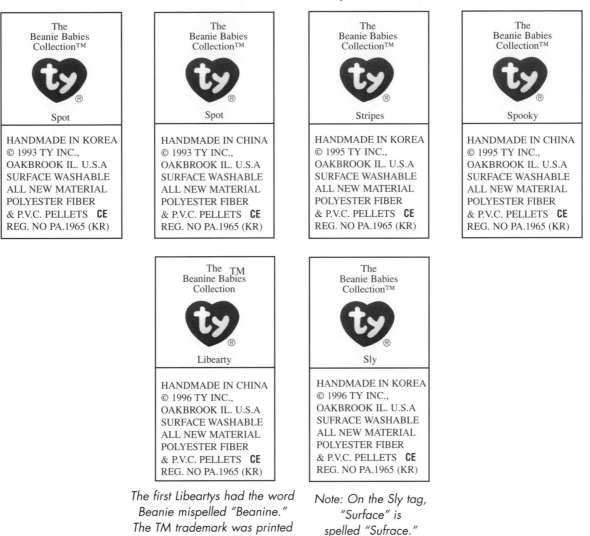

The
Beanie Babies
Collection™

ty®

Spot

HANDMADE IN KOREA
© 1993 TY INC.,
OAKBROOK IL. U.S.A
SURFACE WASHABLE
ALL NEW MATERIAL
POLYESTER FIBER
& P.V.C. PELLETS **CE**
REG. NO PA.1965 (KR)

The
Beanie Babies
Collection™

ty®

Spot

HANDMADE IN CHINA
© 1993 TY INC.,
OAKBROOK IL. U.S.A
SURFACE WASHABLE
ALL NEW MATERIAL
POLYESTER FIBER
& P.V.C. PELLETS **CE**
REG. NO PA.1965 (KR)

The
Beanie Babies
Collection™

ty®

Stripes

HANDMADE IN KOREA
© 1995 TY INC.,
OAKBROOK IL. U.S.A
SURFACE WASHABLE
ALL NEW MATERIAL
POLYESTER FIBER
& P.V.C. PELLETS **CE**
REG. NO PA.1965 (KR)

The
Beanie Babies
Collection™

ty®

Spooky

HANDMADE IN CHINA
© 1995 TY INC.,
OAKBROOK IL. U.S.A
SURFACE WASHABLE
ALL NEW MATERIAL
POLYESTER FIBER
& P.V.C. PELLETS **CE**
REG. NO PA.1965 (KR)

The ᵀᴹ
Beanine Babies
Collection

ty®

Libearty

HANDMADE IN CHINA
© 1996 TY INC.,
OAKBROOK IL. U.S.A
SURFACE WASHABLE
ALL NEW MATERIAL
POLYESTER FIBER
& P.V.C. PELLETS **CE**
REG. NO PA.1965 (KR)

The
Beanie Babies
Collection™

ty®

Sly

HANDMADE IN KOREA
© 1996 TY INC.,
OAKBROOK IL. U.S.A
SUFRACE WASHABLE
ALL NEW MATERIAL
POLYESTER FIBER
& P.V.C. PELLETS **CE**
REG. NO PA.1965 (KR)

The first Libeartys had the word Beanie mispelled "Beanine." The TM trademark was printed above the word "Babies."

Note: On the Sly tag, "Surface" is spelled "Sufrace."

FOURTH VERSION TUSH TAGS

These fourth version tush tags were introduced in mid-1997. While permanent tush tags were being produced, temporary stickers with a star printed on them were used.

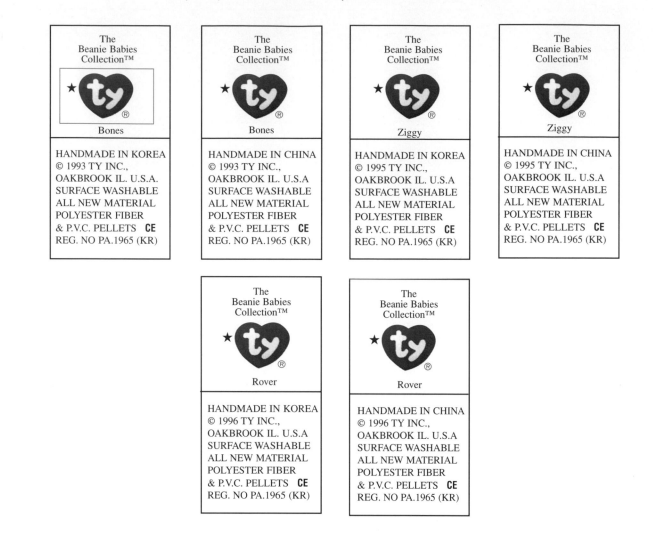

The Beanie Babies Collection™ ★ **ty** ® Bones	The Beanie Babies Collection™ ★ **ty** ® Bones	The Beanie Babies Collection™ ★ **ty** ® Ziggy	The Beanie Babies Collection™ ★ **ty** ® Ziggy
HANDMADE IN KOREA © 1993 TY INC., OAKBROOK IL. U.S.A. SURFACE WASHABLE ALL NEW MATERIAL POLYESTER FIBER & P.V.C. PELLETS **CE** REG. NO PA.1965 (KR)	HANDMADE IN CHINA © 1993 TY INC., OAKBROOK IL. U.S.A SURFACE WASHABLE ALL NEW MATERIAL POLYESTER FIBER & P.V.C. PELLETS **CE** REG. NO PA.1965 (KR)	HANDMADE IN KOREA © 1995 TY INC., OAKBROOK IL. U.S.A SURFACE WASHABLE ALL NEW MATERIAL POLYESTER FIBER & P.V.C. PELLETS **CE** REG. NO PA.1965 (KR)	HANDMADE IN CHINA © 1995 TY INC., OAKBROOK IL. U.S.A SURFACE WASHABLE ALL NEW MATERIAL POLYESTER FIBER & P.V.C. PELLETS **CE** REG. NO PA.1965 (KR)

The Beanie Babies Collection™ ★ **ty** ® Rover	The Beanie Babies Collection™ ★ **ty** ® Rover
HANDMADE IN KOREA © 1996 TY INC., OAKBROOK IL. U.S.A SURFACE WASHABLE ALL NEW MATERIAL POLYESTER FIBER & P.V.C. PELLETS **CE** REG. NO PA.1965 (KR)	HANDMADE IN CHINA © 1996 TY INC., OAKBROOK IL. U.S.A SURFACE WASHABLE ALL NEW MATERIAL POLYESTER FIBER & P.V.C. PELLETS **CE** REG. NO PA.1965 (KR)

FIFTH VERSION TUSH TAGS

The fifth version tush tag has the "Beanie Babies" now ® registered and the name of the Beanie Baby is ™ trademarked. They started appearing October 1997.

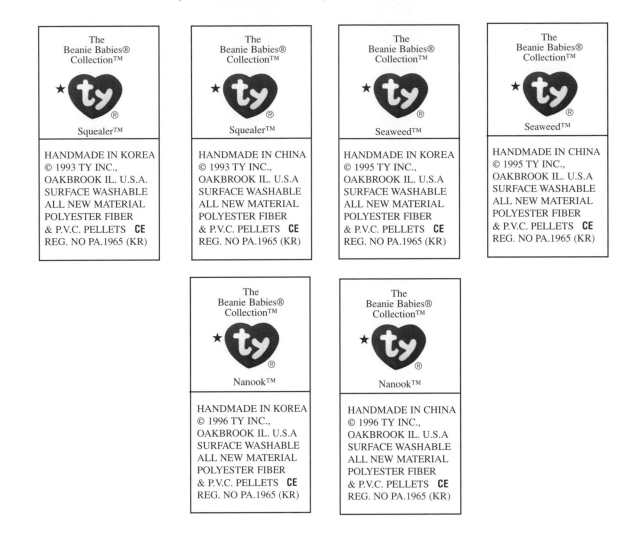

The
Beanie Babies®
Collection™

★ ty ®

Squealer™

HANDMADE IN KOREA
© 1993 TY INC.,
OAKBROOK IL. U.S.A.
SURFACE WASHABLE
ALL NEW MATERIAL
POLYESTER FIBER
& P.V.C. PELLETS CE
REG. NO PA.1965 (KR)

The
Beanie Babies®
Collection™

★ ty ®

Squealer™

HANDMADE IN CHINA
© 1993 TY INC.,
OAKBROOK IL. U.S.A
SURFACE WASHABLE
ALL NEW MATERIAL
POLYESTER FIBER
& P.V.C. PELLETS CE
REG. NO PA.1965 (KR)

The
Beanie Babies®
Collection™

★ ty ®

Seaweed™

HANDMADE IN KOREA
© 1995 TY INC.,
OAKBROOK IL. U.S.A
SURFACE WASHABLE
ALL NEW MATERIAL
POLYESTER FIBER
& P.V.C. PELLETS CE
REG. NO PA.1965 (KR)

The
Beanie Babies®
Collection™

★ ty ®

Seaweed™

HANDMADE IN CHINA
© 1995 TY INC.,
OAKBROOK IL. U.S.A
SURFACE WASHABLE
ALL NEW MATERIAL
POLYESTER FIBER
& P.V.C. PELLETS CE
REG. NO PA.1965 (KR)

The
Beanie Babies®
Collection™

★ ty ®

Nanook™

HANDMADE IN KOREA
© 1996 TY INC.,
OAKBROOK IL. U.S.A
SURFACE WASHABLE
ALL NEW MATERIAL
POLYESTER FIBER
& P.V.C. PELLETS CE
REG. NO PA.1965 (KR)

The
Beanie Babies®
Collection™

★ ty ®

Nanook™

HANDMADE IN CHINA
© 1996 TY INC.,
OAKBROOK IL. U.S.A
SURFACE WASHABLE
ALL NEW MATERIAL
POLYESTER FIBER
& P.V.C. PELLETS CE
REG. NO PA.1965 (KR)

SIXTH VERSION TUSH TAGS

The sixth version tush tag now has the phrase "The Beanie Babies Collection" ® registered.
They started appearing December 1997. Handmade in Indonesia was printed on some of these tush tags.

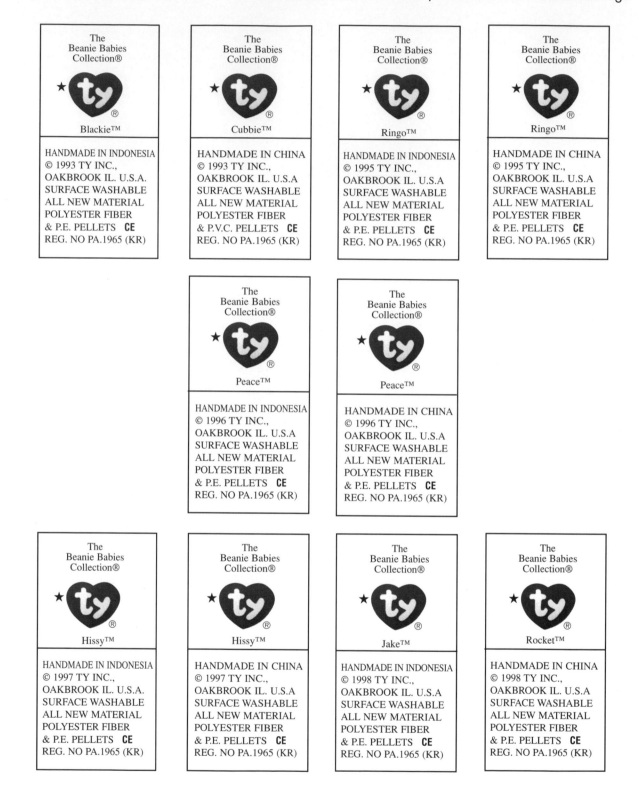

The
Beanie Babies
Collection®

★ **ty** ®

Blackie™

HANDMADE IN INDONESIA
© 1993 TY INC.,
OAKBROOK IL. U.S.A.
SURFACE WASHABLE
ALL NEW MATERIAL
POLYESTER FIBER
& P.E. PELLETS **CE**
REG. NO PA.1965 (KR)

The
Beanie Babies
Collection®

★ **ty** ®

Cubbie™

HANDMADE IN CHINA
© 1993 TY INC.,
OAKBROOK IL. U.S.A
SURFACE WASHABLE
ALL NEW MATERIAL
POLYESTER FIBER
& P.V.C. PELLETS **CE**
REG. NO PA.1965 (KR)

The
Beanie Babies
Collection®

★ **ty** ®

Ringo™

HANDMADE IN INDONESIA
© 1995 TY INC.,
OAKBROOK IL. U.S.A
SURFACE WASHABLE
ALL NEW MATERIAL
POLYESTER FIBER
& P.E. PELLETS **CE**
REG. NO PA.1965 (KR)

The
Beanie Babies
Collection®

★ **ty** ®

Ringo™

HANDMADE IN CHINA
© 1995 TY INC.,
OAKBROOK IL. U.S.A
SURFACE WASHABLE
ALL NEW MATERIAL
POLYESTER FIBER
& P.E. PELLETS **CE**
REG. NO PA.1965 (KR)

The
Beanie Babies
Collection®

★ **ty** ®

Peace™

HANDMADE IN INDONESIA
© 1996 TY INC.,
OAKBROOK IL. U.S.A
SURFACE WASHABLE
ALL NEW MATERIAL
POLYESTER FIBER
& P.E. PELLETS **CE**
REG. NO PA.1965 (KR)

The
Beanie Babies
Collection®

★ **ty** ®

Peace™

HANDMADE IN CHINA
© 1996 TY INC.,
OAKBROOK IL. U.S.A
SURFACE WASHABLE
ALL NEW MATERIAL
POLYESTER FIBER
& P.E. PELLETS **CE**
REG. NO PA.1965 (KR)

The
Beanie Babies
Collection®

★ **ty** ®

Hissy™

HANDMADE IN INDONESIA
© 1997 TY INC.,
OAKBROOK IL. U.S.A.
SURFACE WASHABLE
ALL NEW MATERIAL
POLYESTER FIBER
& P.E. PELLETS **CE**
REG. NO PA.1965 (KR)

The
Beanie Babies
Collection®

★ **ty** ®

Hissy™

HANDMADE IN CHINA
© 1997 TY INC.,
OAKBROOK IL. U.S.A
SURFACE WASHABLE
ALL NEW MATERIAL
POLYESTER FIBER
& P.E. PELLETS **CE**
REG. NO PA.1965 (KR)

The
Beanie Babies
Collection®

★ **ty** ®

Jake™

HANDMADE IN INDONESIA
© 1998 TY INC.,
OAKBROOK IL. U.S.A
SURFACE WASHABLE
ALL NEW MATERIAL
POLYESTER FIBER
& P.E. PELLETS **CE**
REG. NO PA.1965 (KR)

The
Beanie Babies
Collection®

★ **ty** ®

Rocket™

HANDMADE IN CHINA
© 1998 TY INC.,
OAKBROOK IL. U.S.A
SURFACE WASHABLE
ALL NEW MATERIAL
POLYESTER FIBER
& P.E. PELLETS **CE**
REG. NO PA.1965 (KR)

CANADIAN TUSH TAGS

The Canadian tush tag is a larger black and white tag. It is attached to all Beanie Babies that were produced exclusively for Canada. The information on this tag is written in English and French.

Not to be removed until delivered to the consumer	Ne pas enlever avant livraison au consommateur
This label is affixed in compliance with the Upholstered and Stuffed Articles Act	Cette étiquette est apposée conformément à loi sur les articles rembourrés
This article contains NEW MATERIAL ONLY	Cet article contient MATÉRIAU NEUF SEULEMENT
Made by Ont. Reg. No. 97K7293	Fabrique par No d'enreg. Ont. 97K7293
Made in China Content:Polyester Fibres	Fabriqué en Corée Contenu:Fibres Polyester

(a)

Not to be removed until delivered to the consumer	Ne pas enlever avant livraison au consommateur
This label is affixed in compliance with the Upholstered and Stuffed Articles Act	Cette étiquette est apposée conformément à loi sur les articles rembourrés
This article contains NEW MATERIAL ONLY	Cet article contient MATÉRIAU NEUF SEULEMENT
Made by Ont. Reg. No. 97K7293	Fabrique par No d'enreg. Ont. 97K7293
Made in China Content:Polyester Fibres	Fabriqué en Chine Contenu:Fibres Polyester

(b)

These were the first Canadian tush tags attached to Beanie Babies. Note: Tag (a) indicates, "Made in China" and "Fabriqué en Corée" (Made in Korea) on the same tag. Tag (b) indicates, "Made in China" and "Fabriqué en Chine" (Made in China) on the same tag.

Not to be removed until delivered to the consumer	Ne pas enlever avant livraison au consommateur
This label is affixed in compliance with the Upholstered and Stuffed Articles Act	Cette étiquette est apposée conformément à loi sur les articles rembourrés
This article contains NEW MATERIAL ONLY	Cet article contient MATERIAU NEUF SEULEMENT
Made by Ont. Reg. No. 20B6484	Fabrique par No d'enrg. Ont. 20B6484
Contents: Plastic Pellets Polyesters Fibers Made in Korea	Contenu: Boulette de plastique Fibres de Polyester Fabriqué en Corée

Not to be removed until delivered to the consumer	Ne pas enlever avant livraison au consommateur
This label is affixed in compliance with the Upholstered and Stuffed Articles Act	Cette étiquette est apposée conformément à loi sur les articles rembourrés
This article contains NEW MATERIAL ONLY	Cet article contient MATERIAU NEUF SEULEMENT
Made by Ont. Reg. No. 20B6484	Fabrique par No d'enrg. Ont. 20B6484
Contents: Plastic Pellets Polyesters Fibers Made in China	Contenu:Boulette de plastique Fibres de Polyester Fabriqué en Chine

In 1995, new Canadian tush tags appear with the registered number 20B6484.

EMBROIDERED TUSH TAG

This embroidered cloth Ty tush tag has also been found attached to some Beanie Babies. The majority of Beanie Babies that have this tush tag, also have the 2nd version heart tag, as well as, the Canadian tush tag. The embroidered tag is primarily used for other Ty products such as the plush line. Because of human error and language differences, this tag was accidentally attached to some Beanies Babies when a changeover was being made from a plush production run to a Beanie Baby run.

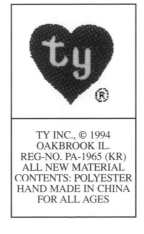

TY INC., © 1994
OAKBROOK IL.
REG-NO. PA-1965 (KR)
ALL NEW MATERIAL
CONTENTS: POLYESTER
HAND MADE IN CHINA
FOR ALL AGES

WATERMARK

During June of 1998, these red, oval markings started appearing on the inside of the tush tag attached to Beanie Babies made in China. The Chinese lettering and the number, indicate the factory where that particular Beanie Baby was produced.

SPECIAL TUSH TAGS

In addition to the special heart tag, Princess also has a special tush tag. Instead of the standard print used on other Beanie Baby tush tags, her name is written in script.

Clubby's tush tag is the same as a 6th generation tush tag, except that it has a two-digit number located next to the upper right-hand corner of the heart.

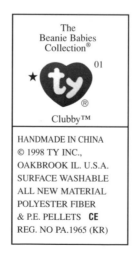

TAG CONDITION AND VALUATION

When buying a Beanie Baby, not only does a collector look at the condition of the Beanie Baby, but the tags as well. The value of the Beanie Baby decreases by approximately 55% to 65% if there is no heart tag. Because of the importance of the tag, even a slight crease diminishes the value of the Beanie Baby. If there are creases in the heart tag, the collector can deduct anywhere from 5% to 60% off the value of the Beanie Baby. If a heart tag was taken off, but is otherwise in mint condition, there is a deduction of about 5%. Many stores and Beanie Baby dealers have hand held tag attachers and will reattach the tag free of charge if you supply them with the plastic fastener. Many Beanie Babies arrive with additional plastic fasteners. Take the additional fastener off carefully and store it until you need it.

The overall value of a Beanie Baby, when the tush tag and heart tag are removed, depreciates by approximately 80%. This is obviously a significant amount especially if the Beanie Baby is retired.

HEART TAG CONDITION AND VALUATION

Mint Tag:
This is a tag that looks like it just came off the printing press. There are no creases, writing or stickers anywhere on this tag. It is absolutely perfect. Some collectors even refer to them as "Museum Quality." Price guides usually list mint tag values.

Mint Tag

Slight Crease:
This is a crease that could be caused by the pressure of the plastic tag fastener or a crease that is usually no more than a 1/4 inch in length. For a slight crease, deduct approximately 5% to 10% off the value of the Beanie Baby.

Slight Crease

Noticeable Crease:
This is a crease that usually runs the length of the tag in either direction. For a noticeable crease, deduct approximately 20% to 25% off the value of the Beanie Baby.

Noticeable Crease

Numerous Creases:
This tag has many creases running throughout the tag. For numerous creases, deduct approximately 35% to 45% off the value of the Beanie Baby.

Numerous Creases

Mangled Tag:
This tag looks as if it was crumpled in one's hand. For a mangled tag, deduct approximately 45% to 60% off the value of the Beanie Baby.

Mangled Tag

HEART TAG CONDITION AND VALUATION-continued

Damaged tag

Writing on tag

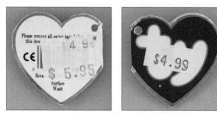

Price sticker on tag

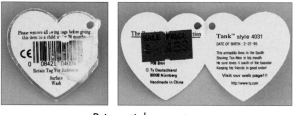

Price sticker on tag

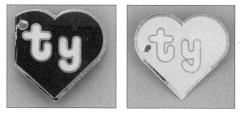

Faded tag

Damaged Tag:

These tags are damaged in some way and need to be evaluated on a case by case basis. Rips, scratches, words missing, or ink fading are some of the items that can be included in this category. The seller must describe the defect in detail. Sending a copy or scan of the tag can help the buyer understand the type of damage, so both parties can agree on a fair price. The price deduction can range anywhere from 5% to 65% off the value of the Beanie Baby.

Writing on Tag:

A deduction in price should also be taken when there is writing on the heart tag. If the heart tag is in mint condition and there is writing on the heart tag, deduct approximately 20% to 40% off the value of the Beanie Baby.

Price Sticker on Tag:

Although less desirable to most collectors, a price sticker on the backside of a heart tag should not affect the value of the Beanie Baby. The sticker is part of the "history" of the Beanie, and removal of it can cause damage to the heart tag.

However, price tags on the front of the heart tag, in the inside of the tag or remnants left on any part of the heart tag, usually result in about a 10% to 20% deduction in value if the heart tag itself is in mint condition.

Many collectors have become quite proficient at taking off price tags and glue remnants with the help of a hair dryer and small amounts of products such as Goo Gone, UnDo, Vaseline or lighter fluid. Be extremely careful though. Some of the products used to remove price tags will cause smearing and discoloration of the heart tag if used improperly!

Faded Tag:

If a Beanie Baby heart tag is exposed to the sun for an extended period of time, the red heart tag will change to a pink color.

If the tag is exposed to the sun over a longer period of time the tag will fade from a red to a cream color and the gold lining to a silver color. This has happened to tagged Beanie Babies kept on a car dashboard, by the rear window, or on a window ledge in the house. This damage to a tag can result in a 45% to 55% price deduction, even if the heart tag is in otherwise mint condition.

TUSH TAG CONDITION AND VALUATION

Tush tag condition also determines the value of the Beanie Baby. Even though tush tags withstand more use because they are made of durable fabric, their condition should also be considered when determining the value of a Beanie Baby. If the tush tag is missing, the value of the Beanie Baby decreases by approximately 55% to 65%, if the heart tag is otherwise attached and in mint condition.

Writing on Tag:
A deduction in price should also be taken when there is writing on the tush tag. The average deduction for writing on a tush tag is approximately 20% to 40% off the value of the Beanie Baby, if the tush tag is otherwise in mint condition.

Writing on tag

Frayed Tag:
A deauction in price should be taken when the tush tag is so worn that the material is starting to fray. The average deduction is about 20% to 30% off the value of the Beanie Baby.

Frayed tag

Damaged Tag:
These tags are damaged in some way and need to be evaluated on a case by case basis. Rips or ink fading are some of the items that can be included in this category. The seller must describe the defect in detail. Sending a copy or scan of the tag can help the buyer understand the type of damage, so both parties can agree on a fair price. The price deduction can range anywhere from 5% to 65% off the value of the Beanie Baby.

Damaged tag

BUYER BEWARE

When purchasing a Beanie Baby sight unseen, either from the Internet or through newspaper ads, it is very important to ask appropriate questions about the condition of the Beanie Baby as well as the swing and tush tags.

- Does the Beanie Baby have both tags?
- What is the condition of the tags?
- Are they mint or creased tags?
- Is there writing on the tush or hang tag?
- Is there a sticker or sticker residue left on the tag?
- What is the condition of the Beanie Baby?
- Is the Beanie Baby in mint condition or is it used? If the Beanie Baby is used, have the seller describe the condition of the Beanie Baby in detail.

When you are spending a large sum of money for a Beanie Baby, do not be afraid to ask questions. Make sure that the Beanie Baby you purchase lives up to your expectations.

HEART TAG AND TUSH TAG CHRONOLOGY

Tush tag examples:

- © 1993 TY INC. OAKBROOK IL U.S.A. ALL RIGHTS RESERVED HAND MADE IN KOREA
- © 1993 TY INC. OAKBROOK IL U.S.A. ALL RIGHTS RESERVED HAND MADE IN CHINA SURFACE WASHABLE
- © 1993 TY INC. OAKBROOK IL U.S.A. ALL RIGHTS RESERVED HAND MADE IN CHINA SURFACE WASHABLE
- ALL NEW MATERIAL POLYESTER FIBER & P.V.C. PELLETS PA. REG #1965
- ALL NEW MATERIAL POLYESTER FIBER & P.V.C. PELLETS PA. REG #1965
- ALL NEW MATERIAL POLYESTER FIBER & P.V.C. PELLETS FOR AGES 3 AND UP PA. REG #1965 CE

Style No.	Beanie Name	Heart/Tush 1st Ver.	2nd Ver.	3rd Ver.	4th Ver.	5th Ver.	BBC 1st version	BBC 2nd version	BBC 3rd version	BBC 4th version	BBC 5th version	BBC 6th version
4032	Ally, the alligator	X	X	X	X		1993	1993	1993	1993		
4195	Ants, the anteater				X	X						1998
4074	Baldy, the eagle			X	X	X			1996	1996	1996	1996
4035	Batty, the brown bat				X	X				1996	1996	1996
4109	Bernie, the St. Bernard			X	X	X			1996	1996	1996	1996
4009	Bessie, the brown and white cow			X	X	X	1995		1995	1995	1993	1993
4011	Blackie, the black bear	X	X	X	X	X	1993	1993	1993	1993	1993	
4163	Blizzard, the black and white tiger				X	X			1996	1996	1996	1996
4001	Bones, the brown dog	X	X	X	X	X	1993	1993	1993	1993	1993	1993
4067	Bongo, the monkey brown tail - r/w tush / no name			X								
4067	Bongo, the monkey brown tail - r/w tush / name			X				1995				
4067	Bongo, the monkey tan tail - b/w tush			X			1995					
4067	Bongo, the monkey tan tail - r/w tush / no name								1995			
4067	Bongo, the monkey tan tail - r/w tush / with name				X	X			1995	1995	1995	1995
4601	Britannia, the brown bear-Union Jack flag-embroidered					X						1997
4601	Britannia, the brown bear-Union Jack flag-sewn on					X						1997
4085	Bronty, the brontosaurus			X			1995	1995				
4010	Brownie, the brown bear	X					1993					
4183	Bruno, the terrier					X						1997
4078	Bubbles, the black and yellow fish			X	X		1995	1995	1995	1995		
4016	Bucky, the beaver			X	X			1995	1995	1995	1995	
4045	Bumble, the bumble bee			X	X		1995	1995	1995	1995		
4071	Caw, the crow			X			1995	1995				
4012	Chilly, the white polar bear	X	X	X			1993					
4121	Chip, the calico cat				X	X			1996	1996	1996	1996
4015	Chocolate, the moose	X	X	X	X	X	1993	1993	1993	1993	1993	1993
4019	Chops, the lamb			X				1995	1995			
4083	Claude, the tie-dyed crab				X	X			1996	1996	1996	1996
n/a	Clubby, the BBOC royal blue bear				X	X						1998
4160	Congo, the gorilla				X	X			1996	1996	1996	1996
4079	Coral, the tie-dyed fish			X			1995	1995	1995			
4130	Crunch, the shark				X	X			1995	1996	1996	1996
4010	Cubbie, the brown bear	X	X	X	X		1993	1993	1993	1996	1996	1996
4052	Curly, the brown napped bear			X	X	X			1993	1993	1993	1993
4006	Daisy, the black and white cow	X	X	X	X	X	1993	1993	1993	1993	1993	1993
4008	Derby, the coarse-mane horse			X	X	X	1995	1995	1995	1995	1995	1995
4008	Derby, the coarse-mane horse-star					X						1995
4008	Derby, the fine-mane horse			X			1995	1995				

HEART TAG AND TUSH TAG CHRONOLOGY

Tush tag header boxes:

- © 1993 TY INC., OAKBROOK IL. U.S.A. ALL RIGHTS RESERVED HAND MADE IN KOREA — ALL NEW MATERIAL POLYESTER FIBER & P.V.C. PELLETS PA. REG #1965
- © 1993 TY INC., OAKBROOK IL. U.S.A. ALL RIGHTS RESERVED HAND MADE IN CHINA SURFACE WASHABLE — ALL NEW MATERIAL POLYESTER FIBER & P.V.C. PELLETS CE FOR AGES 3 AND UP PA. REG #1965
- © 1993 TY INC., OAKBROOK IL. U.S.A. ALL RIGHTS RESERVED HAND MADE IN CHINA SURFACE WASHABLE — ALL NEW MATERIAL POLYESTER FIBER & P.V.C. PELLETS CE PA. REG #1965

Style No.	Beanie Name	Heart 1st Version	Heart 2nd Version	Heart 3rd Version	Heart 4th Version	Heart 5th Version	Tush 1st version	Tush 2nd version	Tush 3rd version	Tush 4th version	Tush 5th version	Tush 6th version
4027	Digger, the orange crab	X	X	X			1993					
4027	Digger, the red crab				X	X		1993	1993	1993		1996
411C	Doby, the Doberman				X	X			1996	1996	1996	1996
4171	Doodle, the tie-dyed rooster				X				1996	1996		
4100	Dotty, the dalmatian with black ears				X	X			1996	1996	1996	1996
4190	Early, the robin					X						1998
4018	Ears, the brown rabbit			X	X	X		1995	1995	1995	1995	1995
4180	Echo, the dolphin				X	X			1996	1996	1996	1996
4186	Erin, the green bear with white shamrock					X						1997
4189	Fetch, the golden retriever					X						1998
4021	Flash, the dolphin	X	X	X	X		1993	1993	1993	1993		
4125	Fleece, the napped lamb					X			1996	1996	1996	1996
4012	Flip, the white cat			X	X			1993	1993	1993		
4113	Floppity, the lavender bunny				X				1996	1996	1996	1996
4043	Flutter, the tie-dyed butterfly			X			1995	1995				
4196	Fortune, the panda-sitting					X			1998			1998
4066	Freckles, the leopard				X	X			1996	1996	1996	1996
4051	Garcia, the tie-dyed bear			X	X			1993	1993	1993		
4191	GiGi, the poodle					X						1998
4188	Glory, the white bear with red/blue stars					X						1998
4034	Gobbles, the turkey				X	X					1996	1996
4023	Goldie, the goldfish	X	X	X	X	X	1993	1993	1993	1993	1993	1993
4126	Gracie, the swan				X	X			1996	1996	1996	1996
4092	Grunt, the razorback hog			X	X			1995	1995			
4061	Happy, the gray hippo	X	X	X			1993					
4061	Happy, the lavender hippo			X	X	X	1993	1993	1993	1993	1993	1993
4119	Hippity, the mint green bunny				X	X			1996	1996	1996	1996
4185	Hissy, the snake					X				1997		1997
4073	Hoot, the owl			X	X			1995	1995	1995		
4117	Hoppity, the rose bunny				X	X			1996	1996	1996	1996
4060	Humphrey, the camel	X	X	X			1993					
4038	Iggy, the iguana-Rainbow tags-collar					X				1997		1997
4038	Iggy, the iguana-Iggy tags-spikes					X				1997		1997
4044	Inch, the inchworm with felt antennae			X	X		1995	1995	1995	1995		
4044	Inch, the inchworm with yarn antennae					X		1995	1995	1995	1995	1995

HEART TAG AND TUSH TAG CHRONOLOGY

Tush tag material labels:

- © 1993 TY INC., OAKBROOK IL, U.S.A. ALL RIGHTS RESERVED HAND MADE IN KOREA / ALL NEW MATERIAL POLYESTER FIBER & P.V.C. PELLETS PA. REG #1965
- © 1993 TY INC., OAKBROOK IL, U.S.A. ALL RIGHTS RESERVED HAND MADE IN CHINA SURFACE WASHABLE / ALL NEW MATERIAL POLYESTER FIBER & P.V.C. PELLETS FOR AGES 3 AND UP PA. REG #1965 CE
- © 1993 TY INC., OAKBROOK IL, U.S.A. ALL RIGHTS RESERVED HAND MADE IN CHINA SURFACE WASHABLE / ALL NEW MATERIAL POLYESTER FIBER & P.V.C. PELLETS PA. REG #1965 CE

Style No.	Beanie Name	Tush 1st	Tush 2nd	Tush 3rd	Tush 4th	Tush 5th	Heart 1st	Heart 2nd	Heart 3rd	Heart 4th	Heart 5th	Heart 6th
4028	Inky, the pink octopus			X	X	X		1993	1993	1993	1993	1993
4028	Inky, the tan octopus with a mouth		X	X			1993					
4028	Inky, the tan octopus without a mouth	X	X				1993					
4197	Jabber, the parrot					X						1998
4199	Jake, the mallard duck					X						1998
4082	Jolly, the walrus			X	X	X			1996	1996	1996	1996
4070	Kiwi, the toucan			X	X		1995	1995	1995			
4192	Kuku, the cockatoo					X			1996			1998
4085	Lefty, the donkey with American flag				X					1993		
4020	Legs, the frog	X	X	X	X		1993	1993	1993			
4057	Libearty, the white bear with American flag				X				1996			
4057	Libearty/Beanine, the white bear with American flag				X				1996			
4033	Lizzy, the blue lizard with black spots			X	X	X	1995	1995	1995	1995	1995	1995
4033	Lizzy, the tie-dyed lizard			X			1995					
4040	Lucky, the ladybug with 7 felt dots	X	X	X			1993	1993	1993			
4040	Lucky, the ladybug with approx. 11 dots				X	X			1993	1993	1993	1993
4040	Lucky, the ladybug with approx. 21 dots				X				1995			
4088	Magic, the white dragon-hot pink stitching				X				1995			
4088	Magic, the white dragon-light pink stitching			X	X		1995	1995	1995	1995	1995	
4081	Manny, the manatee			X	X			1995	1995			
4600	Maple/Maple, the white bear with Canadian flag				X	X			1996	1996	1996	1996
4600	Maple/Pride, the white bear with Canadian flag				X				1996			
4600	Maple/Special Olympics, the white bear-Canadian flag				X				1996			
4162	Mel, the Koala				X	X			1996	1996	1996	1996
4007	Mystic, the unicorn with iridescent horn					X	1993				1993	1993
4007	Mystic, the unicorn with tan horn		X	X	X	X	1993	1993	1993	1993	1993	1993
4007	Mystic, the unicorn with tan horn/fine-mane	X	X	X			1995		1995			
4067	Nana, the monkey with tan tail - b/w tush											
4104	Nanook, the Siberian Husky				X	X			1996	1996	1996	1996
4003	Nip, the all gold cat with pink ears (no white)	X		X			1993		1993			
4003	Nip, the gold cat with white face and belly		X	X			1993	1993	1993			
4003	Nip, the gold cat with white paws			X	X	X	1993		1996	1996	1996	1996
4114	Nuts, the squirrel				X	X			1996	1996	1996	1996
4025	Patti, the deep fuchsia platypus	X					1993					
4025	Patti, the fuchsia platypus			X	X	X		1993	1993	1993	1993	1993
4025	Patti, the magenta platypus			X			1993		1993			
4025	Patti, the raspberry platypus	X	X				1993	1993				
4053	Peace, the tie-dyed bear				X	X			1996	1996	1996	1996

158

HEART TAG AND TUSH TAG CHRONOLOGY

Style No.	Beanie Name	Tush 1st Version	Tush 2nd Version	Tush 3rd Version	Tush 4th Version	Tush 5th Version	Heart 1st version	Heart 2nd version	Heart 3rd version	Heart 4th version	Heart 5th version	Heart 6th version
4053	Peace, the pastel tie-dyed bear					X						1996
4062	Peanut, the light blue elephant			X	X	X	1995	1995	1995	1995	1995	1995
4062	Peanut, the royal blue elephant			X			1995					
4013	Peking, the panda-laying	X	X	X			1993					
4026	Pinchers, the red lobster	X	X	X	X	X	1993	1993	1993	1993	1993	1993
4072	Pinky, the pink flamingo			X	X	X	1995	1995	1995	1995	1995	1995
4161	Pouch, the kangaroo				X	X			1996	1996	1996	1996
4122	Pounce, the brown tie-dyed cat					X						1997
4123	Prance, the gray striped cat					X						1997
4300	Princess, the purple bear with white rose					X						1997
4181	Puffer, the puffin					X						1997
4106	Pugsly, the Pug dog				X	X			1996	1996	1996	1996
4026	Punchers, the red lobster	X					1993					
4024	Quacker, the duck with wings		X				1993					
4024	Quacker, the duck without wings		X				1993					
4024	Quackers, the duck with wings			X	X	X	1993	1993	1993	1993	1993	1993
4024	Quackers, the duck without wings	X					1993					
4091	Radar, the black bat			X	X		1995	1995	1995			
4037	Rainbow, the chameleon-Iggy tags-spikes					X						1997
4037	Rainbow, the chameleon with tongue-Iggy tags-spikes					X						1997
4037	Rainbow, the pastel chameleon with tongue-Iggy tags-spikes					X						1997
4037	Rainbow, the pastel chameleon with tongue-Rainbow tags-collar					X						1997
4086	Rex, the tyrannosaurus			X			1995	1995	1995			
4086	Righty, the elephant with American flag				X							
4014	Ringo, the raccoon			X	X	X		1995	1995	1995	1995	1995
4069	Roary, the lion			X	X	X			1996	1996	1996	1996
4202	Rocket, the bluejay					X						1998
4101	Rover, the red dog				X	X			1996	1996	1996	1996
4107	Scoop, the pelican				X	X			1996	1996	1996	1996
4102	Scottie, the Scottish terrier				X	X			1996	1996	1996	1996
4029	Seamore, the seal		X	X	X		1993	1993	1993	1993		
4080	Seaweed, the otter			X	X	X		1995	1995	1995	1995	1995
4031	Slither, the snake	X	X				1993					
4115	Sly, the brown-belly fox				X				1996			
4115	Sly, the white-belly fox					X				1996	1996	1996

© 1993 TY INC., OAKBROOK IL. U.S.A. ALL RIGHTS RESERVED HAND MADE IN KOREA — ALL NEW MATERIAL POLYESTER FIBER PA. REG #1965

© 1993 TY INC., OAKBROOK IL. U.S.A. ALL RIGHTS RESERVED HAND MADE IN CHINA SURFACE WASHABLE — ALL NEW MATERIAL POLYESTER FIBER & P.V.C. PELLETS PA. REG #1965 **CE** FOR AGES 3 AND UP

© 1993 TY INC., OAKBROOK IL. U.S.A. ALL RIGHTS RESERVED HAND MADE IN CHINA SURFACE WASHABLE — ALL NEW MATERIAL POLYESTER FIBER & P.V.C. PELLETS PA. REG #1965 **CE**

HEART TAG AND TUSH TAG CHRONOLOGY

Tush tag legend (left column):

- © 1993 TY INC. OAKBROOK IL. U.S.A. ALL RIGHTS RESERVED HAND MADE IN KOREA — ALL NEW MATERIAL POLYESTER FIBER & P.V.C. PELLETS PA. REG #1965
- © 1993 TY INC. OAKBROOK IL. U.S.A. ALL RIGHTS RESERVED HAND MADE IN CHINA SURFACE WASHABLE — ALL NEW MATERIAL POLYESTER FIBER & P.V.C. PELLETS **CE** FOR AGES 3 AND UP PA. REG #1965
- © 1993 TY INC. OAKBROOK IL. U.S.A. ALL RIGHTS RESERVED HAND MADE IN CHINA SURFACE WASHABLE — ALL NEW MATERIAL POLYESTER FIBER & P.V.C. PELLETS **CE** PA. REG #1965

Style No.	Beanie Name	Heart 1st	Heart 2nd	Heart 3rd	Heart 4th	Heart 5th	Tush 1st	Tush 2nd	Tush 3rd	Tush 4th	Tush 5th	Tush 6th
4039	Smoochy, the frog with single thread mouth					X						1997
4039	Smoochy, the frog with double thread mouth					X						1997
4039	Smoochy, the frog with felt mouth					X						1997
4120	Snip, the Siamese cat				X	X			1996	1996	1996	1996
4002	Snort, the red bull with cream paws				X	X			1995	1995	1995	1995
4201	Snowball, the snowman				X	X			1996		1996	
4100	Sparky, the dalmatian				X	X			1996			
4030	Speedy, the turtle	X	X	X	X		1993	1993	1993	1993		
4060	Spike, the rhino			X	X	X			1996	1996	1996	1996
4036	Spinner, the striped spider				X	X					1996	1996
4036	Spinner/Creepy, the striped spider					X						1998
4022	Splash, the orca whale	X	X	X	X		1993	1993	1993			
4090	Spook, the ghost		X				1995	1995				
4090	Spooky, the ghost		X	X	X				1995	1995	1995	
4000	Spot, the black and white dog with a spot		X	X	X		1993	1993	1993	1993		
4000	Spot, the black and white dog without a spot	X	X				1993	1993				
4184	Spunky, the cocker spaniel					X						1997
4005	Squealer, the pig	X	X	X	X	X	1993	1993	1993	1993	1993	1993
4087	Steg, the stegosaurus		X	X			1995	1995				
4077	Sting, the ray			X	X		1995	1995	1995			
4193	Stinger, the scorpion					X						1998
4017	Stinky, the skunk			X	X	X	1995	1995	1995	1995	1995	1995
4182	Stretch, the ostrich					X						1997
4065	Stripes, the black and orange tiger			X			1995	1995	1995			
4065	Stripes, the black and tan tiger				X	X				1995	1995	1995
4171	Strut, the tie-dyed rooster				X	X				1996	1996	1996
4002	Tabasco, the red bull			X	X		1995	1995	1995			
4031	Tank, the 7-line armadillo			X	X		1995	1995	1995			
4031	Tank, the 9-line armadillo				X				1995			
4031	Tank, the armadillo with shell				X				1995	1995		
4200	Teddy, the 1997 light brown holiday bear				X						1996	
N/A	Teddy, the employee bear-green ribbon							1993/1995				
N/A	Teddy, the employee bear-red ribbon							1993/1995				
4050	Teddy, the new face-brown bear		X	X	X		1993	1993	1993	1993		
4052	Teddy, the new face-cranberry bear		X	X			1993	1993				
4057	Teddy, the new face-jade bear		X	X			1993	1993				
4056	Teddy, the new face-magenta bear		X	X			1993	1993				
4051	Teddy, the new face-teal bear		X	X			1993	1993				

HEART TAG AND TUSH TAG CHRONOLOGY

Style No.	Beanie Name	Heart 1st Version	Heart 2nd Version	Heart 3rd Version	Heart 4th Version	Heart 5th Version	Tush 1st version	Tush 2nd version	Tush 3rd version	Tush 4th version	Tush 5th version	Tush 6th version
4C55	Teddy, the new face-violet bear			X			1993					
4C50	Teddy, the old face-brown bear	X	X				1993					
4C52	Teddy, the old face-cranberry bear	X	X				1993					
4C57	Teddy, the old face-jade bear	X	X				1993					
4C56	Teddy, the old face-magenta bear	X	X				1993					
4C51	Teddy, the old face-teal bear	X	X				1993					
4C55	Teddy, the old face-violet bear	X	X				1993					
4198	Tracker, the basset hound					X						1998
4C42	Trap, the mouse	X	X	X			1993					
4C76	Tuck, the walrus				X				1995			
4108	Tuffy, the terrier					X			1996	1996	1996	1996
4C76	Tusk, the walrus			X	X	X	1995		1995	1995	1995	
4C68	Twigs, the giraffe			X	X	X		1995	1995	1995	1995	
4C58	Valentino, the white bear with red heart		X	X	X	X	1993	1993	1993	1993	1993	1993
4C58	Valentino/Special Olympics, the white bear-red heart					X						1993
4C64	Velvet, the panther			X	X		1995		1995	1995		
4075	Waddle, the penguin			X	X		1995	1995	1995	1995	1995	
4084	Waves, the orca whale				X	X			1996	1996	1996	
4C41	Web, the spider	X	X	X			1993					
4C13	Weenie, the dachshund dog			X	X	X		1995	1995	1995	1995	
4194	Whisper, the deer					X						1998
4187	Wise, the graduation owl					X						1998
4103	Wrinkles, the bulldog				X	X			1996	1996	1996	
4063	Ziggy, the zebra with thin stripes			X	X	X	1995		1995	1995	1995	
4063	Ziggy, the zebra with wide stripes				X	X		1995		1995	1995	
4004	Zip, the all black cat with pink ears (no white)			X			1993					
4004	Zip, the black cat with white face and belly		X	X			1993					
4004	Zip, the black cat with white paws			X	X	X	1993	1993	1993	1993	1993	1993

© 1993 TY INC.,
OAKBROOK IL, U.S.A.
ALL RIGHTS RESERVED
HAND MADE IN KOREA

ALL NEW MATERIAL
POLYESTER FIBER
& P.V.C. PELLETS
PA. REG #1965

© 1993 TY INC.,
OAKBROOK IL, U.S.A.
ALL RIGHTS RESERVED
HAND MADE IN CHINA
SURFACE WASHABLE

ALL NEW MATERIAL
POLYESTER FIBER
& P.V.C. PELLETS CE
FOR AGES 3 AND UP

© 1993 TY INC.,
OAKBROOK IL, U.S.A.
ALL RIGHTS RESERVED
HAND MADE IN CHINA
SURFACE WASHABLE

ALL NEW MATERIAL
POLYESTER FIBER
& P.V.C. PELLETS CE
PA. REG #1965

HEART & TUSH TAG REFERENCE CHART

This chart indicates which tush tag corresponds to each heart tag.

Through our extensive research on the evolution of the tag generations, we were able to identify which Beanie Baby was produced with which tush and hang tag generations. This information is copyrighted in our first book Beanie Mania that was published July 1997.

1st Version	2nd Version	3rd Version	4th Version	5th Version
© 1993 TY INC., OAKBROOK IL. U.S.A. ALL RIGHTS RESERVED HAND MADE IN KOREA PA. REG #1965 — ALL NEW MATERIAL POLYESTER FIBER & P.V.C. PELLETS © 1993 TY INC., OAKBROOK IL. U.S.A. ALL RIGHTS RESERVED HAND MADE IN CHINA SURFACE WASHABLE — ALL NEW MATERIAL POLYESTER FIBER & P.V.C. PELLETS CE PA. REG #1965 FOR AGES 3 AND UP **1st Version**	© 1993 TY INC., OAKBROOK IL. U.S.A. ALL RIGHTS RESERVED HAND MADE IN CHINA SURFACE WASHABLE — ALL NEW MATERIAL POLYESTER FIBER & P.V.C. PELLETS CE PA. REG #1965 FOR AGES 3 AND UP **1st Version**	© 1993 TY INC., OAKBROOK IL. U.S.A. ALL RIGHTS RESERVED HAND MADE IN CHINA SURFACE WASHABLE — ALL NEW MATERIAL POLYESTER FIBER & P.V.C. PELLETS CE PA. REG #1965 FOR AGES 3 AND UP © 1993 TY INC., OAKBROOK IL. U.S.A. ALL RIGHTS RESERVED HAND MADE IN CHINA SURFACE WASHABLE — ALL NEW MATERIAL POLYESTER FIBER & P.V.C. PELLETS CE PA. REG #1965 **1st Version**	The Beanie Babies Collection™ ty® Beanie Name **3rd Version**	The Beanie Babies Collection® ★ty® Beanie Name™ **6th Version**
1993	1993	1993, 1995	1993, 1995, 1996	1993, 1995, 1996, 1997, 1998
		ty® **2nd Version**	The Beanie Babies Collection™ ★ty® Beanie Name **4th Version**	
		1993, 1995	1993, 1995, 1996	
			The Beanie Babies® Collection™ ★ty® Beanie Name™ **5th Version**	
			1993, 1995, 1996	

162

Beanie Mania II

BEANIE BABY MISTAKES

Classical Mistakes

Garcia

Peace

Tag Misprints

Spook

Spooky

Mistagged Beanies

Ziggy with Pinky tush tag

Tag Cover-ups

Ty's web site covered up

Oddities

Gobbles with one leg

Beanie Mania II

BEANIE BABY MISTAKES
MISTAGGED

When Beanie Babies were first produced, mistakes were seldom made. However, since January, 1997, as more Beanie Babies were mass-produced to accommodate the insatiable demand, more of these mistakes have appeared at an increasing rate.

Beanie Baby mistakes are classified into four categories: <u>Mistagged Beanie Babies</u>, <u>Classical Mistakes</u>, <u>Tag Misprints</u>, <u>Tag Cover-Ups</u> and <u>Manufacturing Oddities</u>.

MISTAGGED BEANIE BABIES

Because of the mass production of more than 60 different Beanie Babies in countries where English is not a primary language (China, Korea and Indonesia), it has become quite common to find Beanie Babies with either an incorrect heart tag, an incorrect tush tag, or both.

Heart Tag: (swing tag)
Although some people like to collect mistagged Beanie Babies, those that do, tend to stay away from Beanie Babies with incorrect heart tags. There are several reasons for not collecting Beanie Babies with incorrect heart tags:

- Heart tags are easy to remove; therefore they can be switched easily. There is no way of proving that an incorrect heart tag was put on at the factory or at a later date.

- Part of the fun of getting Beanie Babies, especially for children, is to have a record of the birthday and poem of that particular Beanie Baby, not those of another.

- Once the heart tag is removed from a mistagged Beanie Baby, that Beanie Baby can no longer be considered unusual or unique.

- An incorrect hang tag can actually reduce the value of a Beanie Baby, especially once the Beanie is retired.

Tush Tag: (body tag)
Prior to January, 1997, incorrect tush tags were quite uncommon. Up until then, the only mistake was the occasional appearance of the embroidered tush tag reserved for use on other Ty products. However, once tush tags came out with the Beanie Babies' name on them, all kinds of mistagged Beanie Babies have appeared on the market.

When some of these "mistakes" first appeared, collectors thought they were unique and were willing to pay more for a mistagged Beanie. This slowly changed over time, as collectors began to realize how extremely common these mistakes were. An incorrect tush tag can actually reduce the value of a Beanie Baby, especially once it is retired.

CLASSICAL MISTAKES

Some tag mistakes are considered "classical" mistakes. A classical mistake is one that is well known and that occurred during a specific time period. Such mistakes do not negatively affect the value of a Beanie Baby, and may even increase it. Classical mistakes include those involving wrong style numbers, name changes, retirement name changes, and switched tags.

Wrong Style Numbers

Colored Teddys:

The colored Teddy bears all have identical heart tags except for the style number. The name on the tag simply says "Teddy" and does not indicate what color bear it is. For this reason, it is not uncommon to find a colored Teddy with the wrong style number on it. Until the proliferation of information about Beanie Babies years later, most people never realized that their Teddy even had a wrong style number on it.

Name Changes

To date there have been four instances where a Beanie's name has been changed after tags were printed. In each instance, there are limited numbers of these tags with the original names on them, and all are highly sought after by collectors. No physical changes were made to the Beanies when their names were changed. Therefore, without these special swing or tush tags, the Beanie automatically becomes the more commonly named version. These Beanies are not considered mistagged Beanies as there are no other Beanies that bear these particular names.

Heart Tags: (swing tags)

Brownie/Cubbie:

One of the "Original Nine" Beanie Babies, Cubbie made his first appearance under the name of "Brownie." Brownie was produced in Korea in 1993, but prior to his official introduction on the market, his name was changed to Cubbie.

Nana/Bongo:

Another name change took place in 1995 prior to the release of Bongo the monkey. Bongo was originally named "Nana." Swing tags with the Nana name on them had already been printed up when Ty apparently thought that Bongo was a more appropriate name. He therefore had stickers made up with the name Bongo on them, and placed over the word Nana.

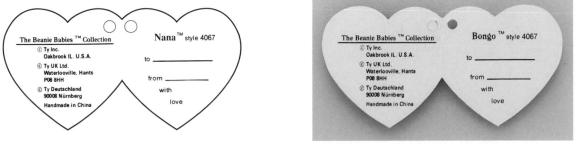

BEANIE BABY MISTAKES
CLASSICAL

Tush Tags: (body tags)
Pride/Maple:
A notable tush tag mistake occurred in 1997 when Ty Canada released the Canadian bear, Maple. Maple was originally to have been named Pride, but underwent a name change before being released to the public. However, about 3,000 had already been made with the Pride name on the tush tag and were distributed with a Maple swing tag.

Creepy/Spinner:
During the spring of 1998, Spinner, the spider, started showing up with Creepy tush tags. It was originally thought that Spinner was going to be renamed Creepy, or that there would be a new "Creepy" Beanie Baby in the next set of releases. When the May announcement came and went without a new Beanie Baby named Creepy, the answer to the origin of Creepy remained a mystery. Spinner/Creepy is made in Indonesia and is primarily found in the United Kingdom.

Retirement Name Changes
Tabasco/Snort:
Tabasco was retired January, 1997, and replaced by Snort. Because they had the same style number, birthday and almost identical poems and body designs, a quantity of the newest released Snorts had Tabasco swing tags on them.

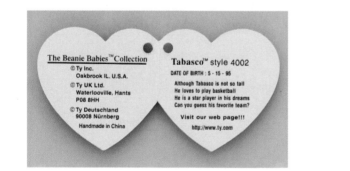

BEANIE BABY MISTAKES
CLASSICAL

Sparky/Dotty:

A notable tush tag mistake occurred in April, 1997, when Sparky the dalmatian started showing up with Dotty tush tags. This mistake instantly alerted the public that a new Dalmatian, although not announced or released yet, was already in production by Ty, Inc. Interestingly, well after Sparky was retired, a large number of Dottys appeared on the market with Sparky swing tags.

Garcia/Peace:

On May, 1997, Garcia was retired and replaced by Peace. The only physical difference between the two Beanies was the addition of the peace symbol to Peace. Peace's style number, birthday and poem are also different from Garcia's. Because Peace did not go into production until well after Garcia was retired, relatively few instances occurred where Peace showed up with a Garcia swing or tush tag. In July, 1998, Peace underwent a subtle color change and started appearing with new tie-dyed pastel colors.

Doodle/Strut:

In August of 1997 Doodle was replaced by Strut. Unlike Snort and Dotty, there were no physical changes made to distinguish Doodle from Strut. The only difference between the two is the name on the swing and tush tags. Because of this, a number of Strut appeared with either a Doodle swing or tush tag. Because of the timing of these tag mistakes, it has been presumed that the Beanie itself is Strut, and the incorrect tag is the Doodle tag.

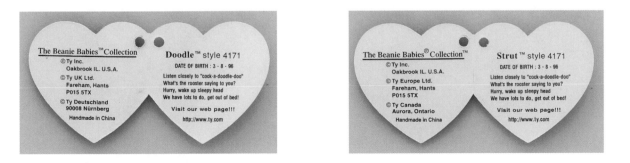

BEANIE BABY MISTAKES

Switched Tags

Echo/Waves:
When first introduced in May, 1997, the entire production run of Echo and Waves had both their swing and tush tags switched with each other. This mistake was corrected during the second production run of Echo and Waves.

Rainbow/Iggy:
Switched tags happened again in January, 1998, when Rainbow and Iggy were introduced. The entire first production run of Rainbow and Iggy had both their swing and tush tags switched with each other. Although these two lizards went through a second production run where a tongue was added to Rainbow, the names continued to be switched according to Ty's web site and catalog. See page 30 for a detailed chronology of Rainbow and Iggy.

TAG MISPRINTS

A large number of typographical and grammatical errors have been found on Beanie Baby swing and tush tags. We are not sure where the tags are printed, but it is most likely in China, Korea or Indonesia where Beanie Babies are made. These misprints are primarily a result of tags being typed up by people whose primary language is not English. In some cases, these errors were corrected on the next production run for that tag, and sometimes new errors were made.

Heart Tags: (swing tags)
Misspelled Names
Unlike common spelling or grammatical mistakes on a swing tag, the misspelling of a Beanie's name can affect its value in a positive way. The Beanies to date that have appeared with misspelled names on the swing tag:

- The earliest Beanie to have a misspelled name was Pinchers. When first produced for sale in the United Kingdom, its name was spelled "Punchers."

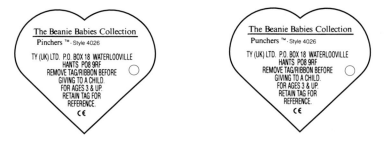

- Quackers was the second Beanie to have an incorrectly spelled name on its swing tag. The 2nd generation swing tag for Quackers, both with and without wings, has its name spelled "Quacker."

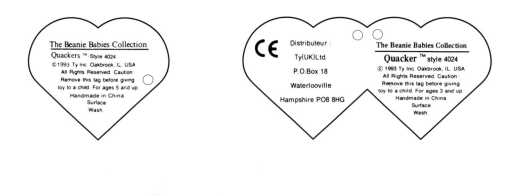

- Spooky was the next to appear with a misspelled name. Its name is spelled "Spook" on the 3rd generation swing tags.

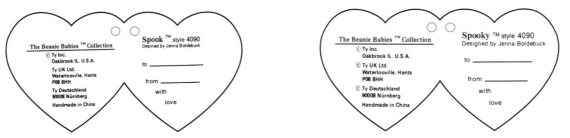

- Not long afterwards, Tusk came out with his name spelled "Tuck" on some of its earlier 4th generation swing tags.

Poem Variations

An interesting printing mistake involves the Beanies' poems. It is not clear why some poems have changed from one production run to the next, but there are actually some Beanies that have more than one version poem.

The most unique is Tusk that actually has four different poem endings.
According to Ty, Tusk's poem should read:

"Tusk brushes his teeth everyday
To keep them shiny, it's the only way
Teeth are special, so you must try
And they will sparkle when you say "Hi"!"

In addition to this version, Tusk has also been found with three other poem endings:

- So they sparkle when you say "Hi"!

- So they will sparkle when you say "Hi"!

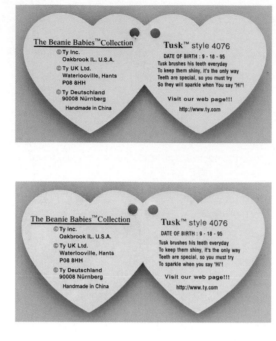

- To sparkle when you say "Hi"!

Sparky, the dalmatian, is another Beanie Baby with several endings to his poem.
Ty lists his poem as:

"Sparky rides proud on the fire truck
Ringing the bell and pushing his luck
Gets under foot when trying to help
He often gets stepped on and lets out a yelp!"

Sparky has also been found with these poem endings:

- He often gets stepped on crying yelp!

- Step on him and he'll let out a yelp!

- Often gets stepped on crying yelp!

Following are some more Beanies that have more than one version poem:

Bones with the 4th line reading:
- "But that all stopped, when his teeth fell out!"
- "That stopped, when his teeth fell out!"

Digger with the 4th line reading:
- "Basking in the sun, riding the tide!"
- "Basking in the sun and riding the tide!"

BEANIE BABY MISTAKES

- Stripes with the 3rd line reading, "Jungle life was hard to get by" or "Jungle life was hard getting by"

Grammatical and Typographical Errors

The biggest source of tag misprints is grammatical or typographical errors. In some instances the tags will be correct for one production run, and then corrected on the next production run, vice versa, or never corrected at all.

Well-known examples of grammatical errors are:

- Garcia's poem that says: The Beanies "use to" follow him around instead of "used to".

- Squealer's poem that at one time read: Squealer "like" to joke around. When this was corrected on later tags to "likes", an error was made in the last line: "There is no doubt he'll will make you smile!"

- With Libearty, the first issue swing tag has the name Libearty capitalized, but uncapitalized on on all subsequent tags.

Other examples of typographical or grammatical errors are:

• Chops' poem where "surely" is spelled "surly"

• Hoot's poem where "quite" is spelled "qutie"

• Scottie's poem where "always" is spelled "slways"

• Bones' poem with "Your" instead of "You're"

• Tank's poem where "border" is spelled "boarder"

• Chocolate's poem with "moose" spelled "rnoose" (with r and n instead of the letter m)

• CLAUDE and TUFFY's name in all capital letters

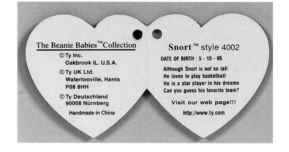

During July, 1997, Snort appeared with Tabasco's poem inside the swing tag. The majority of these were produced for Canadian distribution.

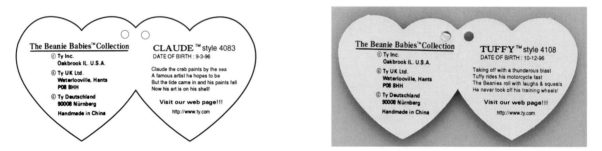

BEANIE BABY MISTAKES
MISPRINTS

At the beginning of 1998 when the 5th generation swing tags were first readily available, some of the tags had two misspelling errors on them. On the tags of:

- Blackie
- Floppity
- Peace
- Tuffy
- Curly
- Hippity
- Roary
- Valentino
- Ears
- Hoppity
- Squealer

The word "ORIGINAL" on the front was spelled "ORIGIINAL" and the word "Surface" on the back was spelled "Suface".

Different Birthdays

It has often been thought that some Beanie Babies have a misprinted birthday because at one time or other the date on the tag did not match the birthday list printed on the Ty website. Actually, there are only two Beanie Babies that have appeared with more than one birthday on their swing tag.

- Freckles can be found with the dates 7-28-96 or 6-3-96

Freckles™ style 4066
DATE OF BIRTH : 7-28-96

From the trees he hunts prey
In the night and in the day
He's the king of camouflage
Look real close, he's no mirage!

Visit our web page!!!
http://www.ty.com

Freckles™ style 4066
DATE OF BIRTH : 6 - 3 - 96

From the trees he hunts prey
In the night and in the day
He's the king of camouflage
Look real close he's no mirage!

Visit our web page!!!
http://www.ty.com

- Scottie can be found with the dates 6-15-96 or 6-3-96

Scottie™ style 4102
DATE OF BIRTH : 6 - 15 - 96

Scottie is a friendly sort
Even though his legs are short
He is slways happy as can be
His best friends are you and me!

Visit our web page!!!
http://www.ty.com

Scottie™ style 4102
DATE OF BIRTH : 6 - 3 - 96

Scottie is a friendly sort
Even though his legs are short
He is always happy as can be
His best friends are you and me!

Visit our web page!!!
http://www.ty.com

Tush Tags: (body tags)

One of the more notable tush tag misprints occurred when Libearty was first released, and on its tush tag the word Beanie was misspelled "Beanine". The misspelling was eventually corrected, but not until after the market had been fairly saturated with the Beanine version of Libearty. While the Beanine Libearty originally was sought after by collectors, and is helpful in dating whether Libearty was produced earlier versus later in 1996, it is thought that Libearty with "Beanie" spelled correctly may actually be the more rare of the two.

Another tush tag misspelling occurred on all Beanies that were in production in mid-1996. On the tush tag, surface washable is spelled "sufrace washable."

BEANIE BABY MISTAKES
COVER-UPS

HEART TAG COVER-UPS

There are several tag "cover-ups" that have appeared on the Ty swing tags since Beanie Babies were first introduced. It appears that when a need arose to change information on a particular tag, rather than throw out what was in stock, Ty printed up small stickers with the correct information, and covered up the old information.

The earliest evidence of such a cover-up appears on numerous first version heart tags that have Ty Inc. information covered up with Ty (UK) LTD information.*1 This practice was discontinued when the second version heart tags were produced, providing each country with their own individual tag.*2 Another instance of a tag cover-up occurred on some of the old-face Teddies. Ty used already printed heart tags that said "Made in China", and covered the words with stickers saying "Made in Korea."*3

The next instance of a tag cover-up appeared on Bongo the monkey early in 1995. It appears that Ty originally planned on calling Bongo by the name of "Nana", and then decided to change it to Bongo. Since tags were already printed up saying "Nana™ style 4067", small stickers were printed saying, "Bongo™ style 4067" and placed over Nana's name and style number. A few tags, however, did make it into circulation with the name Nana uncovered.*4

The largest tag cover-up concerns Ty's web site. Beginning in 1996, Ty had the web site "http://www.ty.com" printed on the Beanie Babies' swing tags. However, at the time that the tags were printed, Ty did not have the rights to the www.ty.com domain name, as it had been granted in early January to a business called Tech Yard. In late January, Ty offered to buy the domain name from Tech Yard, but the gentleman who was using it refused to give it up. Then Ty sued, and the case turned to the courts with Ty defending his claim that Ty was a registered trademark. Ty eventually won the case.

However, until the case was legally settled, Ty had to cover up the www.ty.com web page address on their tags. It is not uncommon to find tags with the web site covered up with specially cut white stickers, or with the web site completely cut off the bottom of the tag. For a brief period during the summer, when the first set of tags were depleted, and the case was still unresolved, newly printed tags either said "visit our web page!" with no address given, or there was no mention of a web page whatsoever. Tags without the web site, or with the web site covered up, appear on Beanie Babies that were in production mid-1996. The first web site cover-up appeared on Libearty. Originally Libearty's date of birth read "Summer Olympics 1996." Due to possible copyright infringement the word "Olympics" was covered up as well as the web site.

Web site and Olympics covered up

Libearty™ style 4057
DATE OF BIRTH: Summer : 1996
Atlanta, Georgia, USA

I am called Libearty
I wear the flag for all to see
Hope and freedom is my way
That's why I wear flag USA

Visit our web page!!!

Web site tag bottom cut off

Libearty™ style 4057
DATE OF BIRTH: Summer 1996
Atlanta, Georgia USA

I am called libearty
I wear the flag for all to see
Hope and freedom is my way
That's why I wear flag USA

Visit our web page!!!

Tag with "Visit our web page!!!"

Libearty™ style 4057
DATE OF BIRTH: Summer 1996
Atlanta, Georgia USA

I am called libearty
I wear the flag for all to see
Hope and freedom is my way
That's why I wear flag USA

Visit our web page!!!

Tusk™ style 4076
DATE OF BIRTH: 9-18-95

Tusk brushes his teeth everyday
To keep them shiny, it's the only way
Teeth are special, so you must try
And they will sparkle when
You say "Hi"!

Tag with no mention of web site.

*1-3 see page 140
*4   see page 82

BEANIE BABY MISTAKES
COVER-UPS

In January of 1998, several Beanie Babies were produced with the new 5th generation swing tag that had two spelling errors on it. On the front of the tag inside the yellow star, the word "ORIGINAL" was misspelled "ORIGIINAL". On the back of the tag the word "Surface" was misspelled "Suface". This error tag appeared on at least eleven different Beanie Babies:

- Blackie
- Curly
- Ears
- Floppity
- Hippity
- Hoppity
- Peace
- Roary
- Squealer
- Tuffy
- Valentino

In March of 1998, Hoppity started appearing in stores with a sticker on the back of the swing tag covering up the words "Suface Wash" with the correctly spelled "Surface Wash". Soon thereafter, most, if not all of the misspelled tags, also sported these sticker corrections.

MANUFACTURING ODDITIES

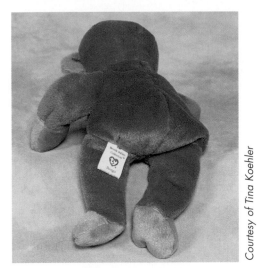

Courtesy of Tina Koehler

Bongo without a tail

Bubbles without eyes

Courtesy of Kathy Yurkunas

Courtesy of Darioush Afshar

Coral without a tail

Coral with corduroy-like material

Courtesy of Dinomates, Inc.

Courtesy of Dinomates, Inc.

Cubbie without a nose

Curly with smooth material on
front of chest and legs

Courtesy of Maxine Winer

MANUFACTURING ODDITIES

Daisy without a spot

Courtesy of Joan Pitner

Derby with an ear on backward

Courtesy of Gregory Pitner

Derby's tail with different colored yarn

Courtesy of Kathy Yurkunas

Glory without a flag

Courtesy of Amanda Kommers

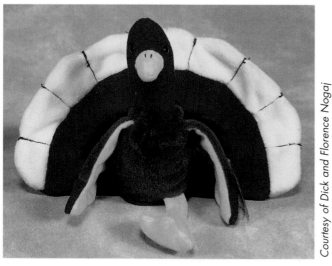

Gobbles with one leg

Courtesy of Dick and Florence Nogaj

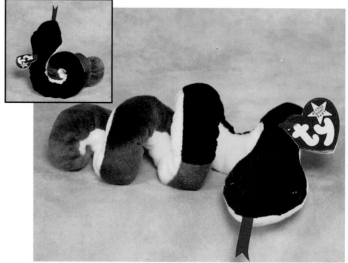

Hissy half black and half blue

Courtesy of Rae Cuykendall

MANUFACTURING ODDITIES

Humphrey with a back leg on backward

Courtesy of Kathy Yurkunas

Inky with 9 legs

Courtesy of Sally Christoffel

Inky with 10 legs

Courtesy of May Casimiro

Lefty without a flag

Courtesy of Chris Wagner

Lefty with a looped mane and tail

Courtesy of John Orozco

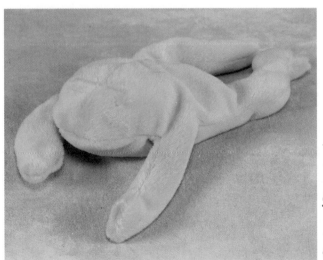

Legs without eyes

Courtesy of Dinomates, Inc.

MANUFACTURING ODDITIES

Libearty without flag

Courtesy of Kathy Yurkunas

Libearty with flag upside down

Courtesy of Chris Estenssoro

Lizzy with a striped tail

Courtesy of Brian Lister

Lucky half 21 dots and half 11 dots

Courtesy of Chris Tozzo

Lucky with 11 dots on one side only

Courtesy of Rose Kutz

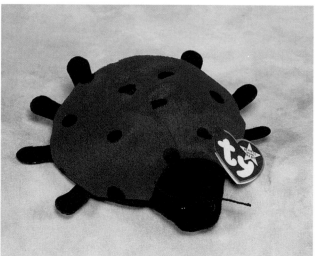

Lucky with 7 legs

Courtesy of Larry & Debbie Paul

MANUFACTURING ODDITIES

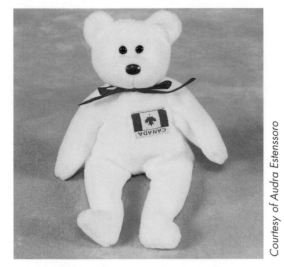

Courtesy of Audra Estenssoro

Maple with an upside down flag

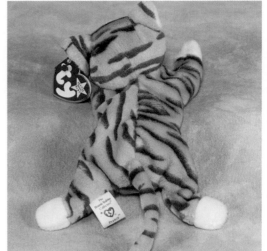

Courtesy of David Lawrenchuk

Prance with stripes running lengthwise

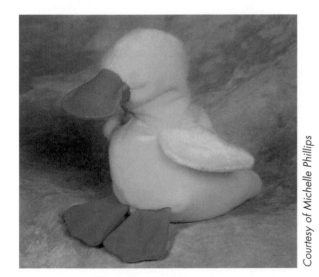

Courtesy of Michelle Phillips

Quackers without eyes

Courtesy of Kerri Hanson

Quackers with a wing on backward

Courtesy of Charles and Felicia Larson

Radar with 3 feet

Courtesy of Kathy Yurkunas

Radar with 3 thumbs and a tush tag for a foot

MANUFACTURING ODDITIES

Courtesy of Kathy Yurkunas

Radar missing a foot

Courtesy of Larry and Debbie Paul

Radar missing an ear

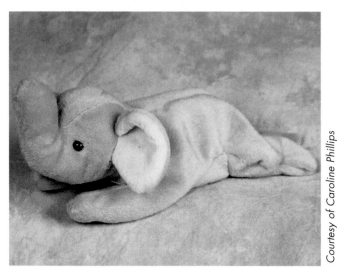

Courtesy of Caroline Phillips

Righty without a flag

Courtesy of Bobbie Meyerson

Righty with an upside down flag

Courtesy of Kathy Yurkunas

Scotty without eyes

Courtesy of Kathy Yurkunas

Snort with 3 ears

MANUFACTURING ODDITIES

Snowball with eyebrows

Courtesy of Dick and Florence Nogaj

Snowball with string on scarf instead of yarn

Courtesy of Gwen McKenzie

Spinner with half of his back fuzzy

Courtesy of Michael Phillips

Splash without eyes

Courtesy of Kathy Yurkunas

Spot without eyes

Courtesy of Rae Cuykendall

Spot with an all white face

Courtesy of Cesar Garcia

MANUFACTURING ODDITIES

Stinky without eyes

Courtesy of Kathy Yurkunas

Sting with a white face

Courtesy of John Hendron

Stretch with a foot on backward

Courtesy of Cynthia Huspeck

Stripes with a fuzzy belly (right)

Courtesy of Matthew Estenssoro

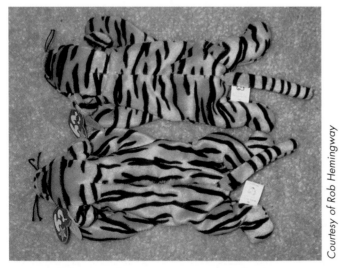

Stripes with stripes running lengthwise

Courtesy of Rob Hemingway

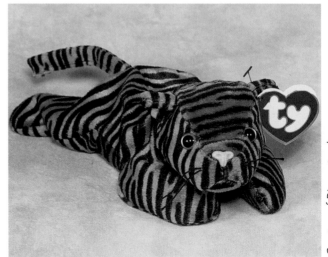

Stripes with a fuzzy head

Courtesy of Dinomates, Inc.

MANUFACTURING ODDITIES

Courtesy of Dinomates, Inc.

Tank with 7 lines of stitching instead of 9

Courtesy of Kathy Yurkunas

Tank without horizontal stitching on shell

Courtesy of Dinomates, Inc.

Tank with light grey material

Courtesy of Lisa Teague

Valentino without a red heart

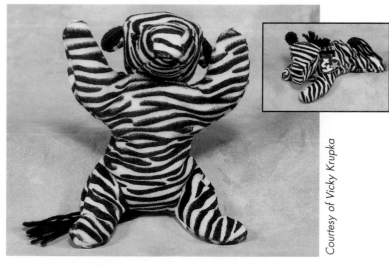

Courtesy of Vicky Krupka

Ziggy with a thin and wide striped fabric
Ziggy with left ear on crooked (inset)

Courtesy of Dawn Fries

1997 Teddy with a red and green ribbon

TY'S
TEENIE BEANIES BECOME HOTTEST TOY GIVEAWAY IN
McDONALD'S
HISTORY

Illustration by Carlton Bjork

1997 - TEENIE BEANIES

On Friday, April 11, 1997, McDonald's introduced Teenie Beanies, a miniature version of the full-sized Beanie Babies made by Ty, Inc., in their Happy Meals.

As April 11th approached, McDonald's realized that they had seriously underestimated the number of toys that were going to be needed. They hoped to avert the problem by taking a "low key" approach in advertising. Instead of a "Big Mac sized" advertising campaign like the company used in other promotions, McDonald's had only in-store displays, which weren't put up until the day the promotion started. They commissioned only three 30-second "mini" TV commercials, which aired on a limited basis starting the day before the promotion.

Despite ordering 100 million toys, McDonald's underestimated the demand and high collectibility of these toys; a direct result of the Beanie Baby frenzy sweeping the country. Individual restaurants reported sales of Happy Meals at 6 to 10 times the normal rate and many were entirely sold out of Teenie Beanies within the first week.

By the end of the first week, McDonald's announced that the promotion would officially end April 25th, three weeks early, and issued a national public apology in the form of TV and radio commercials, as well as full-page newspaper ads.

The Teenie Beanie promotion featured 10 animals which were intended to be released two per week, for 5 weeks, in the following order: #1 Patti, #2 Pinky, #3 Chops, #4 Chocolate, #5 Goldie, #6 Speedy, #7 Seamore, #8 Snort, #9 Quacks and #10 Lizz.

These miniature Teenie Beanies are made of a polyester velour, and are filled with plastic pellets and stuffing. Their facial features are embroidered on, making this toy safe even for very young children. Each Teenie Beanie came individually packaged in a clear plastic bag with its name and item # on it.

1997 - TEENIE BEANIES
TEENIE BEANIE PROTOTYPES

During initial design stages, several prototypes of each Teenie Beanie were made. From those prototypes the final selection of the Teenie Beanie that was to be part of the McDonald's promotion, was chosen. Listed on each prototype is the production number and the design approval date. *Example: Pinky the Flamingo has the following information listed on the prototype: 11834.PF.002 8.16*

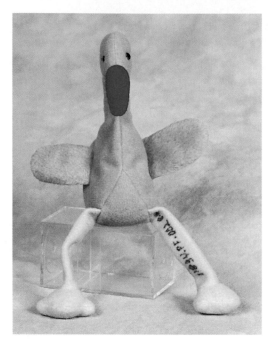
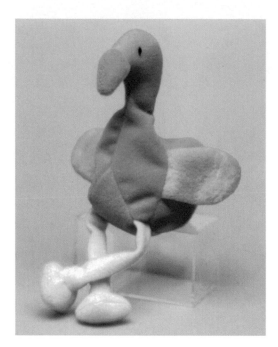

Pinky the flamingo

This Pinky prototype (left) is larger in size, is a lighter pink color and has a red beak. The prototype information is written on its left leg.

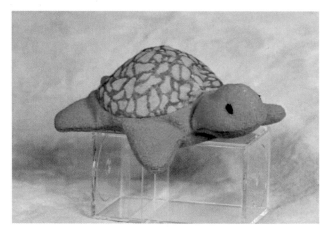

Speedy the turtle

This Speedy prototype (left) has the same body design as the Teenie Beanie, but the shell is green and covered with a yellowish green pattern. The eyes are stitched vertically in contrast to the horizontal stitching on the Teenie Beanie. The prototype information is written on its bottom.

1997 - TEENIE BEANIES
TEENIE BEANIE PROTOTYPES

Chocolate the Moose

This Chocolate prototype (right) has the same body design as the Teenie Beanie, but the color of the body and antlers are slightly darker. The eyes are stitched vertically in contrast to the horizontally stitched eyes on the Teenie Beanie. The prototype information is written on its bottom.

Seamore the Seal

This Seamore prototype (right) is slightly larger in size than the Teenie Beanie. It is a duller white color and its facial features are more pronounced. The prototype information is written on its bottom.

Patti the platypus is a fuchsia colored platypus. She has a yellowish-gold beak, yellowish-gold feet, and black eyes.

Pinky the flamingo is a bright pink flamingo with pale pink legs. She has an orange beak, two-tone wings, and black eyes. The topside of her wings is made out of the same plush material as the Beanie Babies.

Chops the lamb is a cream-colored lamb with a black face and two-tone ears. He has a pink nose and blue eyes.

Chocolate the moose is a brown moose with orange antlers and black eyes.

Goldie the goldfish is an orange fish with black eyes and two rows of orange stitching on each fin.

1997 - TEENIE BEANIES

Beanie Mania II

Speedy the turtle is a green turtle with black eyes and a brown shell consisting of darker brown spots "flocked" onto a lighter brown background.

Seamore the seal is a white seal with a black nose, eyes, and eyebrows.

Snort the bull is a red bull with cream colored horns, two-tone ears, black eyes, and two black nostrils that are sewn onto his cream-colored snout.

Quacks the duck is a yellow duck with black eyes and eyebrows. He has an orange beak and orange feet. The top side of his wings is made of the same plush material as the Beanie Babies.

Lizz the lizard is a dark blue lizard with black spots scattered on top of her body and a solid orange belly. She has a red felt forked tongue and black eyes.

1997 - TEENIE BEANIES
TEENIE BEANIE RENDERINGS
These are color photocopies of the original designs of the 10 Teenie Beanies.

The name Teenie was originally going to be called Teeny. Tabasco was later changed to Snort, Quackers was changed to Quacks, and Lizzy was later spelled Lizz.

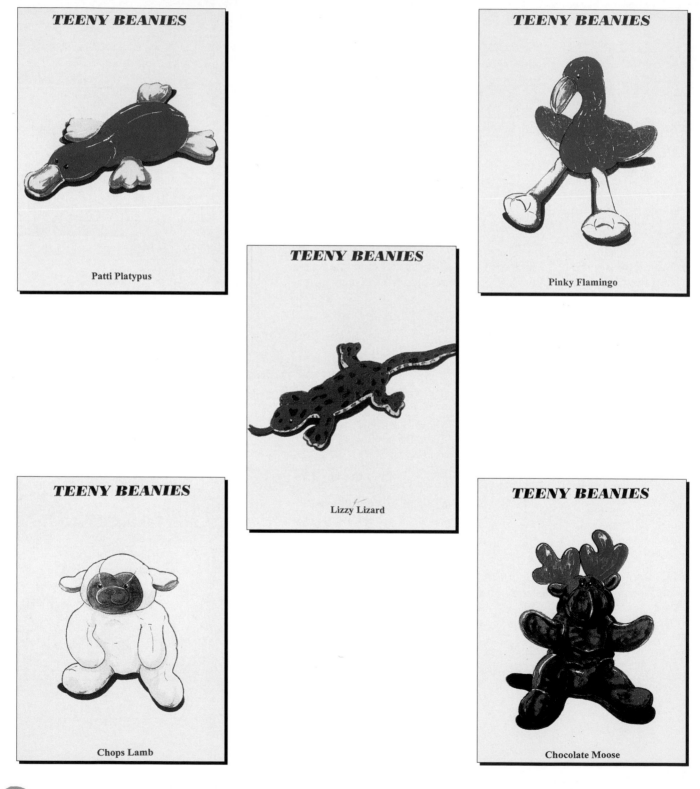

1997 - TEENIE BEANIES
TEENIE BEANIE RENDERINGS

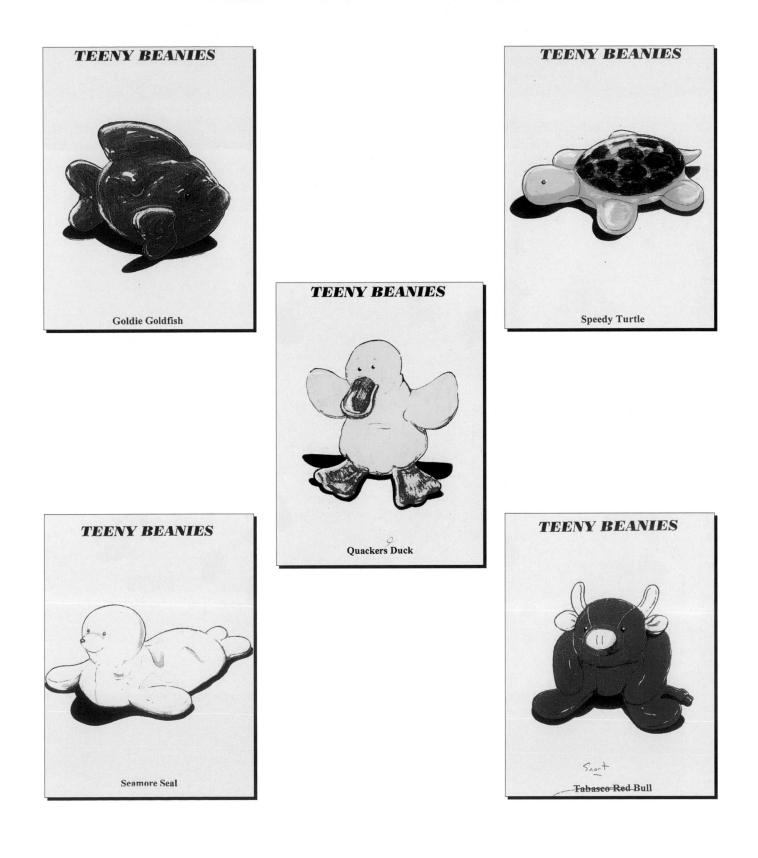

TEENY BEANIES

Goldie Goldfish

TEENY BEANIES

Speedy Turtle

TEENY BEANIES

Quackers Duck

TEENY BEANIES

Seamore Seal

TEENY BEANIES

Snort

Tabasco Red Bull

1997 - TEENIE BEANIES

3-D LOGO

After the filming of the three McDonald's "mini" commercials was completed, several production items were donated for an auction to be held at McDonald's annual convention on May 3, 1997, in St. Louis, Missouri. Proceeds of the auction were donated to Ronald McDonald House Charities. The items donated included the three original storyboard drawings, all signed by the artist; the production book made by the film company, which included scripts and storyboards; the 3-D Teenie Beanie Logo; black and white printouts of scenes from the commercial; photoboards of the finished commercials; color photos of the Beanie logo; color photocopies of the original designs of the 10 Teenie Beanies; an audio cassette of the commercials' music; and a videotape of the finished commercials.

1997 - TEENIE BEANIES

MEDIA KIT

Two hundred and fifty Media Kits were given out around the country to the media and McDonald's executives. The Media Kit holds all ten Teenie Beanies in separate compartments and includes a special photo of the set.

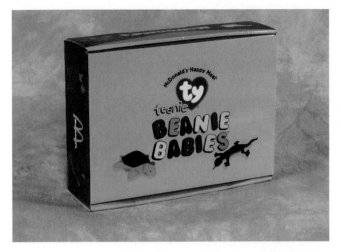

Media Kit – outside

Media Kit – inside

TRANSLITE

*This translite was located near
the McDonald's drive thru menu.*

1997 - TEENIE BEANIES

HAPPY MEAL SACKS

Two different Happy Meal sacks were featured in the 1997 promotion. These Happy Meal sacks pictured all the Teenie Beanies: Pinky, Patti, Chops, Chocolate, Goldie, Speedy, Seamore, Snort, Quacks and Lizz.

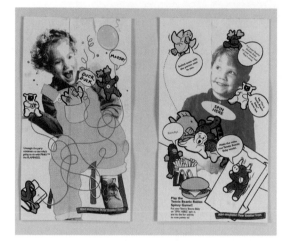

DISPLAYS

This display and 77
Beanie Babies were
raffled off at
McDonald's restaurants
with the proceeds
going to charity.

The 10 Teenie Beanies were on display
at all of the McDonald's restaurants.

1997 - TEENIE BEANIES
Tush Tags: (body tags)

The Teenie Beanies were produced for McDonald's through their own manufacturing sources, under the terms of a licensing agreement with Ty, Inc. Ty had no involvement or responsibility in the manufacture and distribution of Teenie Beanies. McDonald's contracted with two different companies to produce the Teenie Beanies - Simon Marketing Inc., in Los Angeles, California and MB Sales in Westmont, Illinois.

Having two manufacturers of the Teenie Beanies accounts for the differences found in the tush tags. Simon Marketing produced five of the Teenie Beanies - Pinky, Chops, Chocolate, Speedy, and Seamore. Their tags have red printing on one side of the tag and black on the other. MB Sales produced the other five - Pattie, Goldie, Snort, Quacks, and Lizz. Some of their tags have black printing on both sides, and some red printing on one side of the tag and black on the other. All of the Teenie Beanie tush tags have "©1993 TY INC." on the front and "©1996 McDonald's Corp." on the back. Some of the tags also have code numbers stamped on them. These refer to production bag and tag numbering sequences.

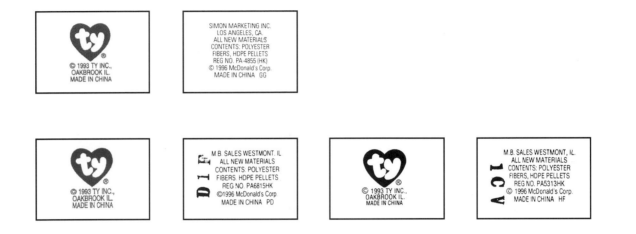

Teenie Beanies produced exclusively for Canada have slightly larger tush tags, and have the additional black and white tush tag with the manufacturer's information printed in both French and English.

1997 - TEENIE BEANIES

Heart Tag: (swing tag)

Attached by red thread to each Teenie Beanie is a single sided Ty heart tag similar to the third version BEanie Baby heart tag found on Beanie Babies. The backside of the tag bears the trademark "Teenie Beanie Babies TM/MC" and the individual Teenie Beanie's name.

This button was given to McDonald's employees after the Teenie Beanies' promotion.

1998 - TEENIE BEANIES

On Friday, May 22, 1998, McDonald's restaurants across the country began offering Teenie Beanies once again in Happy Meals. Last year's Teenie Beanies were the first ever miniature Beanie Babies offered. Introduced April 11, 1997, they became the most successful Happy Meal tie-in in the company's history. One hundred million Teenie Beanies, ten million of each design, were given away in less than a week! Due to the overwhelming success of the 1997 promotion, McDonald's doubled the quantity of Teenies produced for the 1998 promotion to 20 million each - 240 million Teenie Beanies!

As a result of last year's overwhelming success, McDonald's did not have to provide much fanfare before the release of their second round of Teenie Beanies. News conferences unveiling the twelve new Teenie Beanies were given only two days before the promotion was scheduled to begin. Advertising was limited to a 15-second spot targeted to kids (Leo Burnett USA, Chicago); a 30 second spot targeted to Hispanic families (Del Rivero Messianu, Coral Gables, FL); and a print ad targeted to African-American moms (Burrell Communications, Chicago).

1998 - TEENIE BEANIES

Despite the attempts at secrecy, two months prior to the actual release date, an Internet site published the names of all twelve 1998 Teenie Beanie Babies, the Happy Meal sack they would come in, and a few pictures of actual Teenies. Because last year's matching full-sized Beanies flew off the shelves, this Internet information proved to be an advantage to those collectors who wanted to make sure they had matching full-sized Beanies for making sets, especially beneficial since Ty retired eight out of the twelve Teenie counterparts on May 1, 1998.

The twelve different Teenie Beanies produced this year were:

- Doby the Doberman
- Bongo the Monkey
- Twigs the Giraffe
- Inch the Worm
- Pinchers the Lobster
- Happy the Hippo
- Mel the Koala
- Scoop the Pelican
- Bones the Dog
- Zip the Cat
- Waddle the Penguin
- Peanut the Elephant.

Three Teenie Beanies were scheduled to be distributed each week with only one type available at a time. But by early morning of the first day, many stores had already run out of the first two Teenie Beanies, Doby and Bongo, and completely sold out within a week.

Due to the overwhelming success of the Teenie Beanie promotions, according to the June 8, 1998, issue of Advertising Age, McDonald's Corp. is turning the Teenie Beanies promotion into an annual event, with a third offering slated to begin April 23, 1999.

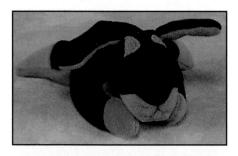

Doby the doberman is a black dog with medium brown eyes, paws, belly, and muzzle. The underside of his ears and patches above his eyes are medium brown. He has a black nose.

Bongo the monkey is a medium brown monkey with a tan tail, face, ears, hands, and feet. He has black eyes and a "V" stitched nose.

1998 – TEENIE BEANIES

Twigs the giraffe is made of orange and yellow flocked material. He has black eyes and dark brown feet and mane. The inside of his ears is dark brown.

Inch the inchworm has multi-colored segments consisting of yellow, orange, green, royal blue, and fuchsia. He has black eyes and antennae.

Pinchers the lobster is a red lobster with black eyes and knotted thread whiskers.

Mel the koala is a gray koala with a white belly and ears. He has black eyes, nose, and mouth.

Happy the hippo is a lavender hippo with tiny black eyes and small rounded ears.

1998 - TEENIE BEANIES

Scoop the pelican is a grayish-blue pelican with orange feet and a huge orange beak. He has black eyes and nostrils.

Bones the dog is a light brown dog with a dark brown tail and ears. He has a black nose, eyes, and eyebrows.

Zip the cat is a black cat with white ears, whiskers, and paws. He has a pink nose, white mouth and green eyes.

Waddle the penguin is a black penguin with blue eyes. He has a yellow collar, an orange beak and feet. The underside of his wings and belly are white.

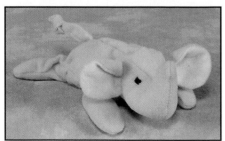

Peanut the elephant is a light blue elephant with pink ears and black eyes.

1998 - TEENIE BEANIES

McDONALD'S EMPLOYEE MERCHANDISE

This year, exclusive merchandise was offered to McDonald's employees. Included were a Collector's Kit of all twelve Teenie Beanies, T-shirts, magnets, hats, and a complete set of twelve Teenie Beanie pins.

Hat

Shirt

Teenie Beanie Pins

Collectors Set

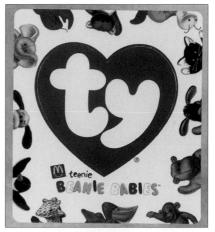

Magnet

1998 - TEENIE BEANIES

MEDIA KIT

Approximately 300 Media Kits were given out to McDonald's executives and the media. The 1998 Media Kits were modeled after the McDonald's Teenie Beanie Happy Meal box but with two pull out compartments that contained the 12 Teenie Beanies. Each Ronald McDonald House was also given two of the 1998 media kits to help with fund raising efforts.

Media Kit

HAPPY MEAL SACKS AND BOXES

Two different Happy Meal sacks were featured in the 1998 promotion. These Happy Meal sacks pictured all the Teenie Beanies: Doby, Bongo, Twigs, Inch, Pinchers, Happy, Mel, Scoop, Bones, Zip, Waddle and Peanut.

Happy Meal boxes, instead of bags, were used as part of a test marketing program at approximately seventy McDonald's restaurants in the Albuquerque, NM and Colorado Springs, CO areas.

1998 - TEENIE BEANIES

RONALD REWARDS CERTIFICATES

In addition to the boxes, Ronald Rewards certificates were also sealed in with the Teenie Beanies. These certificates are redeemable for a variety of prizes such as: Happy Meals, books, videos and CD Roms, each free with the redemption of 25 Ronald Rewards certificates.

TEENIE BEANIE PLASTIC SACKS

Two changes occurred on the Teenie Beanie sacks from the 1997 promotion to the 1998 promotion.
• The 1998 Teenie sacks include the verbiage "Licensed for distribution only by McDonald's restaurants with food purchase. NOT FOR RESALE."
• McDonald's information and child safety warnings are written in English, Spanish and French on the backs of all the sacks, but on some, German is also included.

DISPLAY

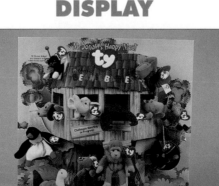

This display with the 12 Teenie Beanies was visable at McDonald's restaurants during the 1998 Teenie Beanie promotion.

1998 - TEENIE BEANIES

DRIVE-THRU SIGN

This sign indicated which Teenie Beanie was available and which ones were sold out.

TRANSLITE

This translite was located near the McDonald's drive thru menu.

BUTTON

This button was given to the McDonald's Employees during the 1998 Teenie Beanie Promotion.

1998 - TEENIE BEANIES
Tush Tags: (body tags)

In 1998, Simon Marketing produced five of the Teenie Beanies: Inch, Mel, Zip, Happy and Pinchers. MB Sales produced seven of the Teenie Beanies: Waddle, Bongo, Doby, Bones, Peanut, Twigs and Scoop. The tush tags on all 12 Teenies are printed with the Ty heart logo, and "(c) 1993 TY INC" in red on the front and "Mfd. for McDonald's" in black on the back. Again, the tush tags have code numbers stamped on them, referring to production numbering sequences. Teenie Beanies for both the 1997 and 1998 promotions were produced for McDonald's through their own manufacturing sources, under the terms of a licensing agreement with Ty, Inc. Ty had no involvement or responsibility in the manufacture and distribution of the Teenie Beanies. McDonald's contracted with two different companies to produce the Teenie Beanies - Simon Marketing Inc., in Los Angeles, California and MB Sales in Westmont, Illinois.

Teenie Beanies produced exclusively for Canada have slightly larger tush tags, and have the additional black and white tush tag with the manufacturer's information printed in both French and English.

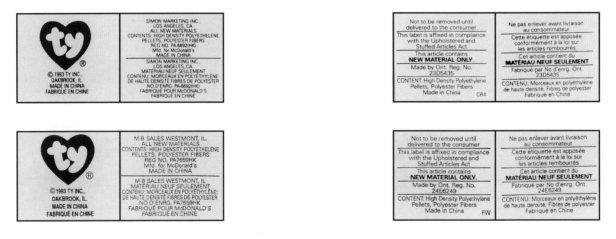

Heart Tag: (swing tag)

Attached by red thread to each Teenie Beanies is a single sided Ty heart tag similar to a third generation Beanie Baby heart tag. The back of the tag is written in the Comic Sans font that is also used on 5th generation Beanie Baby heart tags. It bears the trademark "Teenie Beanie Babies TM/MC/MR", the individual Teenie Beanie's name, and the web site information "www.ty.com."

Courtesy of Rich Seidelman

COMMEMORATIVE SPORTS BEANIES

On May 18, 1997, Ty, Inc. and the Chicago Cubs "teamed" up for the first ever Beanie Baby sports-related promotional event. The Cubs gave the Beanie Baby "Cubbie" to the first 10,000 children, age 13 and under, who entered Wrigley field. That promotion, and a subsequent one on September 6, 1997, where Cubbie was also given out, drew record crowds.

The Cubs' Beanie Baby promotions were so wildly successful that other teams wanted to run similar giveaways. It wasn't until 1998, that Ty, Inc. decided to team up with a number of professional baseball, basketball and football teams. Throughout the spring, summer and fall of 1998, the number of sports teams offering Ty sponsored Beanie Baby promotions grew by leaps and bounds - reaching a point where it became difficult to keep track of what team was giving away which Beanie and when!

These Beanie Baby sports promotions have been aimed primarily at kids 14 years of age and younger, with the number of Beanie Babies and Commemorative Cards given out per event ranging anywhere from approximately 100 to 51,000. Each Beanie Baby has been accompanied by a commemorative card indicating the date of the game, name of the Beanie Baby given out and name of the corporate sponsor. Some of the cards are sequentially numbered.

COMMEMORATIVE SPORTS BEANIES

Wherever possible, the Beanies are "themed" to the team or sport. For example, Batty, Stretch and Peanut are popular with baseball teams. Then there are the ones related to a specific person, such as "Gracie" for Chicago Cubs player Mark Grace, "Rocket" for Roger "Rocket" Clemens of the Toronto Blue Jays and "Chocolate" for Dallas Cowboys fullback Daryl "Moose" Johnston. Still others are related to team names - "Stripes" for the Detroit Tigers, "Valentino" for the New York Yankees and "Blackie" for the Chicago Bears.

With one exception, Beanie Babies given out by sports teams are no different than ones found on store shelves. The exception is Daisy, the cow, given out by the Chicago Cubs on May 3, 1998 when, for the first time in the history of Ty, Inc., a limited edition swing tag was put on a Ty Beanie Baby. In honor of the legendary Cubs sportscaster Harry Caray, a special swing tag was printed up that only appears on the 10,000 Daisys given out by the Cubs. On the inside of the tag is a caricature of Harry Caray and a poem dedicated specifically to Caray. It reads: "A friend to many, a legend to all, the most popular figure in all baseball, crowds would cheer when hearing his name, without you Harry, it won't be the same." Below the poem it says: "In Memory of Harry Caray Ty presents Daisy at Wrigley Field May 3, 1998."

Daisy, the cow, and a commemorative card were given out to the first 10,000 kids 13 and younger.

Hang tag with Harry Caray caricature and a special poem dedicated to Harry.

These sports promotions have captured the attention of the world and have helped to bring families back to the ballparks. The sports teams who sponsor these events are almost guaranteed a sell-out crowd; they have given Ty, Inc. more product exposure; and have brought Beanie Babies back into the hands of kids, for whom they were originally designed.

SPORTS RELATED BEANIE BABY "FIRSTS" INCLUDE:

- **May 18, 1998** - The Chicago Cubs were the first professional baseball team to give away Beanie Babies - Cubbie.

- **January 17, 1998** - The Philadelphia 76ers were the first professional basketball team to give away Beanie Babies - the patriotic Baldy.

- **May 17, 1998** - David Wells, of the New York Yankees, pitched a perfect game during a Beanie Baby giveaway day. In honor of this achievement, his baseball cap, the Beanie Baby - Valentino - and a ticket stub from the game were put on display in the Baseball Hall of Fame.

- **May 31, 1998** - the first retired Beanie Baby was given away at a game. Stripes, who was retired on May 1, 1998, was given out by the Detroit Tigers.

SPORTS RELATED BEANIE BABY "FIRSTS" INCLUDE:

- **June 15, 1998** - The Charlotte Sting became the first women's basketball team to host a Beanie Babies Day. The Sting gave out Curly.

- **July 7, 1998** - Glory was the first Beanie Baby to be given out at an All-Star game. Everyone attending the 69th Annual Major League Baseball All-Star game (attendance of 51,267) was given Glory - the biggest Beanie Baby giveaway ever.

- **August 5, 1998** - The first football related Beanie Baby giveaway (Blackie) was provided by the Chicago Bears in their Kids Fan Club Kits at the National Sports Collector's Convention.

- **September 6, 1998** - The first Canadian Beanie Baby sports promotion took place in Toronto, Canada when Rocket, the blue jay, was given away in honor of Toronto Blue Jay pitcher Roger Clemens.

- **August 19, 1998** - Andres Galarraga, star first baseman of the Atlanta Braves, became the first athlete to be pictured on a Beanie Baby commemorative card. Beanie Baby Chip was given away in his honor.

BASEBALL SPORTS PROMOTIONS

May 18, 1997

Cubbie the bear

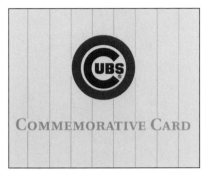

Chicago Cubs vs
San Francisco Giants

*Beanie Baby sports promotions have helped to
bring families back to the ball parks.*

Photographer: Herb Shenkin

September 6, 1997

Cubbie the bear

Chicago Cubs vs.
New York Mets

January 16-18, 1998

Cubbie the bear

Chicago Cubs
Convention

March 10, 1998

Bones the dog

New York Yankees vs.
Toronto Blue Jays

BASEBALL SPORTS PROMOTIONS

March 15, 1998

Ears the rabbit

Oakland A's vs.
Anaheim Angels

May 3, 1998

Daisy the cow

Chicago Cubs vs.
St. Louis Cardinals

May 17, 1998

Valentino, white bear
with red heart

New York Yankees vs.
Minnesota Twins

Jay Leno was on hand to throw out the honorary first pitch for the Beanie Babies
day held at Wrigley Field in honor of Harry Caray.

May 22, 1997

Stretch, the ostrich

St. Louis Cardinals vs.
San Francisco Giants

BASEBALL SPORTS PROMOTIONS

May 31, 1998

Courtesy of Marvin & Karole Frank

Stripes the tiger

Detroit Tigers vs.
Chicago White Sox

May 31, 1998

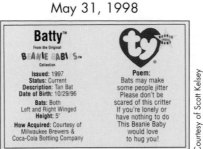

Courtesy of Scott Kelsey

Batty the brown bat

Milwaukee Brewers vs.
Florida Marlins

May 31, 1998

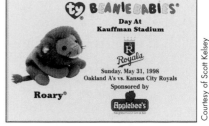

Courtesy of Scott Kelsey

Roary the lion

Kansas City Royals vs.
Oakland A's

June 14, 1998

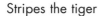

Courtesy of Marvin & Karole Frank

Hissy the snake

Arizona Diamondbacks vs.
St. Louis Cardinals

July 7, 1998

Courtesy of Scott Kelsey

Glory, white bear
with red/blue stars

1998 All-Star game

July 12, 1998

Courtesy of Marvin & Karole Frank

Batty the brown bat

New York Mets vs.
Montreal Expos

July 12, 1998

Blizzard the tiger

Chicago White Sox vs.
Kansas City Royals

Photographer: Herb Shenkin

Frank Thomas, Chicago White Sox first baseman, was on hand to autograph Beanies and baseballs.

July 26, 1998

Courtesy of Bobbie Meyerson

Weenie the dachshund

COMMEMORATIVE CARD

Tampa Bay Devil Rays vs.
Oakland A's

July 31, 1998

Courtesy of Bobbie Meyerson

Lucky the lady bug

Minnesota Twins vs.
Toronto Blue Jays

August 1, 1998

Courtesy of Bobbie Meyerson

Peanut the elephant

Oakland A's vs.
Cleveland Indians

BASEBALL SPORTS PROMOTIONS

August 4, 1998

Courtesy of Marvin & Karole Frank

Pugsly the Pug dog

Texas Rangers vs.
Toronto Blue Jays

August 8, 1998

Courtesy of Marvin & Karole Frank

Stripes the tiger

Detroit Tigers vs.
Seattle Mariners

August 9, 1998

Courtesy of Marvin & Karole Frank

Stretch the ostrich

New York Yankees vs.
Kansas City Royals

August 14, 1998

Courtesy of Marvin & Karole Frank

Waves the whale

San Diego Padres vs.
Milwaukee Brewers

August 14, 1998

Courtesy of Marvin & Karole Frank

Smoochy the frog

St. Louis Cardinals vs.
Pittsburgh Pirates

August 16, 1998

Courtesy of Marvin & Karole Frank

Derby the horse

Houston Astros vs.
Chicago Cubs

BASEBALL SPORTS PROMOTIONS

August 16, 1998

Rover the red dog

Cincinnati Reds vs.
Montreal Expos

August 19, 1998

Chip the calico cat

Atlanta Braves vs.
San Francisco Giants

August 22, 1998

Curly the napped bear

New York Mets vs.
Arizona Diamondbacks

August 23, 1998

Pinky the flamingo

Tampa Bay Devil Rays vs.
Kansas City Royals

August 27, 1998

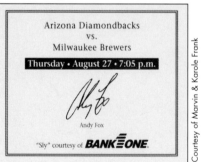

Sly the white belly fox

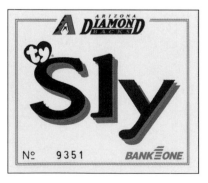

Arizona Diamondbacks vs.
Milwaukee Brewers

August 30, 1998

Tuffy the terrier

San Francisco Giants vs.
Pittsburgh Pirates

Beanie Mania II

BASEBALL SPORTS PROMOTIONS

September 2, 1998

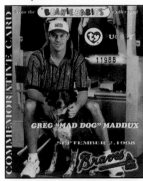

Pugsly the pug dog

September 5, 1998

Chocolate the moose

September 6, 1998

Rocket the blue jay

Atlanta Braves vs.
Houston Astros

Seattle Mariners vs.
Baltimore Orioles

Toronto Blue Jays vs.
Boston Red Sox

September 6, 1998

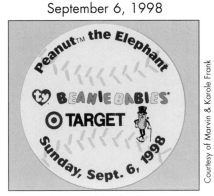

Peanut the elephant

September 13, 1998

Gracie the swan

Oakland A's vs.
Tampa Bay Devil Rays

Chicago Cubs vs.
Seattle Mariners

BASKETBALL SPORTS PROMOTIONS

January 17, 1998

Baldy the eagle

Philadelphia 76ers vs.
Golden State Warriors

April 2, 1998

Strut the rooster

Indiana Pacers vs.
Minnesota Timber Wolves

April 5, 1998

Bongo the monkey

Cleveland Cavaliers vs.
Los Angeles Clippers

April 17, 1998

Chocolate the moose

Denver Nuggets vs.
Portland Trailblazers

April 27, 1998

Curly the napped bear

San Antonio Spurs vs.
Phoenix Suns

April 29, 1998

Pinky the flamingo

San Antonio Spurs vs.
Phoenix Suns

BASKETBALL SPORTS PROMOTIONS

June 15, 1998

Curly the napped bear

Charlotte Sting vs.
Houston Comets

July 11, 1998

Mystic the unicorn

Washington Mystics vs.
Detroit Shock

July 17, 1998

Bongo the monkey

Charlotte Stings vs.
Washington Mystics

Courtesy of Marvin & Karole Frank

July 25, 1998

Mel the Koala

Detroit Shock vs.
Los Angeles Sparks

July 31, 1998

Dotty the dalmatian

Los Angeles Sparks vs.
Phoenix Mercury

August 3, 1998

Mystic the unicorn

Los Angeles Sparks vs.
Washington Mystics

Courtesy of Bobbie Meyerson

BASKETBALL SPORTS PROMOTIONS

August 6, 1998

Scoop the pelican

Augsut 15, 1998

Courtesy of Marvin & Karole Frank

Curly the napped bear

Courtesy of Marvin & Karole Frank

Houston Comets vs.
Phoenix Mercury

Cleveland Rockers vs.
Washington Mystics

FOOTBALL SPORTS PROMOTIONS

Fall 1998

Blackie the bear

September 6, 1998

Chocolate the moose

November 8, 1998

Blackie the bear

Chicago Bears
Kids Fan Club

Dallas Cowboys vs.
Arizona Cardinals

Chicago Bears vs.
St. Louis Rams

December 20, 1998

Curly the napped bear

Chicago Bears vs.
Baltimore Ravens

HOCKEY SPORTS PROMOTIONS

October 12, 1998

Blackie the bear

October 24, 1998

Waddles the penguin

November 21, 1998

Waddles the penguin

Boston Bruins vs.
New York Islanders

Pittsburgh Penguins vs.
Toronto Maple Leafs

Pittsburgh Penguins vs.
Tampa Bay Lightning

November 24, 1998

Gobbles the turkey

March 22, 1999

St. Louis Blues vs.
Nashville Predators

St. Louis Blues vs.
Carolina Hurricanes

Ty Sports Promotion

BASEBALL

	Beanie Baby	Game Date	Issued	Heart Tag Version	Tush Tag Version
Chicago Cubs	Cubbie	May 18, 1997	10,000	4	3
Chicago Cubs	Cubbie	September 6, 1997	10,000	4	4
Chicago Cubs - 1st Convention	Cubbie	January 16-18, 1998	100	4	5
New York Yankees	Bones	March 10, 1998	3,000	5	6
Oakland A's	Ears	March 15, 1998	1,500	5	6
Chicago Cubs - Harry Caray	Daisy	May 3, 1998	10,000	special	5, 6
New York Yankees	Valentino	May 17, 1998	10,000	5	6
St. Louis Cardinals	Stretch	May 22, 1998	20,000	5	6
Detroit Tigers	Stripes	May 31, 1998	10,000	5	6
Kansas City Royals	Roary	May 31, 1998	13,000	5	6
Milwaukee Brewers	Batty	May 31, 1998	12,000	5	6
Arizona Diamondbacks	Hissy	June 14, 1998	6,500	5	6
All Star Game	Glory	July 7, 1998	51,000+	5	6
Chicago White Sox	Blizzard	July 12, 1998	20,000	5	6
New York Mets	Batty	July 12, 1998	30,000	5	6
Tampa Bay Devil Rays	Weenie	July 26, 1998	15,000	5	6
Minnesota Twins	Lucky	July 31, 1998	10,000	5	6
Oakland A's	Peanut	August 1, 1998	15,000	5	6
Texas Rangers	Pugsly	August 4, 1998	10,000	5	6
Detroit Tigers	Stripes	August 8, 1998	10,000	5	6
New York Yankees	Stretch	August 9, 1998	10,000	5	6
San Diego Padres	Waves	August 14, 1998	10,000	5	6
St. Louis Cardinals	Smoochy	August 14, 1998	15,000	5	6
Cincinnati Reds	Rover	August 16, 1998	14,000	5	6
Houston Astros	Derby	August 16, 1998	20,000	5	6
Atlanta Braves	Chip	August 19, 1998	12,000	5	6
New York Mets	Curly	August 22, 1998	30,000	5	6
Tampa Bay Devil Rays	Pinky	August 23, 1998	10,000	5	6
Arizona Diamondbacks	Sly	August 27, 1998	10,000	5	6
San Francisco Giants	Tuffy	August 30, 1998	10,000	5	6
Atlanta Braves	Pugsly	September 2, 1998	12,000	5	6
Seattle Mariners	Chocolate	September 5, 1998	10,000	5	6
Oakland A's	Peanut	September 6, 1998	15,000	5	6
Toronto Blue Jays	Rocket	September 6, 1998	12,000	5	6
Anaheim Angels	Mel	September 6, 1998	10,000	5	6
Chicago Cubs	Gracie	September 13, 1998	10,000	5	6

Heart Tags — 4th Version, 5th Version

Tush Tags — The Beanie Babies Collection™ ty® Bones 3rd Version, The Beanie Babies Collection™ ★ty® Bones 4th Version, The Beanie Babies Collection® ★ty® Snowball™ 5th Version, The Beanie Babies Collection® ★ty® Mystic™ 6th Version

Ty Sports Promotion

	Beanie Baby	Game Date	Issued	Heart Tag Version	Tush Tag Version
BASKETBALL					
Philadelphia 76ers	Baldy	January 17, 1998	5,000	4	5
Indiana Pacers	Strut	April 2, 1998	5,000	5	6
Cleveland Cavaliers	Bongo	April 5, 1998	5,000	5	6
Denver Nuggets	Chocolate	April 17, 1998	5,000	5	6
San Antonio Spurs	Curly	April 27, 1998	2,500	5	6
San Antonio Spurs	Pinky	April 29, 1998	2,500	5	6
Charlotte Sting	Curly	June 15, 1998	5,000	5	6
Washington Mystics	Mystic	July 11, 1998	5,000	5	6
Charlotte Sting	Bongo	July 17, 1998	3,000	5	6
Detroit Shock	Mel	July 25, 1998	5,000	5	6
Los Angeles Sparks	Dotty	July 31, 1998	3,000	5	6
Los Angeles Sparks	Mystic	August 3, 1998	5,000	5	6
Houston Comets	Scoop	August 6, 1998	5,000	5	6
Cleveland Rockers	Curly	August 15, 1998	2,000	5	6
FOOTBALL					
Chicago Bears	Blackie	Fall 1998	20,000	5	6
Dallas Cowboys	Chocolate	September 6, 1998	12,500	5	6
Chicago Bears	Blackie	November 8, 1998	10,000	5	6
Chicago Bears	Curly	December 20, 1998	10,000	5	6
HOCKEY					
Hockey Boston Bruins	Blackie	October 12, 1998	5,000	5	6
Pittsburgh Penquins	Waddles	October 24, 1998	7,000	5	6
Pittsburgh Penquins	Waddles	November 21, 1998	7,000	5	6
St. Louis Blues	Gobbles	November 24, 1998	7,500	5	6
St. Louis Blues		March 22, 1999	7,500	5	6

Heart Tags

4th Version   5th Version

Tush Tags

The Beanie Babies Collection™ ty® Bones — 3rd Version

The Beanie Babies Collection™ ★ ty® Bones — 4th Version

The Beanie Babies Collection™ ★ ty® Snowball™ — 5th Version

The Beanie Babies Collection® ★ ty® Mystic™ — 6th Version

MARKET TREND ANALYSIS

In August of 1996, the Ty Co. started the "Beanie Baby Guestbook" internet site (www. ty.com). The Ty Guestbook offered a site where people could communicate with other Beanie Baby collectors from all over the world. In time, other Beanie Baby web sites were created, and collectors were able to buy, sell and trade retired Beanie Babies online. These web sites helped to increase awareness of retired Beanie Babies as a collectible. Soon, demand for retired Beanie Babies surged, and so did the prices.

During September 1996, we were able to compile reliable price data for the first time, thanks in part to the increasing amount of price quotes on the various web sites. Our price data is also based on our own trading activity, both online and at collectors' shows. The following chart starts with September 1996 price data, for retired Beanie Babies that were being actively traded at that time.

The second column of price data is for December 1996. During the period between September and December, many people were completing their collection and prices for most of the "reasonably" priced Beanie Babies were stable. One notable exception was for Teddy, whose prices increased for all 11 of its styles.

At the same time, some significant price decreases occurred for some of the more expensive Beanie Babies, such as Peanut, the royal blue elephant; Zip, the all black cat; Patti, the raspberry platypus; Quacker/Quackers, the wingless duck; and Spot, the dog without a spot. Peanut dropped from $800 to as low as $500. Zip dropped from a September peak of $500 down to a low of $325. Raspberry Patti dropped from $750 to $550. Quacker/Quackers and Spot fell from $1,000 to $750. Other examples include Chilly, Peking, and Slither, who went down in value from $300 to $200.

During this period, collectors were unwilling to pay premium prices for these Beanie Babies because of a prevailing uncertainty about the longevity of the Beanie Baby collection, and concern about values dropping. This uncertainty was due in part to a slower than anticipated 1996 Christmas season. Approaching the Christmas holidays, collectors were sure that the retired Beanie Baby market would be "red hot," but it just didn't happen! There was still buying, selling and trading going on, but it was slow! Many collectors became worried that the market for retired Beanie Babies was going to collapse.

Adding to the uncertainty was a rumor that Ty Warner was going to introduce 13 new Beanie Babies, as well as retire up to 13 others. A fear of an oversupply and too many types of Beanie Babies crept into the market. Everyone wondered how this was going to impact the secondary market. Collectors were scared and prices started to come down for the higher priced, hard to find Beanie Babies.

During December, the market was very quiet. Adding to the problem, the Ty Guestbook web site was not accessible during the last half of December, because it was being upgraded. There were a few other Beanie Baby web sites to visit, but the volume of collector postings was down dramatically. Fortunately, this situation wouldn't last long - due to the power of the Internet!

MARKET TREND ANALYSIS

Determined Beanie Baby fans began searching for new Beanie Baby related web sites, so they could continue to get information and conduct trading activity. As a result, web sites such as "BeanieMom," "Kim's Auction" and "Collector's Corner" became popular. Kim's site was pivotal in increasing the awareness of retired Beanie Babies as a collectible. Tapping into the incredible marketing potential of the Internet, Kim ingeniously linked her site with a variety of other collector web sites. Suddenly, collectors that were previously unaware of Beanie Babies joined in the hunt and Beanie mania was on again! By the middle of January, the Internet "quiet" period was over and the demand for retired Beanie Babies was greater than ever before!

Sparking further interest, Ty Warner used the Internet to make the first ever public announcement of which Beanie Babies were to be retired and which new ones were to be introduced in early 1997. The Ty Guestbook displayed an ad, during its dormant period in late December, that this announcement would be made, and the Ty Guestbook would become active again, on January 1, 1997, at 12 noon.

The Beanie Baby web pages, as well as the retail stores, were buzzing with excitement! Which Beanie Babies were going to be retired? Everyone waited with great anticipation for the January 1st announcement. Just before 12 noon, thousands of collectors were on the Ty Guestbook site, waiting for this important news . We all waited, and waited, and waited but the promised announcement was not there. Nine hours later, around 9:00 p.m., the news was finally posted - on the BeanieMom web site.

During January 1997, the focus of which retired Beanie Babies people were now buying began to change! New collectors, who did not have any of the older Beanie Babies to trade or sell, had to start from rock bottom. There were very few, if any, of the retired Beanie Babies left on the store shelves to buy or use for trade. Purchases had to occur in the secondary market. These new collectors started by acquiring the lower priced retired Beanie Babies, those below $100.00. These included Bronty, Bumble, Caw, Flutter, Inch, Rex, Steg, Stripes, Tank, Web, etc. Due to strong demand, the prices of most of these "reasonably" priced retired Beanie Babies doubled or tripled by the third week of January 1997.

The 1997 "newly" retired Beanie Babies (Chops, Coral, Kiwi, Lefty, Libearty, Righty, Sting, Tabasco, and Tusk) were also in great demand. Store shelves were being cleaned out as more and more collectors joined in on the Beanie Baby mania!

At the same time, the "new" 1997 Beanie Babies (Bernie, Crunch, Doby, Fleece, Floppity, Gracie, Hippity, Hoppity, Mel, Nuts, Pouch, Snip, and Snort) were starting to arrive in stores and people were buying them like there was no tomorrow. Merchants couldn't keep enough Beanie Babies in stock; their shelves were being emptied as fast as they could fill them.

Prices of the retired Beanie Babies continued to escalate, as more collectors searched relentlessly, outbidding others at high prices just so they could complete their collections. As shown on the chart, prices for almost all of the Beanie Babies had increased by February, and many of the more expensive ones were back up near their September value levels.

MARKET TREND ANALYSIS

The frenzy on the Beanie Baby web boards accelerated during February when word leaked out that McDonald's was producing 10 smaller versions of Beanie Babies, called "Teenie Beanies", for a "Happy Meal" promotion. This promotion began on April 11th, and as we all know by now, it was the most successful toy giveaway in history! McDonald's gave away 100 million Teenie Babies in less than two weeks!

If people hadn't heard about Beanie Babies before the McDonald's promotion, they sure did now! It even caught Wall Street's attention, with articles about Beanie Babies being written in prominent business publications, such as the Wall Street Journal, Investor's Business Daily and Barron's. A new group of collectors joined the mania as a result of the Teenie Beanies campaign, and secondary market prices were on the upward climb again.

Ty, Inc. kept the excitement going, when word spread that they were going to retire 9 more Beanie Babies, and introduce 14 new ones, on May 11th (Mother's Day). Once again, their internet site would be used for this announcement. However, there was no specific time promised. To everyone's surprise, the list of the new introductions and retirements unfolded on the Guestbook site, just after 12 midnight.

Repeating the shopping scene after the January 1st announcement, collectors headed out to the stores to buy newly retired Beanie Babies. This time, however, the search was in vain for most people. Store shelves were bare and there were very few Beanie Babies to be found. This scarcity was partially due to a cutback in the supply pipeline from Ty, Inc. During the middle of March, Ty began limiting their retail customers to a maximum allotment of 36 of each Beanie Baby a month. In addition, Ty announced that they would not fill some backorders. One of the reasons for the supply quotas being imposed was due to increased demand for Beanie Babies in Canada, the United Kingdom and new market areas that opened up across the United States.

Because of supply limitations, the price of the May 11th retired Beanie Babies quickly shot up to the level of the January 1st retirements. Even the current $5.00 Beanie Babies were being sold on the secondary market as soon as they left the stores - for $15.00 to $25.00 each!

During the summer of 1997, there was steady growth in the Beanie Baby market, and by the end of the summer, record new high price levels had been reached.

On October 1, 1997, Ty retired eleven more Beanie Babies - Ally, Bessie, Flip, Hoot, Legs, Seamore, Speedy, Spot, Tank, brown Teddy and Velvet - and introduced five more - 1997 Teddy, Batty, Gobbles, Snowball and Spinner. Two of the new Beanies, Snowball and 1997 Teddy, were for the holiday season. It was a prime time for collectors. There was a very positive feeling in the Beanie Baby market. Shows were well attended, collectors were buying and prices were showing a steady increase.

As the holiday season approached, collectors expressed concerns about the future of the Beanie Baby market. What would 1998 hold for the market?

It didn't take long to find out. A whole new group of collectors came on board during the holidays. Experienced collectors were buying the higher priced Beanie Babies to complete collections. On January 1, 1998, Ty Warner retired nine Beanie Babies - 1997 Teddy, Snowball, Spooky, Goldie, Nip, Lizzy, Magic, Bucky and Cubbie. Two of these Beanies, Snowball and 1997 Teddy, were just introduced three months before! There were also eleven new Beanies introduced - Britannia, Bruno, Hissy, Iggy, Pounce, Prance, Puffer, Rainbow, Smoochy, Spunky and Stretch. There was a very positive feeling in the market. It was almost as if history was repeating itself!

MARKET TREND ANALYSIS

But this year things were a little different. In addition to the private collectors, a whole new group of big Beanie Baby dealers were purchasing large amounts of Beanies and holding on. The supply dried up as the demand increased. Prices seemed to skyrocket out of control in February. Some of the higher priced Beanie Babies - Fine-mane Derby, Brownie, Punchers, Humphrey, Nana, Royal Blue Peanut, Slither and all of the new-face and old-face Teddys, doubled in value! Many of the collectors who had been waiting to purchase these final pieces to complete their collection, purchased them at exorbitant prices under the speculation that they might go up even higher.

By April, many of the Beanie Babies had almost tripled in price - quite out of the normal price range for many new collectors. There was uneasiness in the air; collectors couldn't afford the high prices and dealers who were hoarding supplies started to unload! The prices started to come down! Everyone was afraid the Beanie Baby market would crash! During April, the market was starting to correct. In May, the correction continued...Collectors were scared... But...

But then along came McDonald's Teenie Beanies - 240 million of them - gone in most major markets in a few days. And just when the McDonald's campaign was winding down, Ty introduced 14 new Beanie Babies on May 30 - Ants, Early, Fetch, Fortune, GiGi, Glory, Jabber, Jake, KuKu, Rocket, Stinger, Tracker, Whisper and Wise - the first new Beanies since January!

People started coming back to the shows and a large percentage of the people coming to shows were new collectors. They were purchasing the new releases and the Beanie Babies priced under $100.00. Even though the summer months are usually a slow time for buying collectibles, shows were well attended. By July, the market started to stabilize. There was a feeling of calm and hope for the future.

These new collectors who came on board at the beginning of June eventually started buying the higher priced Beanie Babies. By fall 1998, the Beanie Baby market picked up and the excitement that was once felt prior to January again returned.

In order to keep abreast of the ongoing trends in Beanie Baby market values, we recommend that you regularly check our Beanie Mania Price Guide found on the Beanie Mom web site (http://www.beaniemom.com). Our price guide is updated weekly. Other great sources for current Beanie prices and news include our semi-monthly newsletter, the Beanie Mania Bulletin, and our bi-monthly magazine, Beanie Mania. See the subscription ads in the back of this book for more information about Beanie Mania Bulletin and Beanie Mania magazine.

MARKET TREND ANALYSIS CHART

Beanie Name	Sept. 1996	Dec. 1996	March 1997	May 1997	Aug. 1997	Nov. 1997	Feb. 1998	April 1998	July 1998	Oct. 1998
Ally						$15-25	$25-35	$40-50	$40-45	$40-45
Baldy									$12-18	$12-18
Bessie						$20-35	$30-40	$50-70	50-60	50-60
Blizzard									$12-18	$15-20
Bones									$10-15	$10-15
Bongo-brown tail-r/w-no name			$75-100	$75-100	$50-75	$50-75	$75-100	$75-100	$100-125	$100-125
Bongo-brown tail-r/w-name							$25-50	$50-60	$50-70	$50-60
Bongo-tan tail-b/w				$125-150	$100-125	$100-125	$125-150	$150-175	$150-175	$125-150
Bongo-tan tail-r/w-no name				$20-25	$20-40	$35-50	$60-85	$75-100	$75-100	$75-100
Bronty	$30-35		$300-350	$400-500	$375-450	$450-550	$800-900	$1,100-1,300	$900-1,000	$900-1,000
Brownie			$500-800	$700-1,000	$800-1,200	$1,000-1,300	$3,500-5,000	$4,000-4,700	$3,600-3,800	$3,600-3,800
Bubbles				$25-50	$25-40	$45-65	$100-140	$150-200	$125-150	$130-160
Bucky		$35-50					$20-35	$25-35	$30-35	$30-35
Bumble-3rd gen. tag	$20-25	$25-30	$100-125	$125-200	$175-225	$300-350	$475-525	$525-575	$500-550	$500-550
Bumble-4th gen. tag			$100-125		$200-250	$350-400	$525-575	$575-625	$550-600	$550-600
Caw	$30-35	$35-40	$100-125	$150-200	$200-250	$350-400	$550-650	$650-700	$600-650	$600-650
Chilly	$300	$200	$350-450	$600-800	$725-825	$850-950	$1,800-2,200	$2,000-2,300	$1,800-2,000	$1,800-2,000
Chops			$25-35	$45-60	$45-60	$65-85	$125-175	$175-200	$140-170	$145-170
Coral			$25-30	$45-60	$45-60	$70-90	$125-175	$190-225	$160-185	$170-190
Cubbie							$15-30	$20-30	$20-30	$15-20
Derby-coarse (no star)							$8-15	$20-30	$20-25	$20-25
Derby-fine-mane			$50-100	$200-350	$350-450	$750-1,000	$3,500-5,000	$4,000-4,500	$3,500-3,800	$3,400-3,600
Digger-orange	$65-75	$65-75	$150-200	$250-350	$275-350	$350-450	$650-750	$700-800	$700-750	$700-750
Digger-red		$85-95	$100-125	$25-50	$25-40	$40-55	$75-100	$110-125	$90-110	$95-110
Dino Set	$70-75		$450-650	$800-900	$825-925	$1,100-1,400	$2,300-2,700	$3,100-3,400	$2,600-2,900	$2,600-2,900
Doodle						$30-45	$30-40	$40-50	$30-40	$35-45
Ears									$10-15	$8-12
Echo									$10-15	$10-15
Flash				$25-50	$25-45	$45-60	$85-125	$100-125	$90-110	$95-115
Flip					$30-45	$20-30	$25-35	$25-35	$30-35	$30-35
Floppity-lavender									$10-15	$10-15
Flutter	$30-40	$50-65	$300-450	$400-500	$425-475	$500-600	$800-1,000	$1,100-1,200	$900-1,000	$950-1,050
Garcia				$50-100	$40-75	$55-75	$125-175	$175-200	$160-180	$160-175
Goldie							$15-25	$30-40	$30-40	$30-40
Gracie									$10-15	$8-13
Grunt				$25-50	$50-75	$95-120	$125-175	$175-200	$140-180	$150-180
Happy-gray	$65-75	$65-75	$150-200	$250-350	$275-350	$350-450	$700-850	$700-800	$700-750	$700-750
Happy-lavender									$15-20	$15-20
Hippity-mint									$10-15	$10-15
Hoot						$15-25	$20-30	$30-40	$35-45	$35-40
Hoppity-rose									$10-15	$10-15

These charts have been compiled over the past two years from the Beanie Mania price guide that has been posted every week on BeanieMom (www.beaniemom.com).

MARKET TREND ANALYSIS CHART

Beanie Name	Sept. 1996	Dec. 1996	March 1997	May 1997	Aug. 1997	Nov. 1997	Feb. 1998	April 1998	July 1998	Oct. 1998
Humphrey	$125-150	$150-175	$550-650	$700-900	$800-900	$900-1,000	$1,800-2,200	$2,000-2,300	$1,800-2,000	$1,800-2,000
Inch-felt antennae	$10-15	$10-15	$35-50	$50-75	$65-85	$85-110	$125-175	$150-200	$140-170	$150-175
Inch-yarn antennae									$10-15	$15-20
Inky-pink									$20-30	$25-30
Inky-tan-mouth	$65-75	$65-75	$150-200	$225-325	$225-300	$350-450	$600-750	$625-700	$600-700	$600-700
Inky-tan-no mouth	$65-75	$65-75	$175-225	$250-350	$275-350	$400-500	$650-800	$700-800	$700-750	$700-750
Jolly									$10-15	$12-18
Kiwi			$25-35	$40-50	$45-60	$75-100	$125-175	$200-225	$150-180	$160-175
Lefty			$25-30	$50-75	$65-85	$115-130	$300-375	$325-375	$250-300	$250-300
Legs						$15-25	$15-25	$20-25	$15-20	$15-20
Libearty			$25-35	$60-80	$65-85	$125-140	$350-425	$400-450	$330-380	$330-380
Libearty-Beanine			$30-40	$55-75	$60-75	$115-130	$350-425	$400-450	$330-380	$330-380
Lizzy-black/blue							$15-25	$20-30	$15-20	$20-25
Lizzy-tie-dyed	$150-175	$150-175	$250-350	$350-400	$375-425	$425-525	$650-750	$1,000-1,100	$900-1,000	$950-1,050
Lucky-11 dots									$12-18	$15-20
Lucky-21 dots					$225-275	$325-425	$500-600	$600-650	$500-550	$450-550
Lucky-7 felt dots	$15-50	$15-50	$50-90	$50-75	$65-85	$90-110	$125-175	$175-225	$175-195	$175-195
Magic-hot pink stitching							$35-45	$50-60	$40-50	$50-60
Magic-light pink stitching							$25-35	$30-40	$35-40	$35-45
Manny				$25-50	$50-75	$85-110	$125-175	$160-190	$135-165	$145-160
Maple/Olympic			$75-150	$175-225	$225-275	$350-450	$400-500	$400-500	$400-500	$450-550
Maple/Pride							$450-550	$575-675	$500-600	$500-600
Mystic-coarse-tan horn						$12-20	$15-20	$25-35	$25-30	$25-30
Mystic-fine-mane			$55-75	$100-150	$100-150	$125-175	$175-225	$200-250	$225-275	$225-275
Nana	$300-350	$300-350		$600-800	$800-1,200	$1,200-1,500	$3,500-5,000	$4,000-4,700	$3,800-4,000	$3,800-4,000
Nip-all gold	$75-80	$80-95	$400-500	$500-600	$500-600	$650-750	$800-900	$900-1,000	$800-900	$850-950
Nip-white belly			$150-200	$175-225	$200-250	$275-350	$450-550	$450-500	$450-500	$500-550
Nip-white paws							$15-25	$20-30	$20-25	$20-25
Patti-deep fuchsia					$600-800	$650-850	$850-1,200	$850-1,200	$850-1,000	$850-1,000
Patti-fuchsia									$12-18	$15-20
Patti-magenta	$550-600	$500-550	$450-600	$450-600	$450-550	$500-600	$650-900	$650-900	$650-750	$650-750
Patti-raspberry	$750	$550-600	$550-700	$550-700	$550-650	$600-700	$750-1,000	$750-1,000	$800-900	$800-900
Peanut-light blue									$10-15	$12-18
Peanut-royal	$775-800	$500-550	$700-1,000	$900-1,200	$1,100-1,500	$1,900-2,300	$3,500-5,200	$4,500-5,000	$4,800-5,200	$4,800-5,200
Peking	$300	$200	$400-500	$500-700	$600-700	$800-900	$1,800-2,200	$2,000-2,300	$1,800-2,000	$1,800-2,000
Pinchers									$10-15	$10-15
Punchers					$800-1,000	$1,000-1,200	$3,500-5,000	$4,000-4,700	$3,800-4,000	$3,800-4,000
Quacker-no wings	$1,000	$750	$750-1,000	$900-1,200	$900-1,200	$1,200-1,400	$1,800-2,300	$2,000-2,200	$1,800-2,000	$1,800-2,000
Quackers-w/ wings									$8-13	$8-13
Radar				$50-75	$50-65	$75-100	$125-175	$175-200	$135-165	$140-165
Rex	$25-30	$25-30	$150-200	$200-250	$225-275	$350-400	$700-800	$900-1,000	$800-900	$800-900

These charts have been compiled over the past two years from the Beanie Mania price guide that has been posted every week on BeanieMom (www.beaniemom.com).

Beanie Mania II

MARKET TREND ANALYSIS CHART

Beanie Name	Sept. 1996	Dec. 1996	March 1997	May 1997	Aug. 1997	Nov. 1997	Feb. 1998	April 1998	July 1998	Oct. 1998
Righty			$25-30	$50-75	$65-85	$115-130	$300-375	$325-375	$250-300	$250-300
Rover									$12-18	$15-20
Scottie									$20-25	$20-25
Seamore						$50-75	$125-175	$125-175	$125-150	$125-150
Slither	$300	$200	$375-450	$500-600	$550-650	$800-900	$1,800-2,200	$2,000-2,200	$1,800-2,000	$1,800-2,000
Sly-brown-belly	$10-15	$10-15	$50-75	$75-125	$75-100	$75-100	$125-150	$125-175	$130-160	$125-150
Snowball				$35-50	$35-45	$45-60	$25-50	$35-50	$30-40	$30-40
Sparky							$100-125	$135-175	$110-130	$115-135
Speedy						$15-25	$15-25	$25-30	$25-30	$25-30
Splash				$25-50	$25-45	$45-55	$85-125	$125-150	$100-125	$110-130
Spook				$150-200	$100-150	$125-175	$225-275	$275-300	$300-350	$350-400
Spooky							$25-50	$30-35	$25-35	$25-30
Spot-no spot	$1,000	$750	$750-1,000	$900-1,200	$1,000-1,300	$1,200-1,400	$1,800-2,200	$2,000-2,300	$1,800-2,000	$1,800-2,000
Spot-with spot						$20-30	$25-40	$50-60	$40-50	$40-50
Squealer	$20-25	$20-25							$20-25	$20-25
Steg			$150-225	$250-350	$250-350	$350-450	$750-850	$950-1,000	$850-950	$850-950
Sting		$15-20	$25-35	$45-55	$50-65	$85-100	$150-200	$200-225	$150-175	$150-175
Stripes-blk/orange	$15-20		$65-100	$150-200	$150-200	$200-250	$250-325	$275-350	$250-300	$300-325
Stripes-black/tan									$10-15	$10-15
Tabasco			$75-125	$125-175	$125-175	$125-175	$200-275	$200-225	$160-185	$160-190
Tank-7-line	$15-20	$15-20	$40-75	$50-75	$65-85	$100-125	$150-200	$150-200	$160-190	$160-190
Tank-9-line	$10-15	$10-15	$40-75	$50-75	$85-100	$100-150	$150-200	$150-200	$180-200	$180-200
Tank-with shell						$35-65	$45-65	$60-75	$60-75	$60-80
Teddy-1997							$25-50	$40-50	$40-45	$40-50
Teddy-Employee-red/green						$2,200-3,200	$3,500-5,000	$4,000-4,500	$4,000-4,200	$4,000-4,200
Teddy-NF brown	$75-100	$100-125	$200-250	$400-500	$450-550	$45-75	$40-65	$65-95	$75-90	$75-90
Teddy-NF cranberry	$75-100	$100-125	$200-250	$400-500	$450-550	$750-950	$1,700-2,200	$1,800-2,200	$1,700-2,000	$1,700-2,000
Teddy-NF jade	$75-100	$100-125	$200-250	$400-500	$450-550	$750-950	$1,700-2,200	$1,800-2,200	$1,700-2,000	$1,700-2,000
Teddy-NF magenta	$75-100	$150-200	$450-550	$550-650	$600-700	$750-950	$1,700-2,200	$1,800-2,200	$1,700-2,000	$1,700-2,000
Teddy-NF teal	$100-150	$150-200	$400-500	$500-600	$600-700	$900-1,100	$1,700-2,200	$1,800-2,200	$1,800-2,100	$1,800-2,100
Teddy-NF violet	$100-150	$100-125	$225-275	$550-650	$600-700	$900-1,100	$1,700-2,200	$1,800-2,200	$1,800-2,100	$1,800-2,100
Teddy-OF brown	$75-100	$100-125	$200-250	$500-600	$550-650	$1,000-1,400	$2,500-3,000	$2,800-3,100	$2,600-2,800	$2,600-2,800
Teddy-OF cranberry	$75-100	$100-125	$175-225	$500-600	$550-650	$750-950	$2,000-2,300	$2,000-2,300	$1,800-2,000	$1,800-2,000
Teddy-OF jade	$75-100	$100-125	$175-225	$300-400	$400-500	$700-900	$1,650-2,100	$1,900-2,100	$1,700-1,900	$1,700-1,900
Teddy-OF magenta	$75-100	$100-125	$175-225	$275-350	$400-500	$700-900	$1,650-2,100	$1,900-2,100	$1,700-1,900	$1,700-1,900
Teddy-OF teal	$75-100	$100-125	$175-225	$300-400	$400-500	$700-900	$1,650-2,100	$1,900-2,100	$1,700-1,900	$1,700-1,900
Teddy-OF violet	$75-100	$125-150	$175-250	$300-400	$450-550	$700-900	$1,650-2,100	$1,900-2,100	$1,700-1,900	$1,700-1,900
Trap				$400-500	$425-500	$550-650	$900-1,100	$1,200-1,500	$1,200-1,400	$1,300-1,500
Tuck			$30-40	$45-55	$45-55	$70-90	$110-135	$125-175	$125-150	$125-150
Tusk			$25-30	$40-50	$40-50	$60-75	$100-125	$125-175	$120-140	$120-140
Twigs									$12-18	$15-20

These charts have been compiled over the past two years from the Beanie Mania price guide that has been posted every week on BeanieMom (www.beaniemom.com).

MARKET TREND ANALYSIS CHART

Beanie Name	Sept. 1996	Dec. 1996	March 1997	May 1997	Aug. 1997	Nov. 1997	Feb. 1998	April 1998	July 1998	Oct. 1998
Velvet						$15-25	$15-25	$20-30	$25-30	$25-30
Waddle									$10-15	$15-20
Waves									$10-15	$12-18
Web	$45-50	$50-75	$300-450	$550-650	$500-600	$600-700	$1,000-1,300	$1,500-1,800	$1,300-1,500	$1,300-1,500
Weenie									$20-25	$20-25
Ziggy									$10-20	$15-20
Zip-all black	$350-500	$325-450	$600-1,000	$900-1,200	$1,000-1,300	$1,200-1,400	$1,800-2,200	$2,000-2,200	$1,700-1,900	$1,700-1,900
Zip-white belly	$80-85	$85-100	$175-225	$200-250	$225-275	$300-375	$475-575	$500-550	$500-550	$550-600
Zip-white paws									$30-40	$35-40

These charts have been compiled over the past two years from the Beanie Mania price guide that has been posted every week on BeanieMom (www.beaniemom.com).

MARKET TREND ANALYSIS GRAPHS

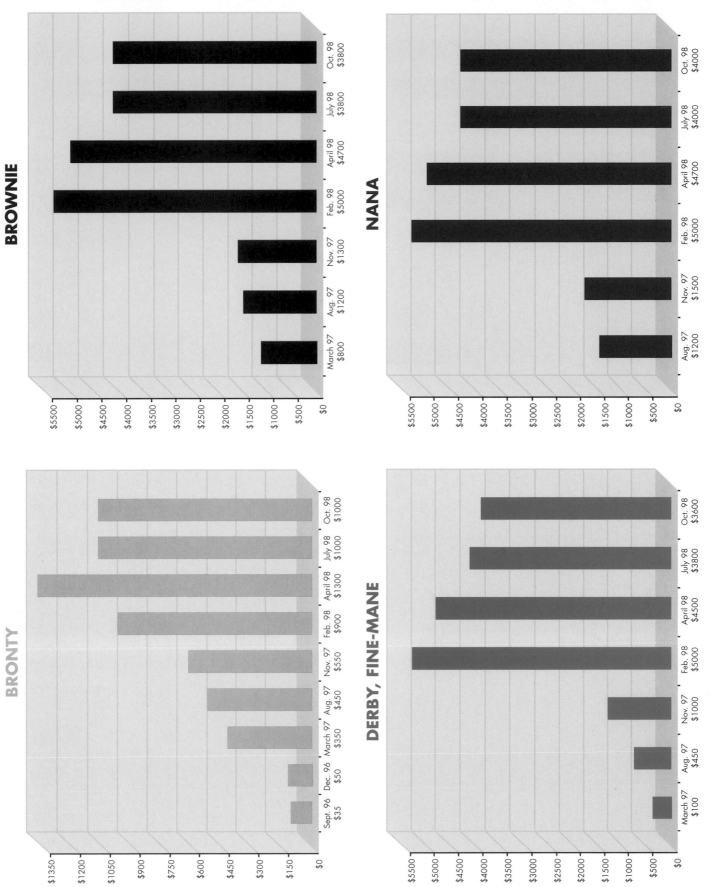

BROWNIE

Oct. 98	$3800
July 98	$3800
April 98	$4700
Feb. 98	$5000
Nov. 97	$1300
Aug. 97	$1200
March 97	$800

NANA

Oct. 98	$4000
July 98	$4000
April 98	$4700
Feb. 98	$5000
Nov. 97	$1500
Aug. 97	$1200

BRONTY

Oct. 98	$1000
July 98	$1000
April 98	$1300
Feb. 98	$900
Nov. 97	$550
Aug. 97	$450
March 97	$350
Dec. 96	$50
Sept. 96	$35

DERBY, FINE-MANE

Oct. 98	$3600
July 98	$3800
April 98	$4500
Feb. 98	$5000
Nov. 97	$1000
Aug. 97	$450
March 97	$100

MARKET TREND ANALYSIS GRAPHS

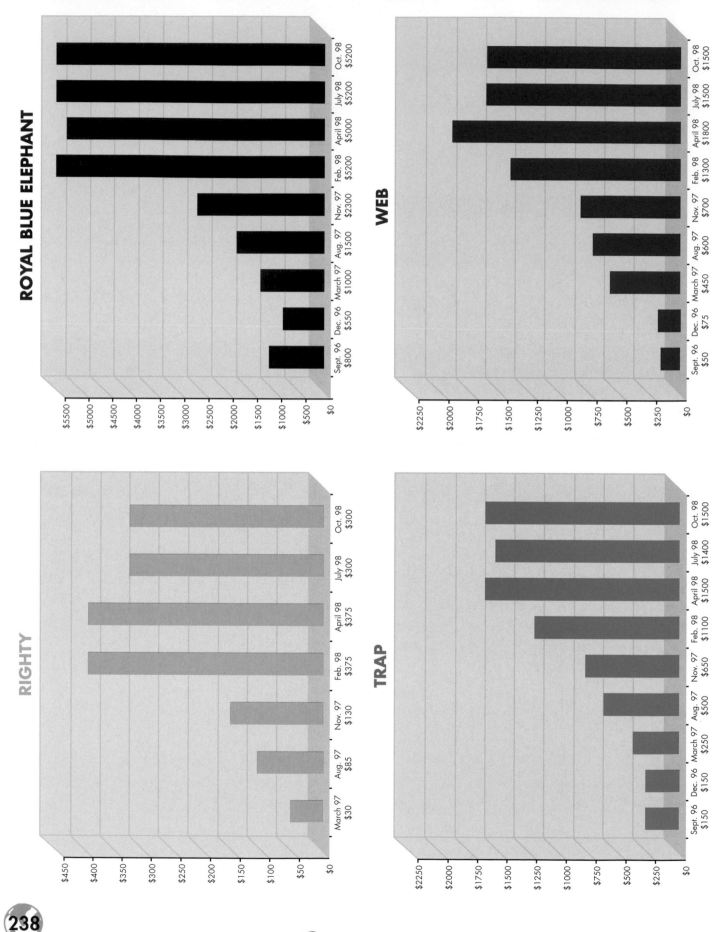

ROYAL BLUE ELEPHANT

Oct. 98	$5200
July 98	$5200
April 98	$5000
Feb. 98	$5200
Nov. 97	$2300
Aug. 97	$1500
March 97	$1000
Dec. 96	$550
Sept. 96	$800

WEB

Oct. 98	$1500
July 98	$1500
April 98	$1800
Feb. 98	$1300
Nov. 97	$700
Aug. 97	$600
March 97	$450
Dec. 96	$75
Sept. 96	$50

RIGHTY

Oct. 98	$300
July 98	$300
April 98	$375
Feb. 98	$375
Nov. 97	$130
Aug. 97	$85
March 97	$30

TRAP

Oct. 98	$1500
July 98	$1400
April 98	$1500
Feb. 98	$1100
Nov. 97	$650
Aug. 97	$500
March 97	$250
Dec. 96	$150
Sept. 96	$150

238

Beanie Mania II

SELLING, BUYING AND TRADING ON THE INTERNET

Selling Beanies

Once you have decided to sell Beanie Babies on a web site, read all the web site's instructions and meet their pre-selling requirements, you're ready to post your Beanie Baby for sale.

Make sure that you have researched the price and are comfortable selling the Beanie Baby at the price you are listing it for. Once you have posted a price, don't raise it. Nothing causes hard feelings more than someone who offers an item for a certain price, and then retracts it because they find out they can get more money for it.

Give a detailed description of the Beanie Baby. Indicate exactly what condition it is in, whether it has both swing and tush tags, and what condition the tags are in. Describe if the Beanie is in "mint condition", "good condition", or "well-loved". It is important that the buyer be aware of its exact condition. The same applies to the tags. Be sure to indicate any creases, markings, or tears on the tags. See page 153 for detailed descriptions of a variety of tag conditions.

If you have posted your Beanie for sale, it is your responsibility to answer all e-mail offers and inquiries in a timely manner. Even if an offer is made that is totally unacceptable to you, reply with a polite "no thank you" so that the other person knows you have seen their e-mail.

Shipping costs should be mentioned in your post to avoid confusion over price. You can either post that shipping is included in the price of the Beanie, or that shipping is additional. If you have a preferred method of shipping, be sure to inform your buyer of this.

When terms of a sale have been agreed upon, exchange mailing addresses. It is even a good idea to exchange phone numbers. People like to know that there is an additional means of communicating if a problem does occur. It is recommended that you ask the buyer to e-mail you when they have actually mailed the money. If you do not hear from the buyer within a couple of days, e-mail them again to make sure of their intentions. If you have not heard anything from the buyer after a reasonable period of time, a week or more, then it is acceptable to e-mail them again notifying them that the deal has been cancelled.

Once you have made a deal, you have the responsibility to keep your end of the bargain. It is important that you keep in close touch with the person you are dealing with until the transaction is consummated.

Buying Beanies

As a buyer, you should spend time browsing the various Internet sites, paying close attention to who is posting items for sale. If the same person has been posting for several months, that might be a good indicator that they are a reputable dealer. You might even spend time in the Beanie Baby chat rooms, getting to know other Beanie Baby collectors, asking questions, and learning as much as possible about reputable Beanie Baby dealers. The majority of Beanie Baby collectors are very willing to share their knowledge and expertise.

Don't be afraid to ask for references and to contact people that you are referred to.

Most sellers ask for payment in advance, either by money order, check or cashier's check. If you pay by check, the seller will usually wait 5 to 7 days for the check to clear before shipping the item. If you have purchased items from the same seller before and have built up a great rapport, they might send the items immediately upon receipt of the check.

SELLING, BUYING AND TRADING ON THE INTERNET

Most sellers do not like to send C.O.D.; it is more costly for the buyer, requires more paperwork and there is a longer wait for payment. Also C.O.D. does not entitle the buyer to open the package before payment is given; it only stipulates that the buyer has received the package. When mailing your payment, be sure to write on the check/money order: your name, e-mail address and items you are buying.

Mailing Beanie Babies

Package Beanie Babies in a plastic zip lock bag. The Beanie Baby will be protected against damage should the package break open and get wet. Ship the Beanie Babies in a sturdy corrugated box to protect the merchandise. Also include in the bag an invoice with the buyer and seller's address, the items being shipped and the price.

There are several ways of shipping a package - via United Parcel Service, the United States Postal Service, D.H.L., Federal Express, R.P.S., etc. Visit your local post office or call local shippers in your area and ask them to send a packet of shipping information. Shipping costs vary greatly depending upon whether or not the package is delivered overnight, in two days or longer. It is very important to insure the package in case of loss or damage during shipment. This nominal fee is definitely worth the price, knowing that if a problem does occur, the merchandise is insured.

Record Keeping

It is very important to record all transactions including the sale date, the other person's name, e-mail address, the Beanie Babies bought or sold and the price quoted. Once a transaction has been confirmed, you should exchange mailing addresses and phone numbers. The buyer should e-mail or call when the payment has been sent and indicate the method of payment. The seller should notify the buyer when the payment has been received and when the package is shipped. Once the buyer receives the package, a call or e-mail confirming that the package has arrived safely is important. In addition to a hard copy record of all transactions, it is highly recommended that you save all e-mails relating to a transaction until the deal is complete.

Trading Beanie Babies

When making a deal to trade Beanie Babies, agree on all conditions of the deal before exchanging mailing addresses. Both parties should agree to mail out their Beanie Babies on the same day. Once the Beanie Babies are shipped, each party should e-mail the other letting them know that the package has been sent. Upon receipt of the package, each receiving party should again e-mail the other party to let them know that the package has arrived. If for any reason something should occur that causes you to delay your end of the bargain, promptly notify the other person about your situation.

If you follow these important steps, you will save time and money and have a more enjoyable time selling, buying and trading on the Internet.

CARE OF BEANIE BABIES

Washing Your Beanie Baby

If your Beanie Baby has gotten soiled over time, carefully follow these steps to give your Beanie a good cleaning:

1) Remove the hang tag if it is still attached. Pass the plastic fastener with the heart tag through the hole. Then, store the tag in a safe place.
2) Place the Beanie Baby in a clean, white pillowcase. Secure the open end of the pillowcase, so the Beanie will stay safely inside during washing. One way to do this is to slip a rubber band down the pillowcase until it is positioned above the Beanie Baby. Wrap the rubber band around the pillowcase until the Beanie Baby is securely sealed inside.
3) Place the pillowcase, which now contains the Beanie Baby, in the washing machine.
4) Also, put a couple of bath towels in the washing machine. The towels act as a cushion, so that the Beanie Baby will not bang against the agitator, which could possibly scratch its eyes or nose.
5) Use a small amount of non-abrasive soap and wash the Beanie Baby in the gentle cycle.
6) When the washing cycle is done, remove the Beanie Baby from the washer. Take it out of the pillowcase and allow it to air dry for several days. Do not dry the Beanie in the dryer!

Removing A Stain On Your Beanie Baby

If there is a small stain on the Beanie Baby, follow these steps to remove the stain:

1) Dissolve 1/8 teaspoon of mild liquid dish detergent in a cup of warm water.
2) Dab a soft clean cloth into the mixture and gently rub the stain.
3) Use another clean, damp cloth to wipe off any excess soap.
4) Allow the Beanie to air dry.

Other Tips

If the plush fur on your Beanie Baby has matted down over time, or little fuzz balls have accumulated on the fabric, you might want to give it a body lift! You can use a piece of velcro or tape to gently lift the unwanted fur off. We suggest not storing your Beanie Baby in a sealed plastic bag. If there is moisture present, or food on the Beanie Baby, mold might develop.

COUNTERFEIT BEANIE BABIES

When counterfeit Beanie Babies first appeared on the secondary market during the summer of 1997, few people were aware of their existence. These initial fakes quietly made their way into the hands of unsuspecting collectors, primarily through the Internet where there was little chance to personally inspect the Beanies prior to purchase. Since that time, larger numbers and wider varieties of counterfeits have continued to slowly infiltrate the secondary market – not just via the Internet, but at collectible shows and even through legitimate retail stores!

Some of the increased activity in counterfeit Beanie Babies, since the summer of 1997, can be linked to an article by Frank Langfitt of the Baltimore Sun that appeared in newspapers around the country on October 7, 1997. The article detailed how Beanie Babies were being sold cheaply in the markets of Beijing, China, and that, "One outdoor market here has several thousand of the cuddly little critters, selling for nearly one-tenth of the $4.99 U.S. retail price." Unfortunately, what the article did not make known, is that a large number of the Beanie Babies sold in these markets were counterfeit.

As a result of this article and the shortage of Beanie Babies in the United States, visitors to Beijing started searching out Beanies in Beijing's Russian Market and Silk Alley. The Russian Market and Silk Alley are both located about two miles east of Tiananmen Square and the Forbidden City in the center of Beijing. Interestingly, the Russian Market, which derives its name from the Russians and eastern Europeans who buy bulk clothing from there, borders the U.S. Ambassador's Residence compound.

Beanie Babies illegally sold in Beijing, China, at the Russian Market and Silk Alley

Authentic Beijing Beanies?

Understandably, some buyers of Beanie Babies from the Beijing markets assume that Beanies with Ty swing and tush tags are authentic. It is even possible to find, mixed in with the general clutter of a vendor's booth, genuine Ty boxes complete with style number, identifying the Beanies they originally held. However, when Beanies are brought to a vendor's stall in rice sacks, and in units of less than 12, it is pretty much guaranteed they are fakes. Some vendors even openly admit that the Beanies they are selling are counterfeits.

COUNTERFEIT BEANIE BABIES

According to Ty attorney, "Twenty percent of Beanie Babies sold on Beijing streets are the real thing, only stolen. Others are "seconds," put aside at Ty factories because of flaws, but still ending up on the secondary market. The rest are mostly fakes."

Beanie Baby seconds - Snowball with a torn hat and Bruno with a broken arm.

It must be kept in mind that – regardless of whether or not the Beanie Baby is authentic or counterfeit – there are no legal, or authorized sales of Ty Beanie Babies in China. All "authentic" Beanie Babies are first shipped to the Ty warehouses and then distributed from there.

Chronology

The first Beanie Babies to make their way to Beijing's Russian Market were a bit dirty, missing tags and somewhat tattered, but nonetheless were real Ty Beanies. These were factory "seconds" that otherwise could not be sold. Seconds can still be found in Beijing, many of them with small stickers with red arrows on them pointing to a factory identified flaw. As the demand by tourists and expatriates grew for Beanie Babies, so did the number that were stolen from Ty factories. In time, these were followed by counterfeit versions.

Spinner "second" with a red arrow pointing to eye needing repair.

COUNTERFEIT BEANIE BABIES

To better understand a typical mix of Beanie Babies one might find in the markets of Beijing, they can be categorized as follows:

1. Authentic – stolen from the 100+ factories in China
2. Authentic – "over-runs" produced over and above what is sold to Ty
3. Authentic – seconds - flawed or dirty, and not intended for resale
4. Counterfeit – made to resemble Ty Beanie Babies, sometimes even using genuine materials and supplies stolen from the Ty factory
5. Counterfeit – do not resemble Ty Beanies, but have Ty swing and tush tags attached to them

The first known counterfeits were old face teal Teddy, old face violet Teddy and Spotless Spot. These made an appearance in the United States during the summer of 1997. Next to follow were Chilly, and royal blue Peanut. It is thought that these counterfeits went directly from the counterfeiters to the secondary market in the US, bypassing the Beijing markets. By the fall of 1997, fakes were no longer confined to rare retired Beanies, and the secondary market saw a huge influx of counterfeit versions of recently retired Bubbles and Grunts. From there, counterfeits progressed down the line from retired to hard-to-find, current and even newly released Beanies.

Consumer demand for Ty products – especially Beanie Babies, is so great that counterfeiters do not always take care to counterfeit Beanies in great detail. They know that even bad fakes will sell as long as they have Ty tags on them. As a result, we have seen Snowball with green fringe, Jolly with a black mustache, Peanut with peach ears, and a red Pinky! Some fakes don't even resemble Beanie Babies, but instead are other bean bag animals that have had Ty tags attached to them.

*Unknown plush beaver
with TY tush tag*

Counterfeit Red Pinky

*Unknown plush dalmation
with TY tush tag*

Jolly authentic, left, Jolly counterfeit, right

COUNTERFEIT BEANIE BABIES

Beanie Mania II

Counterfeit Beanie Babies have not only been found in the US, but they have also been seen in the Canadian and UK markets. In mid-April 1998, several counterfeit Beanie Babies, such as bluish-green Quackers, Garcia, and a beige colored cat similar to Nip, were first spotted by Canadian Beanie Baby dealers. Not only were the Beanie Babies counterfeit, but so were the tags.

Counterfeit mint green Quackers

Counterfeit Nip

Educate Yourself

If you are purchasing Beanie Babies it is important to educate yourself about the material, features and tags found on Beanie Babies.

MATERIAL:

Examine the material to make sure the fabric, ribbon and yarn are the same as on an authentic Beanie Baby.
- Fabric - correct color, thickness and weight
- Ribbon - correct width, color and double-sided satin
- Yarn - correct color and thickness

Counterfeit Peanut with peach ears (left) and authentic Peanut with pink ears.

Counterfeit Righty (left) with shaggy dark grey fabric and authentic Righty

COUNTERFEIT BEANIE BABIES

FEATURES:

Check the features such as the color of the eyes, nose and whiskers.
- Eyes - correct size, shape and color
- Nose - correct size, shape and color
- Whiskers - correct color and thickness

Authentic Nip in center. Counterfeit Nips found with a larger nose and black eyes.

Authentic Prance in center. Counterfeit Prances found with different colored eyes.

TAGS:

Examine the tush tag and heart tag for quality and accuracy. Use the "Beanie Mania II" tush tag and heart tag chronology to make sure the Beanie Baby is tagged correctly.

Heart Tags: (swing tags)
- Uniformity and color of gold foil
- Thickness of paper
- Brightness of the red and yellow colors
- Correct style number inside and on back
- Correct birthday
- Accurate company and web site information
- Correct generation tag

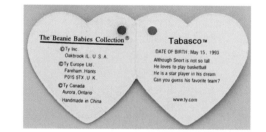

Counterfeit Tabasco swing tag. This tag is written in the 5th gen. style. There is no style number and the birthday is written out. The web site is abbreviated and Snort is mentioned in the poem instead of Tabasco.

Counterfeit tag with a scratched, uneven foil edge

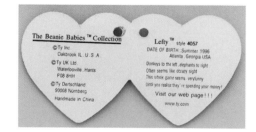

Counterfeit Lefty swing tag with the wrong birthday (Libearty's). There are misspellings in the body of the poem.

COUNTERFEIT BEANIE BABIES

Tush Tags: (body tags)

- Width of tag
- Color of printing
- Correct generation
- Correct copyright date

Pinky is incorrectly Spelled "Pin Ky"

Not to be removed until delivered to the consumer	Ne pas enlever avant livraison au consommateur
This label is affixed in compliance with the Upholstered and Stuffed Articles Act	Cette étiquette est apposée conformément à loi sur les articles rembourrés
This article contains NEW MATERIAL ONLY	Cet article contient MATÉRIAU NEUF SEULEMENT
Made by Ont.Reg. No 20B6484	Fabriqué par No d'envg Ont 20B6484
Content Plastic Pellets Polyester Fibers	Contenu Boulette de plastique Fibres de Polyester
Made in China	Fabriqué en Chine

Counterfeit Canadian tush tag with French verbiage on left side of tag.

Purchase Beanie Babies from reputable dealers who will stand by their product and guide you through your acquisitions.

To insure that your Beanie Baby is a genuine Ty product, purchase your Beanie Babies from authorized Ty retailers.

CATALOG COVERS

1988

1989

1990

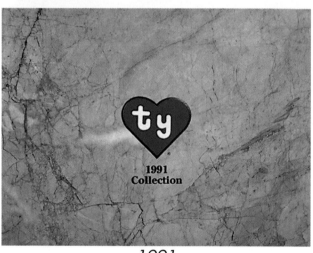

1991

1992

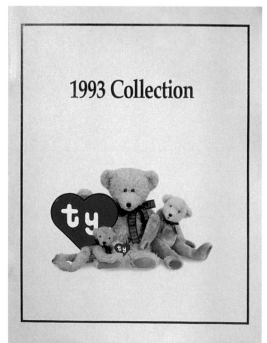

1993

THE 1994 COLLECTION

Beanie Babies were first introduced in this 1994 catalog.

NEW INTRODUCTIONS

THE 1995 COLLECTION

Courtesy of Bears by the Sea, Pismo Beach, California

THE 1996 COLLECTION

Courtesy of Ted E. Bear Shoppe of Florida

Courtesy of Jonathan and Jeremy Wald

Courtesy of Jonathan and Jeremy Wald

BEANIE BABIES POSTER

BEANIE BABIES OFFICIAL CLUB POSTER

Beanie Mania II

1998 BEANIE BABIES OFFICIAL CLUB KIT

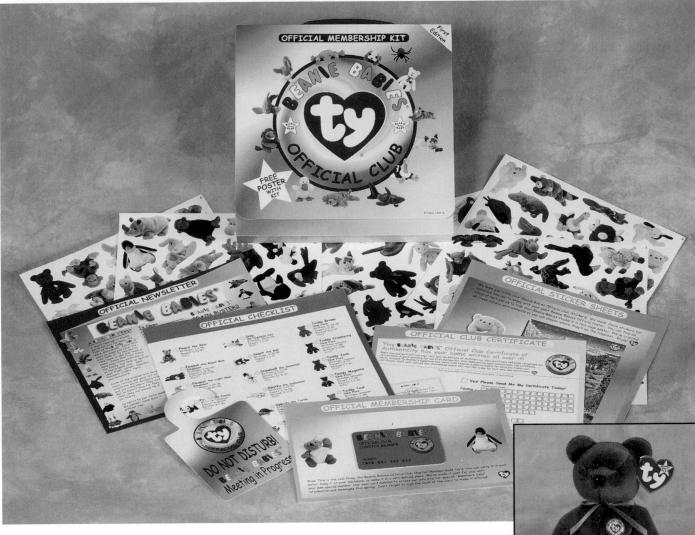

Clubby
1998 BBOC member exclusive

Announced January 2, 1998, Ty Beanie Babies Official Club (BBOC) kits became available at authorized retail stores in mid-March. Individually wrapped in cellophane and marked "First Edition", each kit comes complete with: convenient carrying case with handle and velcro closure; Official Charter membership card; Official Beanie Babies Newsletter; Official Club Certificate of Authenticity offer; Beanie Baby stickers; Official Beanie Babies Checklist; Do Not Disturb sign; and a poster for applying the stickers to. BBOC kits retail for $10 each, and although quite popular, have not been difficult to find at select stores. The number found on the membership cards allows admittance to the BBOC web site accessed through Ty's web page. The Club web site consists of a separate page of games where one can play Tic-Tac Ty, Color the Beanie, Crossword Puzzle, and Photo Frame Riddles. Unfortunately, many have found that the BBOC site is not always easy to access, and Shockwave multimedia software is required to play the interactive games.

In connection with club membership, Ty Inc. announced May 1st the release of Clubby, the BBOC exclusive bear. According to Ty, Clubby is a limited time offer to members only for $5.99 plus applicable state sales tax, shipping, processing and handling. Orders will be limited to only one Clubby per membership card number, so join now! Reminder: As nice as it would be to keep kits in the original wrapper, it is necessary to open them up and send in the enclosed offer along with your charter card number, in order to receive your Official Club Certificate of Authenticity.

Ty-rrific

Ty-rrific storefront at Chicago's O'Hare International Airport.

At first glance, it looks like Beanie Baby heaven. But it's actually a new first-of-its-kind store/museum at O'Hare International Airport – Ty-rrific for WH Smith.

The 700-square-foot store in Terminal 3 features not only the entire line of Ty products (and only Ty products), but a display of Ty Warner's personal Beanie Baby collection of prototypes and never-produced Beanies.

The first historical display, in the cases for the store's May 27 opening, included six versions of Bongo the monkey and several incarnations of Roary the lion – colorful prototypes that preceded the mass-marketed versions. Visitors can also examine four versions of Hissy the snake, some early dinosaurs and several fish that never made it into the line.

Retired pieces of Ty plush will also find a place in the museum display that probably will rotate every three months or so, said Linda DiMaggio, managing director for WH Smith Co. at O'Hare.

The store is as much geared towards children as towards older Ty collectors. Prominently located in the store is a board titled "Ty-rrific Talk" on which letters from children to Ty Inc. are displayed. The notes usually center around kids' suggestions for new Beanies or pictures of their personal collections. One such picture, of a child in a Bumble the Bumble bee Beanie costume on Halloween, was of particular interest to one shopper.

"That child happened to come into the store and see the picture and was so excited," said DiMaggio. The store seems to delight all who enter. Even DiMaggio herself often wanders over to Ty-rrific to brighten her day.

"We all go over there when things are not going well – it's always a lot of fun there. The kids who are often in the store tell us about their Beanie collections and we just love listening to them. So often, they're carrying around their favorite Beanies – you really can tell a Beanie collector from afar!"

Ty-rrific

The idea for the unusual store began about a year ago when the Chicago Department of Aviation asked WH Smith Co. to consider opening a Ty store at O'Hare because there was so much excitement over Beanies.

"We have a long relationship with Ty with both Beanies and plush," said DiMaggio. "So from there, we started thinking of different ideas we had. We didn't want to do just an ordinary toy store. We wanted some type of museum-like toy store. We wanted it to be a place where people could come to see museum pieces, not just to buy plush product."

WH Smith Co. put together a proposal and took it to Ty Inc. DiMaggio says Ty Warner and his employees were enthusiastic immediately. "From there, we moved forward with more ideas and they kept in touch with us and stopped in along the way."

Several brainstorming sessions conducted by employees of WH Smith Co. and Ty Inc. ended with the store being called Ty-rrific by WH Smith. There is no monetary connection, the store is owned and operated by WH Smith Co.

"Ty-rrific, which is open 7 a.m. to 7 p.m. seven days a week, doesn't get priority in the amount or assortment of Beanies it receives," said DiMaggio.

Ty Warner's personal collection of prototypes is prominently displayed throughout the store. All Ty products are sold in the store.

"Our one opportunity is that Smith has 30 stores in the airport and when we need to, we consolidate. But we don't have any priority. I wish we did, that would be nice!" said DiMaggio.

The stores sell all Beanies for $5.99 except for Princess, which is tagged at $19.99 to account for the additional contribution to Princess Diana's charity fund.

"In its first month," DiMaggio said, "Ty-rrific did about twice the anticipated amount of business that Smith officials expected."

"And that's considering that our location isn't what I would consider ideal. It's a very strange location and is attracting more than enough traffic from all over the airport, even though the store has done no advertising."

The terrific early success of the store has Smith officials considering a second location at O'Hare as well as opening similar stores at other airports.

THE COLLIER MUSEUM
BEANIE BABY EXHIBIT

Our complete collection of Beanie Babies was on display at the Collier Museum in Naples, Florida. This was the first time that a complete collection of Beanie Babies was ever exhibited at a museum. In addition to Beanie Babies, also on display were rare prototypes, early Ty plush, Teenie Beanies, oddities, catalogs and special promotional Beanies such as sports commemorative Cubbie and Special Olympics Maple. The museum exhibit took place for seven weeks starting on December 15, 1997 and running through January 31, 1998.

Photographer: Burnell Caldwell

Over 200 Beanie Babies lined the shelves.

Photographer: Burnell Caldwell

Prototypes and oddities were a main attraction.

Photographer: Burnell Caldwell

Princess took "Center stage".

Photographer: Burnell Caldwell

On display was rare Ty Plush and catalogs.

Teenie Beanies had a prominent corner in the room.

Beanie Mania II

THE COLLIER MUSEUM BEANIE BABY EXHIBIT

Beanie Mania II

During the exhibit, visitors to the museum had the opportunity to enter a drawing for Peace or Garcia. To enter they had to answer fifteen trivia questions based on clues placed around the exhibit. Completed entries with correct answers were entered into the drawing. Children, ages 17 and under, entered to win Garcia, and the adults, 18 and older, had the opportunity to win Peace.

A close-up look at some of the rare Beanies

Children searched the room to find answers to the trivia questions.

A panoramic view of the Beanies.

A display of "rare" Teddys.

Photographer: Burnell Caldwell

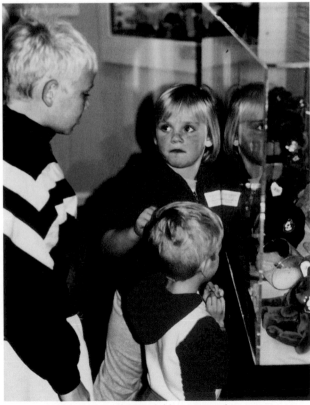

Over 5,000 children enjoyed the Beanie Baby exhibit

THE COLLIER MUSEUM BEANIE BABY EXHIBIT

Mid-way through the exhibit, on January 10, 1998, there was a special three hour presentation given at the Registry Hotel by Becky Phillips, Becky Estenssoro, Vicky Krupka and Sara Nelson (BeanieMom). Over 200 hundred people attended the seminar. We discussed the history of Ty Inc., oddities, Teenie Beanies, collecting tips, and the market outlook. There was also a question and answer session and a book signing.

All visitors received a "SHOW ME THE BEANIES" button when they entered the exhibit

Becky Estenssoro, Sara Nelson, Becky Phillips and Vicky Krupka stand by the welcoming sign.

Over 200 Beanie Baby Collectors attended the 3 hour seminar.

Photographer: Burnell Caldwell

Becky Estenssoro, Becky Phillips, Carrie Teasley, Ron Jamro, curator of museum, Vicky Krupka and Sara Nelson.

Photographer: Burnell Caldwell

TOY FAIR CONGO

In February, 1998, we had the privilege of attending the American International Toy Fair in New York City that ran from February 9-16th. The Toy Fair is an annual event sponsored by the Toy Manufacturers of America, and is the largest toy trade show in the Western Hemisphere. It was attended by over 1,600 exhibitors and 201,000 buyers from the United States and 100 foreign countries.

Ty, Inc. had a very prominent exhibit there, in a prominent location, at the entrance of the Javits Convention Center. We even had the pleasure of meeting Mr. Ty Warner and chatting with him for a while about the secondary market and the new Beanie Babies Official Club.

As part of our display at the Toy Fair we used Congo the gorilla to help promote our first book, Beanie Mania. Congo was displayed hanging from a 4-foot tall replica of New York's famed Empire State Building. With each purchase of 36 books, buyers received Congo and a limited edition card. Around Congo's neck is a red velvet ribbon with the words "Beanie Mania – N.Y. Toy Fair 1998" embroidered in gold thread.

The front of the card accompanying Congo is covered in metallic gold on which is displayed the logo from the cover of the Beanie Mania book, and the words "1998 New York Toy Fair" and a number from 0001 to 1998. (Only 1998 of these cards and ribbons were made). The back of the card is the same as the back cover of the Beanie Mania book - navy blue with a globe in the middle.

1998 Beanie Mania Toy Fair Congo

BEANIE BABY CHECKLIST

	4032	Ally, the alligator		4196	Fortune, the panda-sitting
	4195	Ants, the anteater		4066	Freckles, the leopard
	4074	Baldy, the eagle		4051	Garcia, the tie-dyed bear
	4035	Batty, the brown bat		4191	GiGi, the poodle
	4109	Bernie, the St. Bernard		4188	Glory, the white bear with red/blue stars
	4009	Bessie, the brown and white cow		4034	Gobbles, the turkey
	4011	Blackie, the black bear		4023	Goldie, the goldfish
	4163	Blizzard, the black and white tiger		4126	Gracie, the swan
	4001	Bones, the brown dog		4092	Grunt, the razorback hog
	4067	Bongo, brown tail - r/w tush / no name		4061	Happy, the gray hippo
	4067	Bongo, brown tail - r/w tush / name		4061	Happy, the lavender hippo
	4067	Bongo, tan tail - b/w tush		4119	Hippity, the mint green bunny
	4067	Bongo, tan tail - r/w tush / no name		4185	Hissy, the snake
	4067	Bongo, tan tail - r/w tush / with name		4073	Hoot, the owl
	4601	Britannia, bear-Union Jack flag-embroidered		4117	Hoppity, the rose bunny
	4601	Britannia, bear-Union Jack flag-sewn on		4060	Humphrey, the camel
	4085	Bronty, the brontosaurus		4038	Iggy, the iguana-Rainbow tags-collar
	4010	Brownie, the brown bear		4038	Iggy, the iguana-Iggy tags-spikes
	4183	Bruno, the terrier		4044	Inch, the inchworm with felt antennae
	4078	Bubbles, the black and yellow fish		4044	Inch, the inchworm with yarn antennae
	4016	Bucky, the beaver		4028	Inky, the pink octopus
	4045	Bumble, the bumble bee		4028	Inky, the tan octopus with a mouth
	4071	Caw, the crow		4028	Inky, the tan octopus without a mouth
	4012	Chilly, the white polar bear		4197	Jabber, the parrot
	4121	Chip, the calico cat		4199	Jake, the mallard duck
	4015	Chocolate, the moose		4082	Jolly, the walrus
	4019	Chops, the lamb		4070	Kiwi, the toucan
	4083	Claude, the tie-dyed crab		4192	Kuku, the cockatoo
	n/a	Clubby, the BBOC royal blue bear		4085	Lefty, the donkey with American flag
	4160	Congo, the gorilla		4020	Legs, the frog
	4079	Coral, the tie-dyed fish		4057	Libearty, white bear with American flag
	4130	Crunch, the shark		4057	Libearty/Beanine bear with American flag
	4010	Cubbie, the brown bear		4033	Lizzy, the blue lizard with black spots
	4052	Curly, the brown napped bear		4033	Lizzy, the tie-dyed lizard
	4006	Daisy, the black and white cow		4040	Lucky, the ladybug with 7 felt dots
	4008	Derby, the coarse-mane horse		4040	Lucky, the ladybug with approx. 11 dots
	4008	Derby, the coarse-mane horse-star		4040	Lucky, the ladybug with approx. 21 dots
	4008	Derby, the fine-mane horse		4088	Magic, the white dragon-hot pink stitching
	4027	Digger, the orange crab		4088	Magic, the white dragon-light pink stitching
	4027	Digger, the red crab		4081	Manny, the manatee
	4110	Doby, the Doberman		4600	Maple/Maple, white bear with Canadian flag
	4171	Doodle, the tie-dyed rooster		4600	Maple/Pride, white bear with Canadian flag
	4100	Dotty, the Dalmatian with black ears		4600	Maple/Special Olympics, bear-Canadian flag
	4190	Early, the robin		4162	Mel, the Koala
	4018	Ears, the brown rabbit		4007	Mystic, the unicorn with iridescent horn
	4180	Echo, the dolphin		4007	Mystic, the unicorn with tan horn
	4186	Erin, the green bear with white shamrock		4007	Mystic, the unicorn with tan horn/fine-mane
	4189	Fetch, the golden retriever		4067	Nana, the monkey with tan tail - b/w tush
	4021	Flash, the dolphin		4104	Nanook, the Siberian Husky
	4125	Fleece, the napped lamb		4003	Nip, the all gold cat with pink ears (no white)
	4012	Flip, the white cat		4003	Nip, the gold cat with white face and belly
	4118	Floppity, the lavender bunny		4003	Nip, the gold cat with white paws
	4043	Flutter, the tie-dyed butterfly		4114	Nuts, the squirrel

Retired Beanie Babies are in red

BEANIE BABY CHECKLIST

4025	Patti, the deep fuchsia platypus		4090	Spooky, the ghost
4025	Patti, the fuchsia platypus		4000	Spot, black and white dog with a spot
4025	Patti, the magenta platypus		4000	Spot, black and white dog without a spot
4025	Patti, the raspberry platypus		4184	Spunky, the cocker spaniel
4053	Peace, the tie-dyed bear		4005	Squealer, the pig
4053	Peace, the tie-dyed pastel bear		4087	Steg, the stegosaurus
4062	Peanut, the light blue elephant		4077	Sting, the ray
4062	Peanut, the royal blue elephant		4193	Stinger, the scorpion
4013	Peking, the panda-laying		4017	Stinky, the skunk
4026	Pinchers, the red lobster		4182	Stretch, the ostrich
4072	Pinky, the pink flamingo		4065	Stripes, the black and orange tiger
4161	Pouch, the kangaroo		4065	Stripes, the black and tan tiger
4122	Pounce, the brown tie-dyed cat		4171	Strut, the tie-dyed rooster
4123	Prance, the gray striped cat		4002	Tabasco, the red bull
4300	Princess, the purple bear with white rose		4031	Tank, the 7-line armadillo
4181	Puffer, the puffin		4031	Tank, the 9-line armadillo
4106	Pugsly, the Pug dog		4031	Tank, the armadillo with shell
4026	Punchers, the red lobster		4200	Teddy, 1997 light brown holiday bear
4024	Quacker, the duck with wings		N/A	Teddy, the employee bear-green ribbon
4024	Quacker, the duck without wings		N/A	Teddy, the employee bear-red ribbon
4024	Quackers, the duck with wings		4050	Teddy, the new face-brown bear
4024	Quackers, the duck without wings		4052	Teddy, the new face-cranberry bear
4091	Radar, the black bat		4057	Teddy, the new face-jade bear
4037	Rainbow, the chameleon-Iggy tags-spikes		4056	Teddy, the new face-magenta bear
4037	Rainbow, chameleon with tongue-Iggy tags-spikes		4051	Teddy, the new face-teal bear
4037	Rainbow, pastel with tongue-Iggy tags-spikes		4055	Teddy, the new face-violet bear
4037	Rainbow, pastel w/ tongue-Rainbow tags-collar		4050	Teddy, the old face-brown bear
4086	Rex, the tyrannosaurus		4052	Teddy, the old face-cranberry bear
4086	Righty, the elephant with American flag		4057	Teddy, the old face-jade bear
4014	Ringo, the raccoon		4056	Teddy, the old face-magenta bear
4069	Roary, the lion		4051	Teddy, the old face-teal bear
4202	Rocket, the bluejay		4055	Teddy, the old face-violet bear
4101	Rover, the red dog		4198	Tracker, the basset hound
4107	Scoop, the pelican		4042	Trap, the mouse
4102	Scottie, the Scottish terrier		4076	Tuck, the walrus
4029	Seamore, the seal		4108	Tuffy, the terrier
4080	Seaweed, the otter		4076	Tusk, the walrus
4031	Slither, the snake		4068	Twigs, the giraffe
4115	Sly, the brown-belly fox		4058	Valentino, the white bear with red heart
4115	Sly, the white-belly fox		4058	Valentino/Special Olympics, bear-red heart
4039	Smoochy, frog with single thread mouth		4064	Velvet, the panther
4039	Smoochy, frog with double thread mouth		4075	Waddle, the penguin
4039	Smoochy, the frog with felt mouth		4084	Waves, the orca whale
4120	Snip, the Siamese cat		4041	Web, the spider
4002	Snort, the red bull with cream paws		4013	Weenie, the dachshund dog
4201	Snowball, the snowman		4194	Whisper, the deer
4100	Sparky, the Dalmatian		4187	Wise, the graduation owl
4030	Speedy, the turtle		4103	Wrinkles, the bulldog
4060	Spike, the rhino		4063	Ziggy, the zebra with thin stripes
4036	Spinner, the striped spider		4063	Ziggy, the zebra with wide stripes
4036	Spinner/Creepy, the striped spider		4004	Zip, the all black cat with pink ears (no white)
4022	Splash, the orca whale		4004	Zip, the black cat with white face and belly
4090	Spook, the ghost		4004	Zip, the black cat with white paws

Retired Beanie Babies are in red

September 30, 1998 - Introductions

Beak, the New Zealand kiwi   Style #4211
Birthday: February 3,1998
Isn't this just the funniest bird?
When we saw her, we said "how absurd"
Looks aren't everything, this we know
Her love for you, she's sure to show!

Canyon, the cougar   Style #4212
Birthday: May 29,1998
I climb rocks and run really fast
Try to catch me, it's a blast
Through the mountains, I used to roam
Now in you room, I'll call it home!

Halo, the white angel bear   Style #4208
Birthday: August 31,1998
When you sleep, I'm always here
Don't be afraid, I am near
Watching over you with lots of love
Your guardian angel from above!

Loosy, the goose   Style #4206
Birthday: March 29,1998
A tale has been told
Of a goose that laid gold
But try as she might
Loosy's eggs are just white!

Pumkin', the Jack-o-lantern   Style #4205
Birthday: October 31,1998
Ghosts and goblin are out tonight
Witches try hard to cause fright
This little pumkin is very sweet
He only wants to trick or treat!

September 30, 1998 - Introductions

Roam, the buffalo Style #4209
Birthday: September 27, 1998
Once roaming wild on the american land
Tall and strong, wooly and grand
So rare and special is this guy
Find him quickly, he is quite a buy!

1998 Holiday Teddy Style #4204
Birthday: December 25,1998
Dressed in his PJ's, and ready for bed
Hugs given, good nights said
This little Beanie will stay close at night
Ready for a hug at first morning light!

Santa, the Santa Claus Style #4203
Birthday: December 6,1998
Known by all in his suit of red
Piles of presents on his sled
Generous and giving, he brings us joy
Peace and love, plus this special toy!

Zero, the holiday penguin Style #4207
Birthday: January 2,1998
Penguins love the ice and snow
Playing in weather twenty below
Antarctica is where I love to be
Splashing in the cold, cold sea!

Scorch, the dragon Style #4210
Birthday: July 31,1998
A magical mystery with glowing wings
Made by wizards and other things
Known to breathe fire with lots of smoke
Scorch is really a friendly ol' bloke!

ABOUT THE AUTHORS

Becky Estenssoro and Becky Phillips are the undisputed, world-renowned authorities on all things Beanie. They are the authors/publishers of the highly acclaimed *Beanie Mania - A Comprehensive Collector's Guide* and the updated version - *Beanie Mania II*, and are the co-publishers and editors of *Beanie Mania* magazine and the *Beanie Mania Bulletin* newsletter. Their weekly Market Analysis and Pricing Guide appears on the popular beaniemom.com web site and is widely considered to be the most authoritative secondary market price guide. It is relied upon by Beanie Baby collectors around the world.

The Beckys have been guest speakers on many TV and radio talk and news shows across the country, including Fox News, CBS News, Good Morning Texas, CNN, WGN, KHKS-Dallas, and the Ronn Owens Show. They have been featured in numerous publications, including Time Magazine, Kiplinger's Personal Finance Magazine, Wall Street Journal, Collecting Figures Magazine, the Chicago Tribune, Los Angeles Times and the Dallas Morning News. They attend collector's trade shows across the United States and give seminars on Beanie Baby collecting.

Are you a Beanie Baby collector?
Then take a look at this!

Beanie Mania Bulletin is a newsletter that comes out twice a month!

Printed by the winning combination of Becky Phillips, Becky Estenssoro, and Vicky Krupka, this newsletter is dedicated to keeping you in the know. You get the absolute latest information on what's happening in the Beanie Babies marketplace anywhere in print!

Subscribe to the *Beanie Mania Bulletin* and enjoy:

- **Updated price lists for all Beanie Babies – current, retired, and redesigned.**
- **Beanie Baby news and market analysis**
- **Lists of upcoming Beanie Baby Collector Shows**
- **Collecting tips from Becky, Becky and Vicky**

Finally!
A magazine as collectible as the Beanie Babies themselves!

Becky and Becky bring you:

- Over 100 pages of prices, products, pictures and news
- Tips and commentary from the pros
- Market forecasts and analysis

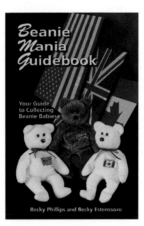